A PSYCHIC BEDSIDE READER

A Psychic Bedside Reader

TIPS, TECHNIQUES, MEDITATIONS,
and HEALINGS *for the* NOVICE *and*
EXPERIENCED READER *and* HEALER

WAYNE MARTIN

Paperback ISBN: 979-8-9902183-0-7
eBook ISBN: 979-8-9902183-0-4

CONTENTS

Grounding

Try this. Sit in a chair. Close your eyes. Take a deep breath. Feet flat on the floor. Hands separated and resting, palms up on each thigh.

Create a grounding cord. This is a line of energy that connects your first chakra to the center of the planet. Chakras are energy centers in your body. Your first chakra is a ball of energy about the size of a quarter that sits just in front of the base of your spine. Your grounding cord attaches to the bottom of that ball of energy.

Grounding makes your body feel safe, so you release energy more easily. Gravity pulls whatever you release, even your own energy, down to the center of the planet. No effort is required on your part. The center of the planet neutralizes the energy and returns it to whoever owns it. No karma for anyone. A virtuous cycle.

Nearly everyone goes to connect to the center of the planet the first time but stops at the soil, often making roots like a tree. This is a method that is taught in some martial arts styles, but it is not the best option for your spiritual development and healing. Shallow grounding can keep the energy you release nearby, and it doesn't neutralize the energy. It stores it.

So, notice the seat of your chair. Take a deep breath. Notice the distance between the seat and the floor. Now notice the distance between the floor and the soil below. Breathe.

Now notice the distance between the soil and the water table underneath. Notice the distance between the water table and the rocky mantle. Notice the distance between the mantle and the molten core below that. Deep breath.

Notice the distance between the molten core and the center of the planet. That ball of light at the very center of the planet is where you connect your grounding cord. Deep breath.

Say hello to the center of the planet. Do you get a hello back?

Notice the color and texture of your grounding cord. It may look like a line of energy, or it may look like something physical: a rope, a wire, a pipe, a tree trunk. Adjust it as needed to be in affinity with your body. If your grounding cord looks like a tree, have the roots of the tree connect to the center of the planet. How your grounding cord attaches is up to you. The important bit is connecting to the center of the planet.

Getting this far means you've already released some energy from your aura and body. Now, it is time to fill in the space that was created when you released that energy.

FILLING IN

Create a gold sun over your head. Have it call back all of your energy from wherever you left it throughout your day and week. Work. School. Online meetings. Video games. Your fantasies about your future. Your regrets about your past. Wherever you've placed your attention. Just watch the energy come back and see if you notice where it came from.

Have the sun burn up and neutralize the energy you've called back. Then bring the sun down into the top of your head. It will automatically flow into the spaces you created. Create a gauge to measure when you're full. Like a fuel gauge. You'll run better if your energy is all the way full. If the gauge doesn't read "full," then create another gold sun, fill it, neutralize the energy, and bring it in.

Continue to ground a little while longer: three minutes, five minutes. That's plenty this first time around.

Now that you're here, at the end of your grounding meditation, create a gold sun over your head. This time, instead of calling back your energy, fill this sun with your highest creative essence, your present time growth vibration, and your affinity for yourself. Your highest creative essence is a healing for you, the spirit. Your present time growth vibration is a healing for your body. Your affinity for yourself is a healing for your affinity in your fourth chakra. Your affinity is how you recognize your own energy.

Take a deep breath. Open your eyes, bend over and touch the floor, draining any tension from the back of your neck, then stand up and stretch. Notice your breathing. Notice your feet and stand on your tiptoes.

If you're ready for more, sit back down and ground some more. Otherwise, have a nice day!

HOW DO YOU APPLY THIS TO YOUR DAILY LIFE?

There is a progression with this technique. After grounding for ten minutes a day for a week or two, at the end of your session, while you're standing with your eyes open, notice your grounding cord. Continue to ground with your eyes open and standing, and bring in another gold sun. Each day, increase the amount of time that you ground standing up with your eyes open.

The first day, maybe you ground with your eyes open for twenty seconds. The next week, you might ground while standing with your eyes open for a full minute and be totally comfortable. Notice the connection to your first chakra and the connection to the center of the planet. Fill in and take a deep breath. The goal is simply to ground with your eyes open and fully out of trance.

Out of trance? Whenever we close our eyes and meditate, at least in this style and many other styles of meditation, we go into a light trance. We are more aware of energy when in a light trance. Learning to use the tools in your daily life makes them more useful.

After a week or two practicing this, add walking while grounding.

Start by standing and grounding with your eyes open. Then take a few steps, stop and notice your grounding. Did your grounding cord stay where it was when you took a few steps? Did it follow you without you thinking about it?

Turn around and walk back to your starting place, stop and notice your grounding again. Notice the connection to your first chakra and the connection to the center of the planet. Check your energy gauge and, if needed, bring in a gold sun to fill in. As this becomes easier, take longer walks inside your house.

When this is comfortable and easy, take a longer walk outside. Notice your grounding cord as you walk. Say hello to the center of the planet while you walk. Bring in a gold sun while you walk. If you lose your grounding cord, stop walking to focus only on your grounding cord and recover it. Closing your eyes while standing can help. If you have to, sit back down and close your eyes and create a new grounding cord.

After short walks outside become comfortable, you're ready to take your grounding cord with you into your daily life. Shopping. Getting coffee. At work. Wherever you go, you can ground and fill in. This, combined with a little amusement about seeing new things on an energy level, will keep you safe and sound.

Ground and fill in. This may be sufficient to prevent you from ever feeling drained again.

Note that with every image you imagine, the gold sun, the grounding cord, the center of the planet, your first chakra, your body parts, you are exercising your clairvoyance. You may be imagining what your tailbone looks like, but you're also creating the image of your tailbone and reading its energy. This is practicing your clairvoyant ability.

Pro Tip: I find it more fun when I'm on a walk to create an electric blue circle around me where my aura touches the ground, and create a grounding cord for that circle. This grounds my aura and helps to keep it closer to my body. It's a good way to break bad habits, like sending your energy home as soon as you leave work, or sending your aura around the corners of alleys or paths in the woods, instead of using your clairvoyance to look for risks.

What's more fun about this? It feels like I'm in a kind of bumper car, LOL! My feet bounce a little more. I rise up on my toes a little more. My body relaxes more because I'm grounded, I'm walking, and my aura is staying close to my body. The cadence of the walking and having my energy close is its own meditation, and I can feel my aura bump into stuff! Trees. Parked cars. People. It's a neat sensation to become aware of.

A useful tip: Read the grounding technique out loud and record yourself with your phone or other device, then play it back as your own guided meditation. This helps you learn the technique faster, and actually gives you useful feedback on your understanding. Here is a simplified version without most of the explanations. Here's how it should sound.

[Recording starts next.]

Sit down. Close your eyes. Take a deep breath and let it out. Rest your hands, palms up, on your thighs. Create a grounding cord from the bottom of your first chakra to the center of the planet. Allow gravity to pull all the energy you are ready to release down your grounding cord and into the center of the planet, where it is neutralized and returned to whoever owns it.

Create a gold sun over your head. Have this sun, like a magnet, pull your energy back to you from wherever you left it throughout your day or night. Bring your energy back into this gold sun. Burn it up to neutralize the energy, and bring the entire sun down through the top of your head and into your space.

Let go of all the problems in your space that aren't yours. Let go of all the communications that you are done with. Let go of all the energy that is not yours. Take a deep breath and release them down your grounding cord.

[Don't record this bit. Allow several minutes of silence to go by, just grounding. If you fall asleep or drift, when you wake up, notice your grounding cord. Check your gauge and if needed, fill in. Resume recording.]

Notice your grounding cord. Notice its connections to the bottom of your first chakra and to the center of the planet. Notice gravity and relax.

Create a gold sun over your head. Fill it with your highest creative essence, your present time growth vibration, and your affinity for yourself. Bring the whole sun down into the top of your head and throughout your body and aura.

Yawn. Stretch. Open your eyes. Bend over and touch the floor, releasing any tension or energy in your neck and shoulders, down your arms and into the floor.

Stand up. Stretch. Yawn and stretch. Stand on your tiptoes, eyes open.

Enjoy the rest of your day and night.

[End recording.]

Grounding
Explained

I find it more fun when I understand how a technique works. This is not how I learn a new technique. I learn best when I experience the technique for myself by trying it out. Then, after I experience a technique that makes my energy change, I have a flood of questions, LOL! That's when I study the details of how things work. These questions tend to be better informed because I experienced the technique first. Other people may learn in other ways, but this is how I learn best, and it's one way that I teach.

Grounding does many things. It provides safety. It's a defensive technique. It protects and serves. It manages your energy. Healing is changing energy from one state to a better state. Grounding can heal you. Grounding raises your awareness by consolidating your energy closer to your body. This leads to a better understanding of yourself and those around you.

Grounding does not require faith, buy-in, a perfect understanding, belonging to a group (though that can be useful), or turning away from things you're familiar with. It is, in one sense, just a storm drain.

The first time I experienced grounding to the center of the planet, it was in a beginning meditation class at the Berkeley Psychic Institute in Berkeley, California. This was in January of 1984. A lovely woman named Hanna Jane was the teacher.

She guided us through a meditation very similar to the one that opens this book. We only tried this for a few minutes, then bent over and touched the floor, and stood up and stretched. She called bending over and touching the floor "dumping out." Bringing in a gold sun of our own energy she called "filling in."

After years of getting mysterious explanations of how energy worked, this pragmatic vocabulary appealed to me a lot.

She also mentioned that grounding this way with our eyes closed helped put us into a light trance. One value of this was teaching us to recognize when we were in trance and when we were not. That way, we'd stop walking around half-tranced. Yes, the jokes were that corny. The point, however, is a valid one. Being all the way out of trance has advantages, as does being all the way in trance.

Think of it like being on and off. This is a useful concept in the beginning because it lines up well with being in trance and not being in trance.

Most of the problems that beginners had when they were feeling overwhelmed by the world came from being half-tranced, i.e. their abilities were turned partially on and they were not aware that their abilities were partially on. This creates a constant input of signals that accumulate until they become a distraction. Distraction? Think of how distracting it would be to be aware of all of the pain around you, for instance, without realizing that it was not your pain. Think of how distracting it would be to be aware of everyone that's zooming anyone within four city blocks of your body. (That's an Aretha Franklin reference. Google 'Who's zoomin' who?' It's a really funny song.)

Being half-tranced also explains a lot of the random nature of beginning abilities, that sense of not being in control of them, which reinforces the idea that your abilities are some kind of gift from some kind of deity that you must prove you are worthy of using instead of an ability that you've been using and refining over many lifetimes.

Eventually, you won't need to be in trance to use your abilities. You'll see or hear something interesting, and just focus slightly, and you are reading the energy. You'll be talking with someone and they'll mention some problem and ask for your opinion, and you'll pause, focus slightly, see their answer in their aura, and give it to them. This can be anywhere, not just in your safe space at home. Easy-peasey.

Hanna asked us to describe our grounding cords and went around the room. Wow! A dozen people had a dozen different grounding cords. She said we could try different images for our grounding cords and notice the differences in how our bodies felt. There wasn't a hard and fast rule to comply with on what your grounding cord should look like. This appealed to me a lot. Years of hard and fast martial arts rules were slipping away.

When she got to me, I told her I couldn't see anything but blackness: no grounding cord, no center of the earth, but I heard it when I connected. I heard the sound of bass voices chanting at the center of the planet. It wasn't human voices. It was like the rock breathing. (Must be those dwarf past lives…)

Even though everyone else had described their grounding cords differently from one another, I was still sure that I'd done something wrong.

Hanna said, "Oh! You're a clairaudient! You hear energy!"

I had no clue what that was but felt fantastic that someone recognized some part of me that until that moment had been invisible. She put a name to it, and I had so many questions my mouth stopped working. And it takes a lot for my mouth to stop working, LOL!

HEADS UP! YOUR GROUNDING CORD WILL NEED TO CHANGE OVER TIME, AND FASTER THAN YOU THINK. JUST KEEP PRACTICING. YOU WILL LEARN TO READ THE ENERGY OF YOUR GROUNDING CORD AND RECOGNIZE WHEN IT'S NOT CONNECTED, OR SPLIT, OR BROKEN, OR IN PAST TIME, OR IN FUTURE TIME, OR PLUGGED UP, OR IN NEED OF AN UPGRADE, AND BE ABLE TO HEAL ALL THOSE CONDITIONS JUST BECAUSE YOU NOTICED THEM.

Hanna had us practice again for five minutes, then we took a fifteen minute break. An hour had already passed.

We came back, grounded two more times, and then were assigned the homework of grounding once a day for ten minutes until the next week's class.

During the next class, she asked what questions we had. I remember there were a lot of questions, and that was fun. Everyone had different questions. Some of us had a few of the same questions. Getting clarification turned out to be fun and useful. So guess what's next...

The following questions come from classes I've taken or taught or controlled for another teacher (controlling is matching energy with the teacher in a specific way, keeping the classroom grounded, but allowing the students to ground themselves. This makes for a safer practice space). Some of the questions are asked often and others are rarely asked, but still important to answer.

WHY DO WE SIT IN A CHAIR? WHY NOT ON THE FLOOR?

The reason we sit in chairs is to eliminate confusion. Lots of different meditations take place sitting on the floor, kneeling, crossed legs, lotus position, lying down. Each change in the geometry of the legs introduces possible changes in the flow of energy and the subsequent awareness of that energy. We want to put ourselves in a position to focus on the connections from our first chakra to the center of the planet. Sitting in a chair accomplishes this.

Can you ground to the center of the planet while in other positions, like lying down on the bed or sitting with one knee down and one knee up under a tree? Absolutely! But from a teaching perspective, having everyone set their bodies on chairs makes it easier for the students to see each other's energy and match the lesson being taught. This makes teaching easier and learning easier.

In the modern world, almost everyone sits in chairs throughout their day. Most other times, they are standing or walking, which makes knowing how it feels to ground while sitting in a chair more useful.

I've taught this technique online and some folks with experience meditating or doing yoga tried sitting in a lotus position on the floor and could not see or feel their grounding. As soon as I asked them to sit in a chair, and they did, all that other energy disappeared and they could see what they were doing. The geometry of the lotus position generates too much energy around the lower chakras for a beginner to see through. This creates confusion.

I read one person online and I could not see them grounding at all when they were in a full lotus. If they were grounding, it wasn't using the technique of a line of energy from their first chakra to the center of the planet. As soon as they sat in a chair, we *both* saw their grounding cord. How cool is that?

Also, some people actually have trouble handling having their butts on the ground. Their first chakras don't handle the earth energy very well, and they need the earth energy to be filtered by coming up their legs first, but put them in a chair and that is a non-issue.

There are some that say that the earth energy will blow out your first chakra. While it's possible for some energy to damage a chakra, the more accurate answer to 'will this blow out my chakra' is 'it depends.' There is a healing technique that runs pure, 100% earth energy up through all seven main chakras. This technique clears out a specific set of energies from your space and feels fantastic. Don't fear the earth and its energy. Learn how it works best for you.

Want to try running 100% earth energy? Wait until after the section called Running Energy.

WHY DO WE NEUTRALIZE THE ENERGY THAT WE BRING BACK INTO THE GOLD SUN? IF IT'S OUR ENERGY, WHY IS THIS NECESSARY?

We live energetic lives. Maybe we have an encounter during our day that triggers us to generate a lot of emotions that we didn't really enjoy. Neutralizing these energies makes it so we don't have to relive that experience when we call our energy back.

Imagine someone saying something about you at work that enraged you so much, you had to go for a walk. At your present level of awareness of your energy, you don't notice that your anger is also covering your desk, the floor, the door to the outside, the lawn and parking lot. The trees are handling your energy by grounding it out, but the machines are becoming reservoirs of your anger. Coworkers might be getting pissed at you and not know why. Bringing that energy that you left scattered all over your workplace directly back into your body without neutralizing it would be distracting at best and more likely deeply disturbing. Instead of filling up your energy reserves, you could prolong and amplify the upset from work by reliving that energy, causing yourself harm in real life.

Let that sink in. Neutralizing energy is one way to avoid reliving an undesirable experience. This is similar to ending karma but on a small, personal scale.

This is rehearsing your ability to end karma with someone else on an energy level instead of going through any additional life experiences to end it. Karma is an agreement. Agreements are energy. Energy can be neutralized. Neutralizing the energy of an agreement ends it. This is a more efficient way of ending your karma with someone, and it's more fun than slashing each other with swords again.

Let the sun neutralize your energy before you bring it into your space.

WHY DO WE NEED THE PROGRESSION?
I JUST WANT TO MEDITATE ONCE
A DAY AND BE DONE WITH IT.

That's fine. So meditate once a day. Everyone is on their own path. Our paths crossed in this book, but you shouldn't live by the book. Be yourself. Being yourself is the greatest gift you can bring into this world, both for yourself and for the rest of us.

But if you find yourself running into more and more energetic situations throughout your daily life, at the doggy park, at work, while shopping or dancing or visiting family, knowing how to ground without going into a trance can be useful. However, there's no requirement to follow the progression before you learn what's next, which is running energy.

Be patient. Some of this just takes time. Some of us have lower energy reserves when starting these exercises than others. You progress at the rate that makes you comfortable. Some of us have more energy to release than others, and this is a different problem from not having enough energy. They are related issues but different. Be patient.

If grounding makes you safe enough to let go and heal yourself, running energy accelerates that process. Running energy is one of the next steps in this book.

Key point: You don't need to ground to read energy. You don't need to ground to heal yourself or someone else. Grounding is a tool that accelerates your growth towards reading and healing more effectively, but it's not a requirement for that growth. This is one way, not *the* way.

All the tools in this book have one thing in common. They help reduce your pain. Pain is the main reason so many people do not open up their awareness. The pain is overwhelming so they stay shut down.

Pain is an energy, and energy tools can help you manage your pain.

WHY DO WE GROUND TO THE CENTER OF THE PLANET? WHY NOT JUST THE SOIL OR A ROCK? ISN'T GRAVITY KIND OF OMNIPRESENT? CAN'T WE JUST LET GO AND EVERYTHING WILL BE FINE?

There are multiple reasons for grounding to the center of the planet.

We ground to the center of the planet for the same reason we hug each other into our chests. That's where the fourth chakras are located in our bodies and bringing them closer together creates a healing. A healing is a change in energy for the better. It can be large or small. The fourth chakra of the planet is at the center of the planet. The first chakra of the planet is also at the center of the planet. Our bodies are part of this planet. Connecting with the center of the planet is a healing for our bodies.

We ground our first chakra to both chakras at the center of the planet. The planet's first and fourth chakras change the energy we release from a defined state to a neutral state, and send it back to whoever created it. Isn't it convenient that two chakras can occupy the same space?

This neutralization of energy and returning it to its owners is a big deal. The energy is neutralized. What does that mean? There's no revenge in it. There's no resistance in it. There's no guilt or blame in it. There's no competition in it. There's no emotion in it. So everyone's energy that you release from your space is neutralized and returned to them. This is why there's no karma created by grounding your body to the center of the planet. In fact, you can release karmic energy from your space and it will be neutralized, ending your part in that karma.

We don't ground our fourth chakra to the planet. Our fourth chakra has multiple purposes, one of which is mediating communication between the three chakras below it and the three chakras above it. Grounding it to the center of the planet can mess with that mediation which can become confusing for you.

Energy can abide in objects, and the soil and crust of the earth are objects, not energy centers. Grounding to the center of the planet neutralizes the energy we release. This is better for everyone than just grounding into the soil or crust or a boulder or a tree. This is good spiritual manners. Don't make a mess and leave it for the next person to clean up. Don't leave your dishes in the sink; put them in the dishwasher at the center of the planet.

There is a Taoist story about monks putting their hands on a large boulder and releasing negative energy into that boulder. Over the centuries, the boulder turned black.

Objects can store up energy like a battery, but they won't change the energy that's stored. At least, not in a timely fashion. The center of the planet neutralizes energy instantly. It's neutralized by the healing power of the planet's fourth chakra.

Taking off your shoes and walking on the soil and grass helps release energy from your space. The blades of grass stimulate the nerve endings and pressure points along the bottom of the foot. This is another form of grounding and it works well, but creating a line of energy to the center of the planet can be done anywhere, anytime, and with your shoes on. This makes grounding cords more useful in your daily life. Still, nothing like leaving the stale office air and taking your shoes off to walk barefoot in the grass for a few minutes. It's refreshing. It cools your feet and clears your head.

Gravity is omnipresent, but it doesn't neutralize energy, and we're so used to it that we're mostly blind to it in our daily life. It's a fantastic reference vector: Down! Don't get caught up in the limitations of our words. We use "down" to mean several things. In the context of this paragraph, it only means grounding, which is a verb meaning to release energy into the ground. Ground yourself!

One benefit of using a grounding cord is it makes gravity new again. All those neat feelings that put that big smile on your face when you are grounding? These are the same feelings we have right after we're born. We don't feel gravity without a body. Everything floats. With a body, everything, including energy, becomes tangible. And that's why we smile. We are here now.

A grounding cord is an energy tool one benefit of which is to remind us that we are here now. Ain't that grand?

WHY DO WE STEP THROUGH DISTANCES? OUR BUTTS TO THE CHAIR, THE CHAIR TO THE FLOOR, THE FLOOR TO THE SOIL, ETC? WHY NOT JUST FIRE OFF A GROUNDING CORD ALL IN ONE SHOT TO THE CENTER OF THE PLANET?

Training you to manage your energy in the body is one goal. Having basic, small bites to chew on one at a time is often easier to learn than throwing the whole meal at you at once. It's a good pedagogy technique, but that's not all.

Stepping through distances is a mindfulness technique. Progressively moving your attention deeper into the planet, step-by-step, focuses your attention on your body and yourself.

We need steps. At every juncture of our lives, we will confront possibly overwhelming energy that's too large for us to take on all at once. Our ability to manage our energy depends on how we've practiced managing our energy in similar situations. Our ability to make decisions that are in our best interests and integral with ourselves depends on our ability to notice we've lost our space, our grounding cord is gone, and our minds are spinning out of control. Then we take that first step again and ground, which calms our body and mind, and then take a look at the energy of what's happening - and then take a look at what needs to happen next, what we want to happen next.

Practicing grounding by gently and slowly lowering our attention a little closer to the center of the planet works really well in high stress environments like hospitals, business meetings, and sporting events. Anything with a bunch of people involved is likely to have a lot of energy involved, and we can lose our space. How do we recover? Okay, there's the floor. I'm standing on the floor. Okay, thirty-four more floors before I reach the ground. Oh! I feel the ground now. Wow. OK. There's the center of the planet.

Sometimes, some random stranger near you starts yelling at the top of their lungs and you grab onto the center of the planet without any effort or forethought. This is a wonderful and useful response. When that doesn't happen, if you can't find the center of the planet right away, you can step down in layers. Now you have two ways to find the center of the planet and connect to it. Stepping down to the center of the planet is a very useful beginning technique.

Guess what? In the advanced clairvoyant classes that I took with Lewis Bostwick, the founder of the Berkeley Psychic Institute, he ended every class with this same simple stepwise grounding of noticing the distance between you and the chair, between the chair and the floor, etc. Why? Because the advanced classes were always the most energy-intense night of the week, and a lot of pictures were blown and energies released. You really don't want to walk out of a class like that at 11:00 p.m. while you're still halfway in a deep trance and swimming through the eddies of the energy in your space. You have a higher chance of falling down the stairs on your way out if you're still in trance than if you slowly return your attention fully onto your grounding of your body and make your body real again.

There are times during meditation and guided meditation and giving or receiving readings that your body disappears from your awareness. You are totally focused on reading or healing energy. It's fantastic, but it's not useful for driving your car, or (as was my case) riding your bike, or crossing the street.

Still not sure about the usefulness of steps? Sometimes doing the opposite thing enhances our understanding of the thing itself.

Try this. Sit in a chair. Close your eyes. Say hello to the moon. Now stand next to the moon. Say hello to Mars. Stand next to Mars. Pick any other planet and stand next to it. Breathe.

Now be at the edge of the solar system. Breathe.

Now be at the edge of the galaxy. Just be there and breathe. Deep breath.

Now be at the edge of the universe. Listen to the sound of the universe creating itself. Deep breath.

Come back to our galaxy and breathe. Come back to our solar system and breathe. Take a victory lap around our sun, stand next to the moon, and breathe.

Notice the soles of your feet. Notice your butt. Notice your backbone and neck and head.

Create a gold sun over your head, filled with your own energy, and bring it down into your body and aura. Take a deep breath and let the energy from the gold sun go wherever you need it to go.

WHY DO WE FILL IN WITH A GOLD SUN OF OUR OWN ENERGY? WHY NOT A DIVINE ENERGY? WHY FILL IN AT ALL? DOESN'T GROUNDING BRING OUR ENERGY BACK ANYWAY? SHOULDN'T ALL THIS BE AUTOMATIC AND INSTANTANEOUS?

Your energy is divine. That doesn't make your energy the same as my energy or the same as the supreme being's energy, eh? And while you can fill in with different energies, one goal of this practice is to help you recognize *your* energy and what you are capable of doing with it.

It becomes more automatic over time for most people that practice this style of grounding and filling in. Some folks it takes more practice, and other folks automate it sooner.

Building small habits like filling in with a gold sun is training your clairvoyance. One day, you may be bopping along, grounding and filling in, and low and behold you see something different in your gold sun. Where did that come from? Has it always been there? Whose energy is it?

As you heal yourself through grounding and releasing energy, your awareness will grow and change. Playing with energy by filling in gives you another useful habit and another chance to read energy.

WHY DO I HAVE TO FILL IN WITH A GOLD SUN? DOESN'T GROUNDING FILL ME IN JUST AS WELL? YOU SAID IT CALLS MY ENERGY BACK. WHY DO I HAVE TO FILL IN "MANUALLY"?

You don't have to. And there will be times when you need to get out of trance, answer the phone or the door, and totally change direction away from meditating on your grounding. This is okay. It's good. Grounding is bringing your energy back to your space without any effort on your part, but it's not usually enough, not in the beginning, and it's usually not as much energy as is possible to bring back. And, creating new energy to fill your space is a useful technique.

Those three energies, your highest creative essence, your present time growth, and your affinity for yourself, are just the beginning. These three help focus your attention on healing three basic things in your space, which heightens your awareness of these things in yourself and in others. As you grow your awareness of specific energies, you can add more energies to your sun. You can play and experiment in the safety of your own chair.

Grounding mostly pulls your aura closer to your body. That's not the only energy that you can leave around during your daily life.

Emotions are a prime example. That joy you surrounded someone with when they told you their good news might stay with them. That frustration you threw at your computer when it crashed and lost all your work might stay with the computer.

The energy you used to protect yourself and own your cubicle at the employer you had before your current employer might stay there.

Attention points are another example. You get curious about something or someone and leave your attention there so you can come back to it later. This isn't necessary as much as it's a common behavior that we learn by copying others in school or in the family who do this. If the teacher has all the answers, we should put our attention into the center of their head, lol. No. Don't do that. It's impolite and does not really work as expected. You want to be in the center of your head and let the information come to you. A separation rose helps accomplish this.

Neutralizing the emotions and energies in a gold sun helps prevent you from re-experiencing them when you call them back. You can ground and pull back all of your energy in a neutral state. It takes intent, but that's easy. It doesn't change the energy you're pulling back. This is not to say that you can't neutralize your own energy on its way back to you, if you wish. Your own energy is in your control, especially when you're grounding. This is only limited by your awareness of your own energy.

So why use a gold sun? The gold sun is a focusing device for your awareness, providing a little ritual that builds good habits.

Filling in with a gold sun lets you learn one of the ways that you create energy. Filling the gold sun with your highest creative essence, for instance, is creating the energy of your highest creative essence *at that moment.*

All of your energies can evolve over time, and the techniques in this book accelerate that evolution. The highest is always relative, i.e. your highest creative essence will be different and better from your perspective with a few months of practice. That's a big benefit of filling in with a gold sun. You're always upgrading your energies!

Using a gold sun to neutralize energy as you call it back allows you to practice reading where that energy is coming back from. This benefits you by building reading skills, which expand your awareness. Doing this daily practice enhances your ability to heal yourself.

You can create other new energies to put into your gold sun. Healing energy. Vacation energy. Peaceful energy. Different energies for your body, like sex energy or endurance energy.

Learning to manipulate and control your energy in this way begins to broaden your perspective. For instance, you'll begin to see karma as just another energy.

The first time I saw the energy of karma, this was a big deal for me. I had spent five intense years immersed in Japanese martial arts and culture, right before starting my basic psychic classes at BPI. From where I was standing, karma was anything but just another energy. It was a system. It had someone or something running the system, if you will.

Then I sat side-chair in my first ever reading, eyes closed like the rest of the readers, looking at a rose that represented the person we were reading. I'm on the left end of a line of readers. I'm doing my best to see an image of a rose. Damn thing kept disappearing, lol. The center chair for this reading, which means the reader with the most experience, was coaching me about what details to look at and what they mean.

It had two leaves on the stem, representing the readee's contracts to have children. The stem was long but without roots, so I was looking at someone that had been on this planet a long, long time, but not all the way back to the creation of the planet. For some reason, that just felt good to see. The flower was open and looking directly into a small, golden sun, meaning the readee was open to the information we were giving. There was one dark ring around the stem…

I'm in a huge field of tall grass. A horse is galloping towards me. On the horse sits a Roman soldier, sword drawn, aiming for me. They are almost on top of me. I can hear the hooves pounding and smell the crushed grass.

Without thinking, I dive off my chair to the left to avoid being crushed by the horse…

The control for the reading is laughing as he helps me back onto my chair. The other readers all have their eyes open and are looking at me. The center chair reads me, describing my past life exactly as I was living it a moment before. Everyone starts laughing. The readee is leaning forward, smiling at me, with a knowing look in her eye. She was that soldier.

The center chair asked me to end my karma with the readee. And I'm like, "What?" And she's like, "Create a stick representing your karmic agreement, hold it in your hands, and break it."

So I did, and a cool rush of energy flowed over me. I opened my eyes to see that the readee had relaxed back into her chair, her shoulders down and her face smiling, looking towards the center chair with great curiosity.

Agreements are energy. Karma is energy. Images of sticks are symbols, which are energy. Breaking the stick ended my karma with a real live person sitting right in front of me.

Practicing creating gold suns is also practicing other psychic abilities.

WHAT IF I CAN'T CREATE A GOLD SUN?
WON'T GROUNDING DRAIN MY ENERGY?

Technically speaking, grounding does drain your space, but it should not feel draining. Not being able to imagine a gold sun of your own energy would be something to take a look at.

If you're a beginner, taking a look for yourself may be difficult. Your clairvoyance may still be unreliable. One way around this is using your hands. You can do this standing or sitting, but not lying down. Lying down, you may leave your body and that will reduce what you're aware of and what you remember.

There is this common exercise of holding your hands in front of you, palms facing but not touching. Make a ball of warm energy between your hands and feel its weight, its density. Just feel the ball of energy come into existence. Now clap your hands together, destroying that ball of energy.

Make another ball of energy, this time a cool, smooth energy. Feel its weight and density. Feel how it moves. Clap your hands gently together and destroy that ball.

Without making a ball, feel the energy of one hand using the other hand. Explore the palm, the fingers, the back of the hand, the wrist. Do the same thing with the other hand.

Take a deep breath, relax your shoulders, and look around you.

Pick the hand that feels like it has more energy. If they feel the same, just pick one. Hold that hand, palm up, in front of you. Create a small ball of golden energy on top of that hand. Allow the golden ball to expand and fill with more energy until it's really large. Keep expanding the ball. Allow it to grow larger and larger. If it falls off your hand, that's OK; let it. Let it fill the room you're in.

Now wave your hand, wiggle your fingers. Shake the energy off of your hand and allow it to dissipate on its own.

Walk around for a minute, just getting the blood flow going, noticing the energy in the room, noticing your backbone from top to bottom, noticing the heels of your feet, the toes of your feet, the arches between the heel and toe.

Now hold your hands out, palms facing but wider apart. Create a gold sun between your hands. Put a magnet inside this sun and have the magnet pull your energy from wherever you left it back into the sun. Allow the sun to burn up and neutralize your energy, freeing it of all emotion and bias.

Squeeze this sun between your hands. Just gather it all together and condense it to the size of a tennis ball. Hold it in one hand. Admire it. Toss it up and catch it.

Smash it into your face like a snowball! Mush it all over your face!

Create a gauge with your hands. Let this gauge measure how much energy you have in your body and aura. There's nothing to fix right away. Just observe and see how high or low your energy reserves are. This gauge is like the fuel gauge in a car. It's just a tool that reads from empty to full.

If your energy gauge reads too low, you can't release energy. Your body will not allow it because that feels more like dying than rejuvenating, and rejuvenation is the goal of this grounding meditation.

Maybe you've been teaching yourself about energy, figuring things out as you grow. Being self taught is an excellent way to learn. Anything another human being can do, you can do. This is a useful assumption. Be curious, not judgmental. Observe your energy. The more aware you become of your energy, the easier it is to manage and change.

If you see a giant booger in your aura, just smile and observe. It's probably been there for longer than you can remember. Just observe and breathe. This almost always means that your awareness has grown enough to be aware of that booger for the first time. Maybe a good laugh will shake it loose.

Breathing gives you oxygen, which makes your brain conscious, which enables you to be more spiritually aware. Breathe.

WHEN WE'RE DONE GROUNDING AND HAVE FILLED IN, WHY DO WE BEND OVER AND TOUCH THE FLOOR?

There is a kind of constant in energy work. Whether we are meditating, doing a healing, doing a reading of energy, reading a book, or working, energy tends to build up on the backs of our necks. Why? Our fifth chakra is located behind the cleft in the throat, just in front of the spinal column. The fifth chakra holds our narrow and broadband telepathy, creativity, direct voice trance mediumship, clairaudience (your ability to hear spirit), and, our inner voice (this is how you hear you). You can see that there's a lot going on in the fifth chakra.

Like some electronics, the fifth chakra develops a charge that causes other energies to stick to it, especially in the back of the chakra and the back of the neck. Everyone who is interested in what you're reading in this book right now more than likely has their attention on the back of your fifth chakra to listen in. Attention points are energy. Cool, eh?

Most of the time, it's a normal operating procedure and we don't pay it any attention. It's like how we treat walking on public sidewalks; we have our attention on the destination or our phone or something else other than the sidewalk, and that works just fine. We don't focus much on what's on the sidewalk.

Sometimes the energy on the back of the fifth chakra becomes too much and can cause muscle aches and headaches. Some massage therapists can tell what kind of work you most likely do all day by feeling your neck and shoulders. Massage therapists are psychic healers in disguise.

So you've been grounding for ten minutes and you've loosened up a lot of energy, including the energy that was on the back of your neck when you began grounding. Bending over and touching the floor grounds off that energy through your arms. This is similar to taking your shoes off and walking on the grass, or the Taoists putting their hands on that boulder.

Bending over and touching the floor also starts bringing you out of trance. When you meditate, no matter the style of meditation, you enter a light trance. Trance means your energy and awareness are more focused in your head or higher, out of the body. It's like being spaced out but with a purpose. With practice, all your awareness is on energy and you barely notice your body.

Bending over begins to put your attention back on your body: feeling the floor with your fingertips, stretching your spine. Standing up and stretching your arms above your head, going on tiptoes, requires more of your attention on your motor skills to maintain your balance. Doing all of this with your eyes open begins to disengage your awareness from your clairvoyance and put it on your physical surroundings. This brings you out of trance. You want to be out of trance before you get behind the wheel of your car or hop on your bike. It's safer that way.

WHAT IF I CAN'T SEE IMAGES? HOW WILL I EVER BE ABLE TO DO THIS?

Don't worry about not seeing the images. Instead, just have the idea that your grounding cord exists, and that you created it out of energy. Have the idea that it has two ends. Have the idea that one end can feel around until it finds its connection to the bottom of your first chakra. Maybe this is a feeling of you sitting on something like a boulder or tree stump. Have the idea that the other end can move around until it finds the connection to the center of the planet. Feel for what changes when your grounding cord finds the center of the planet.

New word: Having an idea that something exists is called a **postulate**. You can create a cord that you see. You can also postulate that a cord just exists. I couldn't see my grounding cord the first several times I tried creating one. For two weeks and two classes, I couldn't see anything but blackness, LOL! Some clairvoyant I was!

Like everyone else in class, eventually I could see a little more clearly, and it became less and less work to see, and that became a lot more fun! What changed during my practice was that more and more of the energy covering up my chakras left my space. That's all. It's like the curtains in a theater slowly dissolving until I could see the stage.

TIMEOUT!

Way before I found BPI and learned these techniques, I was a beginning Aikido player and learned a tiny bit about how to feel someone's energy. My dad called one day to tell me that mom had cancer. I flew into Los Angeles and got to the hospital just before she went into surgery.

We talked. She said the cancer was on her right side (this was the 70s and medical imaging was not like today). I held my hand over her abdomen and felt nothing on her right side. Oh well.

But this thought popped in and I moved my hand over her left side. Whoa!

An image of a gray octopus appeared, as clear as if it was in a tidepool. Its tentacles were wrapped around her descending colon, squeezing it tight. The beak of the octopus was buried in her left ovary.

Later that afternoon, I was allowed into her room and she had an ostomy bag on her left side. Total hysterectomy, plus they took out a third of her colon. Other than the diseased right ovary, her right side was clean.

So why was it so hard for me to see my grounding cord? Energy! Taking my first step in controlling my own abilities seemed to have caught the attention of those that didn't approve of my choices of energy work, LOL! A lot of energy rushed into my space to blot out what I could see, so that other energies could remain safely hidden from my prying eyes.

Also, grounding this way lights up more energy than other styles of grounding. Another way of saying this: if my former style of energy work looked at energy through a window, this style looked at energy through a telescope. The blackness was always there; I needed a bigger lens in order to see it.

TIME IN!

WHAT'S THE FIRST THING TO DO WHEN GIVING SOMEONE A HEALING?

When I was giving someone a healing, the first thing I did was ground them to the center of the planet. How do you do that if you're not in trance and you can't see the center of the planet, even as an imaginary symbol? What I did was postulate that a large bell existed at the center of the planet. I postulated that the bell would ring whenever one of my grounding cords connected to the center of the planet. And you know what? I could hear it! The person I was healing could feel it sometimes!

I used a postulate, hearing a bell, to give me feedback on creating a grounding cord.

When the time came that I could finally see a cord, see the center of the planet, and see the connection (like week three of the healing class), I left the bell there because it was so much fun. I changed the postulate a little. Instead of the bell ringing when the cord connected, I created a rose and dropped it down their grounding cord! It hit the bell and rang out loud and clear!

Key point: almost everyone cannot see energy clearly or consistently in the beginning. Part of your growth by reading this book is learning how to correct that inconsistency.

WORKAROUNDS: A SHORT TANGENT.

Every beginner needs workarounds sometimes. Here's a little tangent that offers up some useful workarounds.

Can't see your grounding cord? Feel it! Use your hands.

All of the abilities in your seven major chakras are mirrored in your hand chakras. A dolphin once told me the only thing he envied about the human body was the hands. He also said it was a shame that human beings walked around with the light of the universe in the palms of their hands, unaware that they could change the world. Even dolphins can get an attitude.

You are now becoming aware of your hands. Somebody throwing energy around and it's affecting your body? Point the fingers of one of your hands down, allow the hand to redirect that energy that's making you uncomfortable down into the ground.

Can't feel your grounding cord this morning? Put the palm of one of your hands between your legs if you're sitting or in front of your crotch if you're standing, and recreate the feeling of being grounded.

Useful tip: Need a quick healing? Use both hands with the palms facing your hips and create your grounding cord with your hands. You can even create a hip-width grounding cord! It feels great, but takes some getting used to.

Notice what's happening when you do that. It's really fast. You don't have to be in trance with your eyes closed. It's easier in the beginning to make really big grounding cords, like hip width grounding cords, or a grounding cord the size of your aura. Your hands automagically use your creative and healing abilities because all of your abilities in your seven major chakras are mirrored in your hand chakras. You'll also start to see different images, or see energy with more clarity. This improvement will spill over to what you see when you're in trance.

FOR THOSE THAT ARE NOT SURE THEY ARE EVEN BEGINNERS YET

I was like that in the beginning. Everyone else appeared to be able to do and see stuff that I couldn't. It's OK. You'll be OK. It just takes practice. Be patient with yourself. Energy accumulates on our chakras. Getting rid of the layers of energy can feel like an impossible task in the beginning. But be patient. You have enough time. You have enough energy. You have the will.

BACK TO THE MAIN STORYLINE

So these are the reasons we do each step in this grounding exercise. Each step has a benefit. Each step compliments and strengthens something else.

Some of you may discover that you have a different grounding than any of the images I shared here. That's wonderful! Play with it. Discover all you can about it. Each of us has our own spiritual information, even if we haven't experienced it yet this lifetime. Most of what we get out of spiritual study is reminding us of something we already know.

When I was studying in the clairvoyant training program, I would change my style of grounding depending on the intensity of the energy in a class or reading. Everything began the same, pretty much using the instructions provided at the start of the book. When the energy in a class got too intense, I'd expand my grounding cord to hip width. This enabled me to manage my space during more rapid changes of energy or through bigger waves of energy.

If the energy in a reading got too intense, and I was one of the readers, I'd take a look at the other readers in the room to see what was happening with them. If one of the readers was new in the program, I might be matching their struggles to keep up, their struggle to stay matched at the crown chakra color for the reading, or their general sense of anxiety. Then I'd blow my matching pictures with them and reset my grounding. Resetting means noticing the connections, top and bottom, and saying hello to the planet again.

If I was controlling a reading and the room began to rock and roll, I would stand on the center of the planet with both feet and just be there until things straightened up. (Notice the new postulate, standing on the center of the planet.) I'd give the readers some time to blow their pictures and reset their energy, rather than heal or protect them or teach them (lol wtf did I know!). Healing them would only slow down their growth and understanding of how to handle their energy in a reading.

Some of you may find that you skip all the steps in the basic grounding exercise and find yourself standing on the center of the Earth. The souls of your feet meld with the center of the planet. This is a really powerful grounding. This might be your past life

information on grounding kicking in! It just *might be*, lol. If this works for you, keep doing it. Running energy will work with this just as well. The choice is yours.

If I was controlling at the female trance medium healing clinic, I would add some brown to my grounding cord. The energy in that clinic was always too intense for a lot of people, especially those with male bodies, but I found myself quite comfortable standing in that energy. Women doing the readings were leaving their bodies and allowing another being to come in and take over their body for an hour or so. This meant these women were running all the combinations of their energy higher than usual, their crown chakras set at a white color, sometimes a silver white, and they had no grounding.

Keeping the room safe and their bodies safe was my job. Grounding my male body with a little extra brown male energy was all it took for me to handle the female trance medium energy bouncing off of everything in the room. It was intense and fun, kind of like a big roller coaster for spirits!

At the trance medium clinics, keeping their bodies safe meant something different. I did not ground their bodies. That would have messed up the vibration they were setting for bringing in a being. What I did was when they picked a being to bring in, I was kinda like that guy at the train station that says, "This train is full. You'll have to wait for the next one." I was saying that to all the other beings a few feet above our heads that really wanted to experience coming into a human body. Sometimes it was quite the rowdy crowd on the ceiling, LOL!

Speaking of controlling, you can ground a room. A room doesn't have a chakra, but if you create cords to all eight corners of a room, meaning the four corners at the ceiling and the four corners at the floor, then join those eight cords to a point in the center of the room, you now own the room. If you then create a grounding cord from that center point to the center of the planet, you now own a grounded room. Both steps are useful. They can be done separately, but I always found them to be more effective when used together.

For instance, all the readers were taught to own the room for themselves. Grab the eight corners and bring them to a point that you create in the center of the room (if the ceiling is 8 feet high, the center point will be 4 feet up from the floor). And that was it. Sit. Close your eyes. Ground and run your energy. Own the room for yourself. Create protection and separation roses. Blow your matching pictures. Read.

Note: you can also ground a room just by connecting the floor with a big grounding cord to the center of the planet. This works, too. Play with both concepts. Make up your own concept for grounding a room. It's a really useful exercise to play with energy this way. Play with grounding the floor vs. grounding the bottoms of the walls vs. owning the room and grounding the center of the room. See what's different in the energy in the room with each method.

One instructor, Hanna Jane, would grab all eight corners of the room and tie them around her waist. This grounded the room through her space. On the plus side, there were fewer grounding cords to keep track of. On the negative side, there were fewer grounding cords and all the energy in the room would pass through her space. She didn't complain about it, and I know she could see how everyone else grounded, so who am I to judge her grounding information? I tried her way once; uh uh. Not for me, lol.

For grounding a car, I grab the four wheels and create grounding cords for each one to the center of the planet. Really useful in the mountains where the visuals and pulls to the side screw with your equilibrium.

There was a gathering of clairvoyant students and graduates of the program. We had a party in the mountains! Music and drink. Lots of conversations, even on topics that were "off the books" so to speak. Why does this instructor behave like that? What happens after graduation? Wow! Look at the group of women creating some mischief over there!

I had arrived with someone, but that person left without me. (Psychics are no different than anyone else sometimes, LOL!) One woman who hadn't been drinking offered a ride home to whoever needed one, and five of us accepted.

The driver's car was a small sedan. Four people agreed that me and my long legs should get the front passenger seat. (Even drunk psychics can be kind, just like anyone else.) Four ladies piled into the back seat, I got into my seat, and away we went.

First thing I noticed was how drunk the ladies in the back seat were. They were loud. They laughed at anything and everything. They pushed and tickled each other. The second thing I noticed was we were going downhill on a mountain road. The third thing I noticed was just how frightened the driver was.

She was doing her best to ground, but the energy from the back seat was fast and overwhelming. She was not intoxicated, just afraid.

We had all had something to drink except the driver, so we were looser than normal. I had a few beers. The ladies in the backseat were hammered on cheap margaritas. The party had been great fun, with dancing and good conversations, so the desire to continue the party energy was strong.

Then the brakes locked up, the tires squealed, and we skidded towards the crash barrier on my side of the road.

The driver eased off the breaks as our speed bled away enough for the wheels to regain traction. She looked at me with a combination of apologetic embarrassment and a plea for help. She had control of the car again, but was seriously shaken. The car was heavier than she was used to.

The laughter from the back seat only got louder and more raucous after the skid. If ignorance is bliss, then drunken ignorance is heaven with slurred speech.

I grounded the driver. She relaxed a little and her energy came back closer to her body. She glanced at me. I grabbed all four tires and grounded them to the center of the planet. I created a bubble around the car and grounded the bubble. I grounded the engine and drive-train for good measure. Blowing a gasket or overheating on a mountain road was not desired. The driver smiled.

I kept one hand between my legs, the palm facing my grounding cord, grounding my body from the first chakra and maintaining a hip width grounding cord. Basically, I slid into a similar kind of control space that we were taught to use in readings, but on steroids, and with one exception: the driver.

In a reading, all the readers ground themselves. If they don't, or they lose their grounding during the reading, the control will remind them but will not create grounding cords for them. This gives the readers good practice with checking on their grounding cord. This helps the readers navigate through, for instance, death pictures in the readee's space from this or past lives. See a death picture? Check your grounding cord next.

The friend driving the car was not doing a reading. The death pictures in her space about falling down a canyon were real, meaning they were a real possibility and an imminent threat. We could do something stupid and die.

So I grounded myself, then grounded her, grounded the four wheels of the car, and grounded the bubble I created around the car.

I did not ground the people in the back seat. As long as the driver remained in control of her car, there was no need. If the passengers had begun to yell at the driver or touch her in a distracting way, then I'd ground them and end the party.

The backseaters had all fallen asleep not long after the car came out of that skid, so the grounding of the car gradually took out the party energy from their spaces anyway, and they passed out.

I created a gold sun over the car and the driver. I filled it with the driver's certainty and control, and brought it down into her space, which actually woke her up more. She knew where everyone lived and delivered each reveler to their home.

One by one, we woke up the people in the backseat and waited for them to untangle themselves and go inside their homes. I grounded the walks and front porches of their homes until they got inside. They had sobered up enough that all but one didn't need my help walking from the car to their front door.

I was the last one she dropped off. I was checking her fatigue levels to make sure she was safe to drive. She smiled a big smile and thanked me for keeping everyone grounded during the last hour and drove away, arriving at her home without incident. I set a timer on the bubble and grounding cords on her car that made them self-destruct and the energy return to me through the grounding of the car.

What was the bubble for? It had a few jobs. One was containing our combined energy to make it easier to keep grounded. So, it was a focus technique. Another was providing some warning of the road conditions in our immediate path. Containing your energy helps focus it on more details inside the containment area. Another was making our situation funny. I used the image of a bumper car when I created the bubble. The same kind of bumper car that's found at carnivals, that are intended to run into each other. This helped remove resistance from the bubble.

There is quite a bit of truth in the saying, "You become what you resist." I didn't want us to be hit head on by another driver for no other reason than we were totally resisting the idea of being hit head on by another driver. Bumper cars bump, but it's fun, not life threatening.

In a very real sense, what I did became a mockup, which is a method for manifesting what you want. A mockup uses your imagination and intent to create an image. I created quite a specific wish or intent, and a vivid image of a safe journey home for us all. I set the energy of our traveling party by grounding us, grounding our immediate surroundings, and having a clear intent provided by an image.

By keeping the mockup at the vibration of amusement, the trip home became more like a fun game than a defensive posture.

WHAT ABOUT KIDS?

My wife and I were visiting my really good friend from my early years and his wife. We learned that he and his wife hadn't had a date since the birth of their second child two years before.

Well, that won't stand! LOL! We offered to babysit for the evening so that they could go have an adult dinner at an adult pace with nothing but adult conversation.

What do you do with a three year old boy and two year old girl? We taught them to ground and play with energy, of course.

I placed a big tree branch at the center of the planet and asked them if they could see it. Their eyes got big and so did their grins. They nodded their heads. I asked if they were sure they could see it, teasing them a little. They laughed and yelled, "yes!"

I asked them to feel their tail bones. Then I asked them to create a monkey tail big enough to wrap around that branch at the center of the planet.

Big eyes got even bigger!

We sat like that, just smiling and enjoying grounding. The boy was the big surprise. He was 'late' growing out of his 'terrible twos' according to my friend. I have no idea what that meant: ADHD? bedwetting? No matter. He and his little sister were grinning and enjoying grounding.

My wife held out her hand, "Can you see the pie I'm holding?" They looked astonished, and then nodded their heads. My wife then hit the boy in the face with the pie and asked him what flavor it was. Wifey is laughing. Boy is laughing. Girl is wondering, "Where's my pie?"

Boy says, "Chocolate!" and laughs more.

I hold out my hand, smiling a wicked smile at the girl. She gets the giggles so bad, she falls off her stool. I tell her that she has to be sitting with her monkey tail holding onto that branch before we can play 'pies.'

She scrambles up and onto the chair, grabs that branch with her tail, and sticks her face out.

I deliver the energy pie and she yells, "Lemon!"

The boy hits me with his pie. "Raspberry!" I yell. The girl hits my wife. It's a pie battle royale!

An hour later, they've laughed themselves out and are asleep for the night. Five hours later, the parents return. We tell them about the evening and the pie game, and they're a little jealous that they didn't get to play. So, naturally, my wife and I hit them in their faces with energy pies!

Notice the flavor. This was a postulate. We created the pies to be the favorite flavor of each kid. We didn't know the kids at all, so guessing was useless, and asking them would spoil the surprise.

I got raspberry pie from the boy. It's not my favorite. The boy didn't know that and wasn't aware of our postulate, but he knew his mom's favorite flavor. He was guessing what I would like based on an adult in his family. Fun!

WHY ARE OUR HANDS RESTING ON OUR LEGS WITH OUR PALMS FACING UP?

Peeking ahead are we? Oh, that's cheating, using your precognition like that! No looking ahead!

Well, maybe a little looking ahead. Alright, I'll tell you. It's preparation for what comes next, which is running energy. Almost next.

So these are the reasons we do each step in this grounding exercise. Each step has a benefit. Each step compliments and strengthens something else.

Grounding began the process of you healing yourself, making your body feel safer, and waking up your spiritual abilities. Running energy accelerates that process. Amusement and being in the center of your head also accelerates that process!

Review of grounding and filling in

Sit in a chair and close your eyes. Take a deep breath and exhale, relaxing your body as your breath leaves your lungs.

Create a grounding cord between your first chakra at the base of your spine and the center of the planet. Your grounding cord can look any way you wish. Allow any energy that is not yours to release and take a deep breath.

Call your energy back into a gold sun and neutralize it, then bring that gold sun down into your space.

Continue to ground and release for ten minutes or so.

Ground. Say hello to the center of the planet. Ground. Say hello to your body. Ground. Allow gravity to heal your space. Ground.

Create a gold sun over your head. Fill it with your highest creative essence, your present time growth vibration, and your affinity for yourself. Bring all of this energy down through the top of your head, letting it go wherever you need it.

Bend over and touch the floor.

Sit up. Open your eyes. Notice the objects closest to your body on either side.

Stand up and stretch up onto your tiptoes. Smile. Laugh. Breathe. Take a break and walk around. Have something to drink, maybe something to eat.

TL;DR: ground from your first chakra to the center of the planet. Call your energy back into a gold sun and neutralize it, then bring that gold sun down into your space. Ground and allow gravity to heal you for ten minutes. Fill in with a gold sun filled with your three new energies. Dump out.

ONE MORE EXERCISE.

Sit down. Close your eyes. Ground yourself and take a deep breath. Release energy for a few breaths. Yawn big! Fill in.

Ground. Create an image of a rose in front of you. Have the flower represent your first chakra, have the stem represent your grounding cord, and have a rock beneath the stem represent the center of the planet.

Notice if the stem connects to the flower. Notice if the stem connects to the rock. Don't move the rock! Just lengthen the stem to connect to the rock, LOL!

This is taking a look at your grounding cord and assessing its health. This is your first simple version of what is called an "energy check." It's the preferred way to diagnose problems with the techniques, or tools, that you are learning in this book. This is tool maintenance.

Over time, you will change your energy. No one can tell how fast you will change, but change you will. What will happen is your tools, in this case your grounding cord, will drift out of sync with your energy.

Change in this context means your energy is rearranging itself to the new configurations created by your release of energy from your space and replacing what was released with new energy of your own.

When enough change happens, your tools can drift into past time and out of sync with where the "new" you vibrates.

If you drop your grounding cord and recreate it without bringing your idea of it into present time with your energy, it won't work as well as it could. Sometimes, it won't work at all. It's like your template for your tools needs to be refreshed and updated on a regular basis.

Every beginner does this. It's not a flaw. It's part of how we learn to manage our energy. Be patient.

By the way, "dropping your grounding cord" means exactly that. Disconnect it from your first chakra, let it go, and gravity will take it away to the center of the planet and neuter… oops! neutralize the energy.

Disconnect your grounding cord and let it go. Listen to the sound it makes as it falls and hits the center of the planet.

The simple act of taking a look at your grounding cord and reading its details brings your attention onto just that tool, and this tends to bring it into the present, which means reading it brings it in sync with your energy and abilities now.

Another cool way to refresh your grounding cord is to drop something.

Grounding works with gravity. Gravity is a constant. In the institute, we had baskets of crayons in every room. This was for coloring in the aura charts during the readings. In class, everyone would pick a crayon out of the basket being passed around. When everyone had a crayon, we were told to drop it on the floor.

How stupid is that!? Everybody had this thought the first time the crayon dropped, LOL!

Then we were told to pick it up and drop it again, observing why it dropped. Oh, that's not nearly as stupid. I can feel something change in my space.

Then we picked it up and dropped it, over and over, for like five minutes. Everyone's energy changed. Everyone became more grounded. Everyone lightened up and smiled.

This is basic tool maintenance. It is normal for your tools to lag behind you in your growth. Sometimes during the clairvoyant training program I would go for weeks without needing to update my tools. Reading so often almost made the updates automatic, but every now and then I would blow a picture that rattled and changed everything. Even worse, every now and then I'd get a picture lit up that I couldn't blow. That's when I needed an energy check the most. It's a mini-reading on the pictures that are affecting your tools.

There's a formal section called Energy Checks which goes into much greater detail, coming up after the tools have all been introduced. If you are curious and want to jump ahead, by all means, please do so!

Amusement!

Why amusement? What is that for? It seems disrespectful or shallow to laugh in a spiritual context.

The energy of amusement is the spiritual Teflon of energies. This is useful, eh? Amusement helps stuck energy get moving again. It's the opposite of disrespect where your energy is concerned. Too bad for everyone else's energy that you release!

You aren't laughing at someone else's energy. The oil in an engine isn't disrespecting the many moving parts of the engine by making them frictionless. You are being amused. This means you are being playful and not taking the energies that you uncover in your space seriously. After all, they've probably been in your space much longer than you've been aware of them, and you still got to where you are.

Amusement is another accelerator.

Most people have had an experience where they felt stuck, frustrated, or helpless. Those feelings are energies and amusement can help break them up. You might have to experience the stuck energies, but finding your amusement about being stuck shortens how long you stay stuck. You may not be able to change the terrible situation you are in, but you can change how you react to it.

For the beginners who aren't even sure they are beginners yet, or for those practitioners who have been seriously pursuing their spiritual goals for far too long without getting what they want, let me reiterate: amusement is another accelerator. Be patient. Things will change faster than you hope.

Grounding accelerates your ability to heal yourself and protect yourself on an energy level. Amusement accelerates grounding. Amusement is your secret weapon that gives you a magic door to escape being stuck. Amusement can control your reactions when you uncover something unpleasant in your space that's been there for a very long time. Taking these kinds of energies seriously tends to make them more stuck.

It's like you're wandering around your grandfather's farm, just washing yourself in the energies from another time, enjoying the overflow of memories, many of them not even yours. You look in the barn and find the most disgusting, rusted piece of farm machinery you've ever seen. You don't know what it's for or why it's still there. You want to move it but everything is rusted solid.

Well, if you put some oil on the rolly bits and come back tomorrow, it might just roll away the way you want.

When you find an energy, black and deadly, hiding in your aura behind your fourth chakra, put some amusement on it and it might just roll away the way you want.

When you run energy (another accelerant), you will quickly begin to uncover more energy in your space that is not yours. Sometimes, the darker the energy is, the longer the energy has been there, stuck. If it's been there a long time, it will seem like it doesn't want to be released. In some cases, that may be true, but bringing in your amusement solves that. When you laugh, it's like taking your internal space through a spiritual car wash. All that stuff just washes off, and the bits that don't wash off you can get in the next wash cycle, which means in your next meditation.

Like the rusty old farm implement, it may just take some time to remove a chunk of stuck energy. Fretting over it can ruin your life in the short term. Being amused that you found something *so stuck* that it's created dependencies on many other layers of energy can enable you to preserve all that's going right in your life while your amusement dissolves those dependencies and begins to release that funky old energy.

Sometimes, when you feel so bad that you don't even want to try to ground, you just want to crash on the couch and disappear, try smiling. You don't even need a reason to smile. Hit that couch and smile. The act of smiling lifts the energy of your body on a neurochemical level. Endorphins or some other fancy word is involved, but there is a deep energy involved as well. So, smile. Lay on the couch and smile.

Then laugh. It's not funny, you say. It hurts like hell, you say. You can't possibly laugh right now. Just go to your room, or look down at your feet, smile, and fake a laugh. Even a slight smile and a chuckle that no one can hear works for you. Fake laughs lead to real laughs as your amusement breaks up the energy that's stuck.

If everything is energy, and if amusement is the slickest spiritual lubricant, then laughter is the trigger that opens the magic escape hatch.

Key point: We tend to think of triggers as always being negative. Why not have a trigger that is positive? That's what amusement is.

Tell yourself a bad joke or a dad joke. Here's a favorite of mine that I made up. "What is the opposite of unbridled lust? Dressage sex."

Horse people either hate this or love it. Or they love it but are embarrassed to admit it. When I recall telling horse people this joke, the memory generates amusement for me.

There is a phrase, "lift your spirits," that is derived from amusement. This can be seen in a progression of helping someone else out who is stuck.

It often begins with you asking them, "what's wrong?" Then, a little later, you follow up with "well, it could be worse," or maybe pivots to "it's not that bad," and soon the smiles and chuckles follow, and then the stuck person returns to the land of the living, their spirits lifted.

You didn't solve any problems on their behalf. In fact, the problems are still as real as ever. A lifted spirit stands above its problems, seeing them from an amused perspective.

Amusement is not the highest energy. I don't really care for hierarchies as they tend to be artificial and program our expectations of what we will see when we read. If your only tool is a hierarchy, then everything in the world looks like a hierarchy, even when it's not. Interesting filter on our spiritual awareness, eh? The better question is, "what's the most useful energy for this task?" For releasing stuck energy, amusement is hard to beat.

Amusement is the slickest energy, which is why the saying, "laughter is the best medicine" makes sense to us. We know, on some level, that amusement helps us heal.

Key point: Amusement is energy. You can create energy. Amusement is an energy that you can create for yourself on demand to heal yourself, protect your perspective, and move through static and strong energies with more grace. You can add some amusement to your gold suns. You can create your raw amusement in the palm of your hand and touch it to your face. You can bathe yourself in your amusement with the palms of your hands.

Amusement enhances your awareness, your sense of safety, and your sense of certainty. Amusement is the gateway energy to enthusiasm. Enthusiasm feels like invincibility.

TELL ME AGAIN WHY WE LAUGH? WHAT'S WITH ALL THE CORNY JOKES AND PUNS? DOESN'T THIS BECOME ANNOYING?

Every student that walks into the institute brings with them something painful. All the students are adults and have had enough life experience to have been bruised or battered in some way. There is a strong need in these beginning students to not have their secret pain exposed.

"Don't take life so seriously. You're not going to get out of it alive!" "Don't walk around half-tranced!" "Yes, it's all your parents' fault, but you mocked it up!" "What's the definition of British foreplay? Forty-five minutes of clearing your throat!" "What's the definition of Irish foreplay? 'Brace yourself, Mary!'"

The crassness is obvious. The purpose of it is not as obvious.

Everyone walking into a psychic institute has secrets, some of them painful. Incest-rape (one of my classmates). Almost beaten to death by an alcoholic parent (another of my classmates). A broken heart and a shattered heart chakra caused by naive relationship expectations and betrayal (not a classmate: me).

None of this pain is safe to expose the first time a student walks into the institute because they don't have the energy management skills to deal with it yet, and yet there are no secrets in a psychic institute.

So what do you do when you're running an institute? You teach the students how to better manage their energy and buy them the time they need by telling lots of jokes to get them laughing. Because just beneath the surface lies that pain, and they need time to learn how to dispose of that pain. Laughter buys them time. Laughter loosens up stuck energy. Laughter makes classes more fun, so the students tend to come back every week to class and make steady progress on their healing of themselves.

Notice that the humor is not targeted at individuals. Groups? Yep. Puns? As silly as possible. Many of the jokes and puns got more groans than laughs.

What did the psychic say to the other psychic when they passed on the street? You're OK. How am I?

In a psychic institute, in my experience, the definition of enlightenment is "Lighten up, dude!" Laughter is part of creating a safe environment in which to do energy work. All energy work is personal.

You're reading a book about energy work. Have fun creating a safe space with as much amusement as you can imagine, and your energy work will flow much more smoothly. Ground and say hello to the center of the planet. It's a different kind of happy place, the center of the planet. Our home is more amused by us than one would expect. It puts some difficulties into a much better perspective.

I reiterate: Amusement enhances your awareness, your sense of safety, and your sense of certainty. Amusement is the gateway energy to enthusiasm. Enthusiasm feels like invincibility. Being amused, especially at yourself, is a kindness. Laughing at yourself is a kind of self care, or self compassion.

Real story: One of my classmates in the clairvoyant training program was attacked in her apartment. Two men followed her home and tried to rape her, but her neighbors intervened and called the cops.

Meanwhile, word got round to me and half a dozen other men in the program and we showed up before the cops. We gave her a healing and a reading, pointing out the past life pictures she shared with her two attackers. Karma was at play.

The cops show up. She's laughing because she already blew the pictures of the trauma she just experienced. One cop said, "If you're not one of the rapists, would you please wait outside?" which cracked us all up!

This is basic energy management in the real world.

Center of the Head

L et's find the center of your head. This is the place where you are most neutral to the energies you see or feel or know, and this gives you a huge advantage as you open up.

Try this. Be in the center of your head. Put all of your attention and awareness in the center of your head.

The center of your head is roughly between the tops of your ears and a line connecting the center of your forehead and the dimple where the back of your neck meets your skull. You can touch the tops of your ears with your fingertips and imagine a line connecting your fingertips. Then touch your forehead and neck dimple and imagine a line. Where the two lines cross is approximately the center of your head. This is in front of and just above your sixth chakra.

The center of your head is not your third eye. The center of your head is not your pineal gland. The center of your head is a place where all information flows towards you, and you are more neutral to that information.

Try this again. Be in the center of your head. Put your attention all on this space.

Another really cool thing that happens when you get into the center of your head is that instead of seeing a single portrait in two dimensions, your focus spreads around you 360 degrees! It's a neat sensation to see behind and in front of you at the same time! And above, below, and to each side. When we read, however, even though we are in the center of our head, our focus narrows down to some detail in the person we are reading or in ourselves.

With practice, you can make the slight shift between focusing on who you're reading and unfocusing to see all around you. This is useful because it allows you to control the room you're reading in more easily.

The primary benefit of being in the center of your head is this space is neutral ground. From here, you can look at anything without judging it. This saves you from resisting something that turns your stomach to see or feel. Not resisting it enables you to more easily release whatever matching energies may be in your space.

For example, if you read or heal someone that has a childhood trauma that is similar to your own childhood trauma, being in the center of your head enables you to release more of the energy of your trauma, ground it out of your space, and have your energy return to you as neutral, fresh energy for you to create something new.

All information tends to flow towards you. The best place to decide what information is important and what is not is in the center of your head.

So you're sitting in the center of your head and can't stay there for long. You feel drowsy until you pop up just outside of your head, and then feel more awake.

What's going on? Welcome to everyone else's energy in the center of your head!

Your energy doesn't put you to sleep or feel unconscious. Your energy wakes you up.

So what's that mean? One explanation that works most of the time is you have more of your energy outside of your body than inside, so getting just outside of your body raises your awareness. It's very common for beginners and those that have practiced some styles of meditation to be just above their body when they begin to ground. Getting you comfortably in your body is more the goal of this book.

Another explanation that works is that everyone else's energy is in the center of your head. "I wonder what <your name goes here> is thinking about?" They put their attention in the center of your head and some or all of the energy of their attention gets stuck there.

Does the teacher have all the answers? Then the students get into the center of the teacher's head. This doesn't happen in all classrooms. Every teacher is different, but it's common enough that you will likely recognize it when you see it during a reading or healing.

Some people have more capacity than others for leading a normal, healthy life with everyone in their friends and families having some energy in the center of their head. Some of us have less capacity in this respect. Having less capacity to lead a normal life with psychic abilities is often described as being a highly sensitive person, or an empath. This is quite manageable, though. Learning to recognize your energy and managing it better is another goal of this book.

Why do you go unconscious when you get in the center of your head? Simple. It's filled with energy that is not yours. You cannot create with it. You cannot heal with it. It doesn't have your awareness in it, and, most importantly to this book, you cannot see or feel energy with it. In your space, someone else's energy usually appears darker than your energy, and more stagnant. The coloring could be anything from white to black to any color in between. The key is you can't control it and it doesn't generally flow like your energy.

Here's a neat way to clean out the center of your head.

Create an image of a rose in front of your body. Take hold of the stem of that rose with your hand. Stick the flower through your forehead and into the center of your head. Swish it around to loosen up the dark energy that you've been staring at.

Have the rose suck up the dark energy and then pull that rose out and throw it on the ground. This is your psychic rinse cycle!

Create another rose and repeat the process. It really helps if you laugh at yourself while doing this. It is kinda silly looking, eh? Imagine doing this while you're sitting in Starbucks, LOL! The looks you will get!

Laughter is a wonderful energy for cleaning other energies out of your space. Imagine yourself doing this hand-to-forehead thing in a really nice restaurant with everyone staring at you thinking God knows what, LOL! The waiter shows up to take your order and you're like, "One moment please, I'm dusting off the center of my head," and your hand is making circles in front of your forehead.

Yeah, don't do that! Instead, use your hand in the privacy of your home until you can create an image of a rose and move it into your head, swish it all around, gather up all the foreign energy, remove it to a safe distance away from your face, and explode that rose. Using your hand when you begin is really powerful. The hand chakras mirror all of the psychic abilities, including all of your healing abilities, in your seven main chakras. Using your hands in the beginning makes learning to clean out your head without having your eyes closed and holding an image of a rose in your hand easier. Easier means faster.

An image of a rose has many uses. That's why I wrote several sections of roses. Does a rose have magical meanings? Maybe. Maybe not. On one hand, it's just a neutral image of a rose. On the other hand, it's as magical as you want it to be.

Notice that nasty pile of roses accumulating at your feet? You've made another mess! It's okay. Just create a grounding cord for your body or notice the grounding cord you already have and then instead of throwing the roses at your feet, you can let them fall down your grounding cord. I like to kick them with my toes like little soccer balls, kicking them to the back of the net before falling down my grounding cord.

Fill in with a gold sun. Especially fill in the center of your head. Shine a little light on that area!

Now be in the center of your head. Is it a little more comfortable this time? If not, don't worry about it. Most beginners have to clean house one layer at a time while they get the hang of these tools. You can't see the dirt for all the dirt on top of the dirt.

Those with more experience doing energy work usually take to this like a duck to water.

Being in the center of your head enables you to be more neutral to all energies. Being neutral to energy means you are much less likely to be disturbed by what you see and get stuck. Getting stuck less often means you grow your skills faster and get what you want faster.

Being in the center of your head is another accelerant.

Now let's begin to run some energy. This also helps with the housekeeping in the center of your head.

Running Energy

RUNNING ENERGY PART 1:

Try this. Sit on a chair. Close your eyes. Rest your hands on your thighs with the palms facing up.

Drop and recreate your grounding cord. Notice its attachment to the center of the planet. Call back your energy from your day into a gold sun over your head. Let that sun burn up and neutralize your energy, then bring it down through your crown chakra and into anywhere in your space that you need it.

Check your energy gauge to see if you're full, and if not, bring in another gold sun.

Be in the center of your head. Create a rose and clean out the center of your head. Bring that rose out in front of you and blow it up.

Notice the bottoms of your feet. Between the ball of each foot and the heel, near the top of the arch, is a small ball of energy called the foot chakra. Allow the earth energy to flow into your feet chakras, fill them up, and spin them, cleaning them out.

There is a channel in each leg for earth energy. It begins at the foot chakra, rises up through the ankle, between the bones of the lower leg, through the knee, through the thigh to the hip, then into the first chakra at the base of the spine. Look at the channel in your left leg. Look at the channel in your right leg.

Allow the earth energy to flow out of your feet chakras up the leg channels, and into the first chakra, filling up the first chakra, spinning it around, and cleaning it out. Then allow it to flow down your grounding cord to the center of the planet, taking everything you've released with it to be neutralized and returned to whoever owns it.

Take a deep breath. Notice your grounding cord. Notice your feet chakras and the energy flowing through your legs to your first chakra and down your grounding cord.

Create a gold sun over your head. Fill it with your highest creative essence, your present time growth vibration, and your affinity for yourself. Bring that gold sun down into your crown chakra and fill in your space.

Bend over and touch the floor. Stand up and stretch with eyes open.

Notice how your body feels. If you need a short break, take it now. If not, just relax completely, take a few deep breaths, and enjoy the moment.

Do it again. Close your eyes. Notice your grounding cord. Notice the bottoms of your feet and your feet chakras. Allow the earth energy to fill up your feet chakras, spinning them and flowing into your leg channels. Watch the earth energy pass the knee, the hip, and flow into your first chakra, filling it up and spinning it.

Allow the earth energy to flow into your grounding cord, letting gravity remove it from your space, down into the center of the planet, where the energy is neutralized and returned to whoever owns it, including you. Just let it go and gravity does the rest.

Create a gold sun over your head. Fill it with your highest creative essence, your affinity for yourself, your present time growth vibration, and a little of your amusement. Bring the sun down into your crown chakra, filling in your space, especially the center of your head.

Bend over. Touch the floor. Breathe. Open your eyes. Stand up and stretch your arms above your head, standing on your tiptoes. Come all the way out of trance and take a short break. Walk around. Get some tea or coffee or water. Walk around some more.

RUNNING ENERGY PART 2:

Notice the top of your head and your crown chakra. Your crown chakra is a ball of energy on the top of your head. Sometimes, it looks like a discus shape. It can cover the whole top of your head or it can close down very small, to the size of a golf ball. It can feel either cool to your fingertips or warm. Sometimes it feels electric.

Feel your crown chakra with your fingertips or the palm of your hand. Move your hand side to side and front to back, passing over your crown chakra and off of it. Feel the difference when your hand is directly over your crown chakra, and when your hand or fingers pass over the edge of your crown chakra.

Chakras are small balls of energy. There are seven main chakras. The first five, starting at the bottom and counting up, are just in front of the spine. The sixth is in the middle of the head. The seventh is on the top of the head.

Try this. Sit on a chair. Close your eyes. Relax your hands on your thighs, palms up. Notice your grounding cord. Notice your feet chakras. Allow the earth energy to flow through your feet chakras, through your leg channels to your ankles, knees, and hips, into your first chakra, filling it up and spinning it, and down your grounding cord.

Notice the golden energy that is above and around you. It stretches in all directions as far as the eye can see. This is the cosmic energy. Cosmic means universal and everywhere. Most folks see this as a soft golden color of energy. Cosmic energy has a specific vibration, but people may see the same vibration as slightly different colors.

Allow the cosmic energy to flow into the back of your crown chakra, down the two channels from your crown chakra through the back of the skull to the back of the neck, down along either side of the spine past each vertebra, down to the tailbone and through the tailbone to the back of the first chakra.

Allow the cosmic energy to fill the first chakra, spinning and mixing with the earth energy, cleaning out the chakra.

Allow a mixture of cosmic energy and earth energy, about 90% cosmic energy and 10% earth energy, to flow out the two channels on the top of the first chakra to the bottom of the second chakra, which is a ball of energy in front of the spine, a little below and behind the navel. Let this mixture fill up and spin the second chakra, cleaning out the chakra.

Allow the mixture to flow up the two channels out the top of the second chakra to the bottom of the third chakra, behind the solar plexus and in front of the spine. Let the mixture fill up and spin the third chakra, cleaning out the chakra.

Allow the mixture to flow up the two channels out the top of the third chakra to the bottom of the fourth chakra, behind the sternum in the center of the chest and in front of the spine. Let the mixture fill up and spin the fourth chakra, cleaning out the chakra.

Allow the mixture to flow up the two channels out the top of the fourth chakra to the bottom of the fifth chakra, behind the cleft at the bottom of the neck and in front of the spine. Let the mixture fill up and spin the fifth chakra, cleaning out the chakra.

There are channels coming off of the sides of the fifth chakra, running across the shoulders and down the arms to the hand chakras in the centers of the palms. Allow some of the earth and cosmic energy mixture to flow down each arm channel, filling up and spinning each hand chakra, and flow out the hand chakras through your palms. Have this energy form fountains out of the hands, filling up your aura and spinning it, cleaning out the hand chakras and your aura.

Allow the rest of the mixture to flow up the two channels out of the top of the fifth chakra and into the bottom of the sixth chakra, near the center of the head, between the tops of your ears and a little towards the back. Allow the mixture to fill up and spin your sixth chakra, cleaning it out.

Take a deep breath.

Allow the mixture of cosmic and earth energies to flow up the two channels out of the top of the sixth chakra and into the bottom of the seventh chakra, filling it up and spinning it, cleaning it out. Allow the mixture to form a giant fountain that reaches all the way to the top of your aura, flowing down the edges of your aura all the way under your feet and down your grounding cord.

Take a deep breath. Notice your grounding cord. Notice your earth energy. Notice your cosmic energy. Notice the fountains coming out of your crown chakra and your hand chakras.

Create a gold sun and fill in. Open your eyes. Bend over and dump out. Stand up and stretch.

Running energy explained.

Running energy is allowing the earth and cosmic energy to flow through your body, in specific channels in the legs, arms, and beside the spine, and up through all the chakras into a fountain out the top of the head. The fountain cleans out the aura and takes whatever you've released down your grounding cord.

This is not kundalini energy, nor does it use the kundalini energy channels. The kundalini channels spiral up from the kundalini amplifier behind and a little up from the first chakra. There are two main kundalini channels that spiral around each chakra, beginning with the second chakra. Looking at the kundalini channels from behind someone, the spiral resembles the caduceus symbol used in the medical profession. The spiral on the caduceus is formed by two snakes. Ancient Greece had a pretty good bead on a lot of different energies.

This is not channeling another spirit or entity. In fact, it's just the opposite. They cannot be in your space when you're running earth and cosmic energy like this. If you're having issues with so-called entity attachments, running energy can help loosen things up and move them along.

Earth energy tends to be seen as greens and blues, just like the planet, but however you see it is how you see it. Some folks see it as pink. Some folks first experience it only as the feeling of something coming up their legs, either as a coolness or a release of pressure.

Cosmic energy tends to be seen as a soft gold with similar first experiences as earth energy. Coolness, release of pressure, the reassurance of something familiar.

Earth energy comes up through the feet chakras, through the leg channels, and into the first chakra, then down the grounding cord.

Cosmic energy comes into the back of the crown chakra on the top of the head, down the back channels to the first chakra, mixes with a small amount of earth energy, then goes up the front channels through each chakra, cleaning them out and spinning them, until it fountains out the crown chakra and cleans out the aura, healing the edges and going down the grounding cord.

There are two channels down the back, one on either side of the spine, and two channels coming up the front, both just going straight up to the next chakra.

Note: most people have four back channels. I have four back channels. If you have four back channels, by all means, run your cosmic energy down through all four. There are the two channels parallel to the spine, and then there are two outside channels that start out parallel to the two channels out of the crown chakra and down the neck, then bow out to the inside ridges of the shoulder blades, then in a 'V' down to the tailbone and in the back of the first chakra.

Key Point: All four back channels are inside of the body. Both front channels are inside of the body. There is a tendency for a few people during the beginning months of practicing running energy to allow the energy to slip outside of the body and, hence, not flow up through the chakras. This is how some folks avoid seeing the unpleasant energies that might be getting flushed from their chakras or their physical bodies. This isn't useful because it prolongs the pain.

Finding the center of your head and being there enables you to find neutrality to whatever energy is coming out of your space. The energies coming out of your chakras tends to be more concentrated. Running energy dilutes these concentrated energies, breaking them up and making them easier to manage.

Finding your amusement and allowing whatever you are releasing to leave your space is the shortest path to having a healthier, more vibrant space in which to live and from which to create what you want.

Creating and destroying roses blows up the pictures coming out of your chakras, preventing them from getting stuck in your aura on the way out. Create a rose. Put a bomb under it. Blow up the rose. Fireworks!

When I was at the institute, they mostly taught just two back channels. When asked why, teachers had different explanations. John Fulton said that everyone had four back channels but the Institute only taught two. Typical John Fulton dry wit, non-answer, LOL!

Lewis Bostwick, the founder, had an explanation that was interesting.

He said most folks had four back channels, but every so often someone with only two channels would come through the program and could not see that others had four, so they would, inadvertently most likely, program everyone else to only see two back channels.

There is this idea that we see what we see in others because we have the same or almost the same things inside us. It's said that this is how we can read so clearly. We have the same or very similar spiritual information and life experiences. We see it this lifetime because we've seen it during or before this lifetime.

In my experience, this idea of only seeing energy and pictures in someone else that we have in ourselves is only true during the first year or two of actively reading others. As we blow our matching pictures, our curiosity begins to take a larger role, and we can see anything we want to see, whether or not we have a matching energy or experience. Curiosity takes over and that's also really fun! This doesn't mean we understand everything we can see, LOL!

No one has experienced everything, so our information varies. We do have something like blind spots. Not every reader and healer knows about pictures.

This is why some readers are not good fits for reading some people. They don't blow their matching pictures and can't see clearly.

This is why some readers experience visceral pain when trying to read certain people. They don't blow their matching pain pictures and experience the pain in the readee themselves.

It's not necessarily the person they're reading doing anything at all. It's the reader's matching pictures getting lit up, just like the resonance between two tuning forks. If you can't wait, go read the section on Matching Energy and Matching Pictures now.

Note: We don't need to experience being raped as a child in order to read victims of child abuse. We only need to see their energy and

pictures clearly enough to read how those experiences and residual energies affect their lives now.

At the fifth chakra, some of the energy branches off into each arm, cleaning out the creative channels, and fountaining out the hand chakras, helping clean out the aura, then goes down the grounding cord. That's three fountains you have for cleaning out your aura, keeping your energy moving, and increasing your energy to create your next step.

One reason for bringing up a little earth energy with the cosmic energy is to enhance the clairvoyant ability in the sixth chakra. Pictures and energy appear more solid and detailed with a little more earth energy. This makes the pictures and energy easier to read.

Key point: a little earth energy mixed with the cosmic energy makes pictures and energy easier to read. If all the images look fuzzy, try increasing the percentage of earth energy in the mix.

All the teachers at BPI said the same thing: "Mix 10% earth energy into your cosmic energy." 10% is easy to teach. It's a clear picture. This was a wise consistency. Not always accurate, but a wise starting point.

I asked many of my classmates what percentage of earth energy was the easiest for them to read with. The answers ranged from 8 to 15%. Just for fun, I did some readings at 50% earth energy. *That* was interesting!

Experiment for yourself and find out what works best for you. Then, after six months, experiment again. A lot can change in six months of grounding and running energy.

It sounds complicated in written form, but it's easier to do than to write it out or read it! Everyone has these channels. For many, they are dormant or just idling along.

Grounding and running energy in this way is useful for developing your awareness of your space (chakras, energy channels, aura, physical body, astral body) and learning how to manage them to get what you want. It wakes you up and changes your energy in a large way the first six months that you practice it.

One funny occurrence often reported by first timers is getting phone calls out of the blue from old friends or family, just checking in, asking how you're doing, what's new, that sort of thing. Some aren't happy that their energy has been moved out of your space. Some are over-joyed for you. It's just like real life, only it's happening because you're grounding and running energy. And it's happening in a more com-pressed timeframe. Fun times!

When you ground and run your energy, you're clearing your space of past time energies, making space to create something new. It begins with grounding to the center of the planet and ends with grounding to the center of the planet. If you have zero experience this lifetime with energy, just a couple weeks of grounding practice is typically all that's necessary to prepare you to run energy.

RUNNING ENERGY EXPLAINED ANOTHER WAY.

It's pretty straight forward, isn't it? Might even seem familiar, eh? You've done this before, when you were born. Babies run energy.

One aspect of newborns that grownups find so beautiful is the baby's energy just flows. This reminds the adults in some way of who they really are, and they heal themselves a little bit, sometimes a large bit.

The pedagogical technique for teaching you to run energy is designed to 1) have you experience running energy, 2) help you heal yourself faster than just grounding alone, and 3) help you remember that, on some level, you already know this stuff. Ain't life grand!

Do you have to practice it this way? No. Do you need to practice it three hours a day like I did for several years? Only if you are as messed up as I was, LOL!

I'm only partly kidding. I was messed up, for sure. But I also loved doing healings, energy work, and readings. It was the most playful time in my adult life, and I love to play with energy. By the end of the clairvoyant training program, I could ground and run energy and read for just about all my waking hours. My 'mess' was also the motivation to learn to read and heal in greater detail and on more technical levels. In every reading, I found one or more matching pictures with the person I was reading, and I blew those pictures, getting back a little more energy each time. In every reading, reading these matching pictures helped me grow my understanding of how my life happened the way it happened.

I also asked how the person I was reading created things in their life. I got to learn how they dealt with life's challenges on an energy level. This gave me ideas for how I might want to change.

There are some patterns that seem to repeat, but you might be surprised just how many different ways, different energies, people use to create their life experiences.

Don't worry. Three hours a day of running energy is not required, nor am I recommending it. This is how I learn stuff this lifetime. I did the same thing with Aikido, turning a part time hobby into a full time adventure. It's just who I am. The shallows are where I start, just like most folks, but I jump into the deep end as soon as possible, usually before I can swim. This is not required. Be yourself.

Key Point: We don't all create in the same ways. It's really fun to take a look at how another spirit creates.

Manners time: if you read someone and really like the way they create, don't steal it, don't climb into it, don't diddle it to see what happens. If you're capable enough to see how they do it on an energy level, you're capable enough to simply make an exact copy of their information in your space. Then you can play with it, take it for a test drive, modify it, or say nope and ground it out of your space.

Helpful hint: if you make a copy of someone else's information to play with in your space, consider as a first step making a backup of your copy. This allows you to start over from the same place. Consider as one of your experiments with someone else's information just bringing it into affinity with you and see what happens. Sometimes we can use a copy to change something in our space, and other times we can change the copy slightly so it fits better in our space.

DOES EVERYONE RUN ENERGY THE SAME WAY?

No. There are many ways, and being the creative humans we are, we will most likely invent more ways to run energy. We learn other ways of running energy from other beings. The human kind and the non-human kind of beings. Mostly, this is accomplished by matching energy. That's how spirits try out new experiences.

Matching energy is a core ability of human beings. The reason you feel energized after a great concert is because the whole audience was matching a great vibe, and that vibe gave you a healing. The reason you feel down at a stranger's funeral comes not from your loss but from matching the down energy of the group attending the funeral. You match the vibration of their loss. The reason you feel excited watching a ballgame is because the crowd is excited about the ballgame and you match it. Sometimes, you are excited about something and everyone else matches you.

Your body is of this Earth. You are of this Cosmos. Running earth and cosmic energy through your body heals both aspects of your reality.

That's a small paragraph with a big punch. Let's look at it again. Your body is of this Earth. Running earth energy heals your body. You are of this Cosmos; a being made of energy organized around awareness, unique in all the universe. Running cosmic energy heals you and your spiritual space in and around your body.

That's as philosophical as I get. While this sounds good and is true, it's incomplete. This combination of earth and cosmic energies does lots more for you. And you get to discover what those things are!

There are some traditions that believe we cannot exist in both worlds, the physical world and the spiritual world. This is an old school thing from the Gypsies, if I recall correctly. I got a reading from one and he was astonished that very young and untrained me had each foot solidly in both worlds. He went on and on about it, and I'm like "Of course I do. Don't you?" It didn't make sense to me to not be in both worlds at once. I knew I wasn't just a body from an early age. I didn't know what that meant or how to express it in words, but I still knew it.

You very likely know this, too. Why else would you pick up a book like this, LOL!

Notice the filter on that Gypsy's world view. Notice the contradiction; he's reading my spiritual energy while sitting in his physical body. He was so close.

DOES RUNNING COSMIC AND EARTH ENERGY DO THE SAME THING FOR EVERYBODY?

Yes. Allowing these energies to flow through your space is a spiritual hygiene routine that heals and maintains your space (physical body, astral body, chakras, all the channels, and aura).

Not everyone, however, is starting from the same place. This means some folks will find running energy very challenging, while others will take to it with ease. Some big factors that determine how easy or difficult your spiritual hygiene experience is comes from either your physical age and/or the kind of life experiences you've had before your first attempt at running energy.

Everyone gets old. The older you are, the more layers of energy you tend to accumulate in your space, which means as you run energy, there can be more hiccups where a chunk of energy breaks loose and it takes you several days to release that.

The more traumatic your life has been, the chunkier the energy in your space may be.

That said, no matter the size or shape of the chunk, or the intensity of trauma, grounding and running energy will lubricate the healing process and accelerate it. It's still just energy.

Amusement takes the edges off the big chunks. You can add amusement to your earth and cosmic energies. Oh! Did I just sneak another technique in there for you to try?

Remember, you are allowing the cosmic and earth energies to flow through your space, not pushing them through your space. This takes no effort, just like allowing gravity to remove energy down your grounding cord.

Cosmic and Earth energies feel gentle and soothing. When they don't feel good, that means you've succeeded in finding some kind of blockage or foreign energy in your space. Just laugh, find the center of your head, blow some roses, and allow the two energies to flow. They will do their jobs.

What does chunky, old energy look like? One vision of it looks like my mother in her 70s, on her death bed with cancer. She was under palliative care, meaning she was snowed with a painkiller called Brompton's Solution, which is a mixture of liquid morphine, cocaine, ethyl alcohol, and simple syrup. She died in the 1980s. Brompton's Solution is now considered obsolete.

I hadn't seen her in a year. I showed up, looked at the ulcers on her legs, felt her clammy forehead and noted that her eyes were staring through a slit between her lids. She didn't respond to my voice or my touch at first. When I moved the covers on her feet, she screamed out in pain, tried unsuccessfully to raise her head, and told me not to do that. The feeling of the sheets moving across her ulcers (bed sores) was excruciating for her.

We were able to talk for a short while after that. The pain of the covers touching her ulcers broke through the morphine stupor. She was crying and talking.

I scanned her space with the palms of my hands. She didn't have enough energy to die. Yes, it takes a lot of spiritual energy to leave your body for the last time. Giving her the basic healings didn't change that. Her chakras were dull and mostly not spinning. Her aura was thin and wispy. Her red dot was pushed in and surrounded by gray.

The red dot is found on the back of the neck, just above the fifth chakra and near the genetic entity (or genetic tapes). It's not a switch. It's an indicator, sort of like those red things that pop up when a turkey is done. Some people see it at the base of the skull on the neck. How you see it is how you see it. The interpretation is the same.

It's bright red and standing a little proud in everyone except those close to death. If the dot is out but has gray or black energy around it, that's most often someone else's death energy, not that person's death energy. Removing the gray or black energy is a nice healing in that case. Trying to remove it when the dot is in and they really are dying is not useful.

In addition to earth and cosmic energies, we have access on this planet to a light, lemon-gold energy. Many cultures know how to use this energy and it has many names. At the Berkeley Psychic Institute, it was called Christ Force. BPI is, after all, the seminary of the Church of Divine Man, which is a Christian denomination based on the Book of Revelations. The Book of Life has seven seals, and these represent the seven major chakras, and when they are opened, your old perspective is replaced with a new one. That is what apocalypse means: an "uncovering." That is literally the death of your old life view and rebirth of your true self, in part or in whole. Those crafty Greeks were pretty astute, eh? Not perfect, but still astute.

This lemon-gold energy can remove all of the foreign energy from someone's body. This is a big deal! We didn't learn about this energy until near the end of the clairvoyant training program because using it eliminates almost all of the learning opportunities, and eliminates the chance to blow all of your matching pictures. Deferring teaching this until the end was a curriculum choice at BPI. Other traditions get to this energy or other similar energies like Supreme Being energy as soon as possible.

The risk with Christ Force energy is creating a messianic cult. This energy existed before Jesus. It's like earth and cosmic energy in that regard. An unethical or confused teacher can heal people with this energy and create a following, even if the teacher's explanations are inaccurate. Just sayin'.

I gently took hold of her feet, getting my hand chakras aligned with her feet chakras. I matched my crown chakra to the vibration of Christ Force and let it flow down my shoulders and arms, and through my hands, into my mother. Technically, this is a kind of channeling. If you have the information for using energy this way, why not use it? If you do not, experiment with different ways of channeling the energy: backs of the hands only, back of the fifth chakra, down the arms and out the hands, back of the fourth chakra and out the front of the fourth chakra, as well as from the fourth through the arms and out the hand chakras.

I did this for a few minutes until her space was full of the lemon-gold energy. As I was finishing up, making separations from mom and the Christ Force energy, she sat up on the bed, took my hands, and said, "I don't know what you did, but I'm proud of you." She kissed my cheek.

Then she passed out.

Those were her last words to me. We had a love-hate relationship. She was so good to me and so bad to me, it's hard to know where I stood.

We were estranged in so many ways, but, in the end, I did something I was happy with, and left her to die with her family.

I share this story with you to let you know what you, too, are capable of. You can be aware of energy and not become a victim of that awareness. You can be a healer and not become sick from healing others. You can thrive in a world that looks and feels broken, and not turn into a meaner, broken version of yourself. There is a toughness to you, a strength, that enables your kindness.

The tools, grounding and running energy, being in the center of your head, blowing matching pictures, reading a spiritual question, giving to yourself, etc., can help you be yourself at every stage of your life. Using the tools becomes like blinking. It's just something you automatically do to refresh your vision and peace of mind.

Now! Before anyone goes making up a rule that you have to master grounding and running energy before you can channel Christ Force energy, or any other kind of healing technique that might pop into your mind, there is no such rule or requirement. If you have the information, please use it. You might as well. You will gain some really useful life experience, even if you don't have the words to describe what you're doing in a rational way or a traditional way. Do not worry about it. The information is yours, not the tradition's. Be respectful but always be yourself.

Before I learned these tools, I was getting calls in the middle of the night to come over and heal a friend of a friend with menstrual cramps, or someone's back spasms. I had very little formal training and no robust explanation for anything. All I knew was that if another human being could do it, so could I.

So can you. Grounding and running energy made my healing abilities faster, more powerful, and more fun. I rarely had any aftereffects from doing a difficult healing or reading once I could ground and run energy and blow matching pictures.

You can ground and run energy and be in the center of your head for as long as you wish AND you can also practice anything else you wish to practice, like yoga and martial arts.

Inside the clairvoyant training program, we were not allowed the same leeway, and with good reason. We wanted and needed a group vibration that reinforced and supported our specific practices. There were a lot of hurdles and blockages to overcome just to get to the beginning classes, and then huge hurdles and challenges to overcome to join and complete the clairvoyant training program. All of those hurdles, by the way, were inside us. The goal was to learn to read for ourselves, and limiting our practices to just those in the institute was useful towards accomplishing that goal.

You, on the other hand, reading my words and following along on an energy level, are not in a clairvoyant training program. You can ground and run energy, and take yoga, martial arts, fast for seven days, compare and contrast seventeen different styles of meditation. Wherever your curiosity takes you, I say, "Have fun!" You will learn how to take a look at energy for yourself.

Remember, most of your growth is going to come from remembering what you already know about energy and spirit. Grounding and running energy are useful in that pursuit because they accelerate the time it takes to get through whatever energy is in between you and your information.

"Time heals all wounds." Bullshit. Healing heals all wounds, except those it can't. Time is about gaining life experience. It's why we incarnate: to have time for life experiences.

That said, be patient with yourself. Something as simple as finding the center of your head takes repetition, which takes time. All of the techniques in this book take some time and practice. How much? Ah! That depends on you. If you remember how to ground and run energy because you read about babies coming out with their energy running, that's wonderful. It didn't take as much time. If this is grounding and running energy is somewhat new to you, it might take a little longer to kick in. If your life experiences are rich and long, or thick and crusty, or whatever, it will take as long as it takes, okay? LOL!

Don't compare yourself. Discover yourself. Comparison is the thief of joy.

Be curious, not judgmental, and you'll progress as fast as you're able.

Matching Pictures and Matching Energy

Take a look at this short video. It's about resonance. You will need to type the url into your browser if you're reading the physical book.

https://www.youtube.com/watch?v=lFWXjzhH8a0

This simple physical phenomena is a great metaphor for what happens to us on an energy level during our daily lives, and oftentimes happens during our healings and readings.

A picture is a static collection of memories, information, and energy, with an energy that binds those three together. The combination of the contents and the "frame" that binds them creates a unique vibration, or pitch. A picture is therefore just like a tuning fork.

Spirits communicate with each other through pictures. Spirits also communicate with bodies through pictures. Bodies perceive pictures. This doesn't mean a body necessarily sees a picture, but a body does become aware of a picture and then creates the emotions that fit with that picture. A scary movie is just a series of fast changing pictures designed to make your body aware of some threat so that your body creates the emotion of fear. Bodies can't tell the difference between a zombie chasing you in the dark and a picture of a zombie chasing someone else in the dark. The characters on the screen might need to remind you of someone in order to make you empathize more, but that's not that difficult to achieve.

Destroying a picture breaks the frame, allowing the energy, information, and memories to go where they belong.

We all have pictures in our space. Each picture has a unique vibration, just like a tuning fork. Having strong pictures in our space is part of how we meet the people we are looking for, so we don't want to destroy our pictures haphazardly. These people have a matching picture with one of our pictures. When a picture has enough energy to light it up, the body becomes aware of it and responds accordingly. A stranger gets our attention and we introduce ourselves and get to know them a little; that's also having a matching picture light up. This is often the explanation for thinking you know someone. It's why we look up just in time to see someone on a bus looking into our eyes.

It is not the goal to destroy all of your pictures. That would not accomplish what you want. The goal is to learn how to manage your pictures by taking the energy off them or by destroying the picture to free up your energy for creating something new.

There are two ways a picture can be lit up and affect a body. One way is for some energy to hit that picture, restimulating it and charging it, which makes the body think that whatever that picture is about is happening right now.

Pictures contain memories, information, and energy, all locked into a geometry inside of a frame. It's that geometry, for lack of a better word, that gives a picture its unique vibration, just like the size and shape of a tuning fork gives it its pitch. The frame is a metaphor for an energy that binds those three things together into a static whole.

So lighting up a picture by throwing some energy at it makes it perceivable by the body, which cascades into the body creating the emotions that go with that picture. Think of a scary movie again and how it excites and manipulates your body's emotions.

The second way a picture gets lit up is resonance. Watch the tuning fork video again. Imagine some person just passing by you in a coffee shop, but you have a bad feeling about this person and get totally distracted from what you were doing before they walked by.

The first tuning fork that is struck with the hammer in the video represents a picture in the space of the stranger walking by you in the coffee shop. The second tuning fork that resonates with the first tuning fork represents a matching picture in your space with that picture in the stranger's space.

And that ping pong ball? That's your body's emotions going bat-shit crazy for no rational reason. Pretty funny, eh?

Let's repeat that idea. A complete stranger can have a picture in their space that matches close enough with a picture in someone else's space for resonance to occur, restimulating and energizing the picture in someone else's space without any intent of doing so. The picture is lit up and the body creates the matching emotions for that picture.

In the weakest case of a matching picture getting lit up, you are distracted. In a moderate case of a matching picture, you can't see clearly during a reading or healing, or your daily life. Everything seems to be just beyond some fog in front of your face. In the strongest case of a matching picture getting lit up, you begin to relive the memory contained in your picture. That can be disturbing.

Notice the intent or lack of it. A picture of yours gets hit with energy thrown by someone else, lighting it up. This requires someone else to choose to throw energy at that picture of yours. That's intent.

Matching pictures don't need an intent and rarely have one associated with them. It's just mechanical resonance on a spiritual energy level.

When someone throws energy at one of your pictures, that carries intent. You may decide that this is an attack and get angry. That might be appropriate. Might not. Knowing that their verbal insult was just lighting up a picture in your space gives you the option to just blow your picture and ignore them altogether. Sometimes no reaction pisses them off even more, which can be fun to watch, lol.

Some empaths think the world is out to get them, when in fact all that's going on is their matching pictures are lit up. This is why recognizing the intent is important. It pulls you back from judgment and belief, and turns the assumed attack into just an energy management opportunity. In other words, knowing your body is reacting to a matching picture maintains your neutrality to the emotions flowing through your body, and you can more easily destroy that matching picture and calm your body quickly.

Note: Narcissists sometimes will create a matching picture in their space to manipulate someone else. Think of this like a phony common ground picture. "Oh! I'm just like you!" Yep. Nope. Narcissists manufacture emotions at will. It's a small step for them to see what pictures you've got in your aura and manufacture the same picture in their aura.

The one flavor of matching pictures that may seem like there's some intent is when a stranger reminds you of someone. This is your picture being lit up enough for you to become aware of the memory enough to recognize the details and buy into your body's emotional response to the picture.

That last sentence is clunky, lol. A short story will clear things up.

My very good friend Paul Ohmart once had a woman come into a healing clinic and sit down to get a healing. Paul was a control at the clinic, so was walking behind the readers, chatting with people, setting the energy with his hands.

This woman got angrier and angrier, such that everyone near her took note of her anger and stopped doing whatever energy work they were doing. She was staring daggers at Paul.

Paul looked at her, saw she had a picture lit up, and asked, "Do I remind you of someone?"

She growled, "Yes! My ex-husband!" Some fear rolled through the readers.

Paul said, "Well I. am. not. him," and smiled broadly.

She stared at him, meeting his eyes for a long moment, her mouth open, then exhaled all her breath and refilled her lungs. Her body shook a little and released all that anger. She smiled quietly and nodded at him.

The readers laughed, began talking among themselves and preparing their spaces to read again.

She blew her matching picture. She didn't know how to describe what she did in terms of matching pictures, but that's exactly what she did.

Blowing a picture means breaking the energetic bonds that hold those memories, information, and energies together in a static pattern. As soon as that energetic bond, or frame, is destroyed, all the energy that lit up that picture is released. Any of your energy that was captured within that frame is released and returns to your reserves. The memories and information go to where they belong in your space.

It's a lovely little healing. Sometimes it's a lovely big healing, but either way, the same things happen. A picture is blown, which removes it from your body's awareness, so your emotions subside. You've changed your state from a less resourceful, distracted, emotional state to a less emotional, more neutral, and slightly more energized state (remember that energy contained in the picture is freed). The more pictures you blow, the more your energy grows.

Grounding, running energy, and blowing your pictures is the psychic trifecta. Doing readings and healings with an intent to blow your matching pictures brings to you more people with more matching pictures, which accelerates your spiritual growth, awareness, and understanding.

The technique for blowing your matching pictures is simply matching the color of your crown chakra to the crown chakra of the person you are reading or healing. This lights up your matching pictures with this person. You blow your matching pictures. Fill in. Then read or heal with much more energy and clarity.

Matching crown chakra colors is one way to match energy with someone else.

There's a good chance that when you match crown chakras, you might light up *all* of your matching pictures, LOL! Be amused and hang on. All that means is the healing you give yourself will be just that much better.

Don't worry about the person you're reading or healing. By consciously blowing your matching pictures with them, you're creating permission for them to blow their pictures, if they so choose and if they are able to at this time. As you read and give to yourself, you are growing at a faster rate than the average. Don't expect the readee to keep up, lol. But also don't expect them not to change their energy right in front of your eyes. Allow them to be exactly where they are and control their own rate of change.

Another way that we match energy is just that. We match energy with someone else or with some group or with an idea. We each have streams of energy in our space, especially in our aura. If you practice martial arts, you will have some energy in your space from martial arts. This is not a picture, but it can resonate with another person with a similar energy just the same.

Dancers have a different energy when they move than gymnasts when they move. Look at a dancer and a gymnast walking side by side and you'll notice there are differences, and not just the structural differences in their bodies. There are energy differences. There will be pictures in their auras that you can read, but your first impression of them is often from the way their energy moves.

We all have our different tells in our energy, just like poker players have in their faces. We aren't usually concerned with hiding our tells like poker players, lol. It's fun to scan a room full of people, look for their tells, and see what we find. This is another way to light up your matching pictures with someone.

This is how we usually notice someone that is in a bad way. The first thing we see is some energy in their aura that dominates all the other energies. Sadness. Anger. Grief. An emptiness.

When I walked home late at night from the Institute in Berkeley, I passed by the People's Park, which was usually filled with the homeless, the addicted, and once in a while, the violent. Having been without an address for most of a year in Alaska, I knew I didn't want a repeat performance of that adventure. It was necessary at that time, but that time had fulfilled itself and I had changed.

I didn't read the people in the park. That was too disturbing right before bed. It would also be a violation of their privacy on some level to read their pictures more than just the surface level that they already showed to the world. It also was not necessary.

What I did was match their crown chakras, one at a time, and blew any matching pictures that lit up in my space. After a few weeks of doing this, no more matching pictures of desperate hope and fear lit up in my space. My memories of Alaska and all the near-fatal risks I took were still as clear as ever, but the energy of the trauma, disgust, disappointment, and fear were gone. The exhilaration was still with me, which is to this day still a fun energy to tap into and heal myself, but the energy of the career alcoholics, the murderers, the dead, and the pain are gone.

DROPPING PICTURES

There are energy games being played and everyone is a player. Adolescents often put their energy into someone else's space just to see what happens. That boy or girl that you just can't stop thinking about? They're in your space.

There's a subtler game that involves dropping a picture in front of someone or in their space. This can be a control game or a flirting game, or both. If the person dropping the picture is successful at capturing your attention in that picture, they can control you in some way. Control in this case is not meant in a bad way.

Some women will drop a sex picture, which gives the people chatting them up or approaching them in a club a reason to keep doing what they're doing. It captures their attention, which freezes them temporarily on an energy level, enabling the woman to slip away gracefully and end the exchange. Most men and women confuse a sex picture that gets dropped on them with an intent to have sex. This is what freezes them. There is no intent to have sex, just an attempt to escape without confrontation.

Models and celebrities are a step up from this dropping pictures game. They learn to carry pictures in their auras. These can be sex pictures, beauty pictures, exotic pictures, innocent pictures. These serve to set expectations, which diverts attention, which is how they control their own energy in a crowd of admirers or fans or paparazzi.

ANOTHER WAY TO MATCH ENERGY

Walk up to any stranger, match your crown chakra to theirs, and say, "Hello!" out loud. That's all. If you do this from the center of your head, with an enthusiastic and neutral hello, you will get their attention. You don't get in their space, either. This works because it is so rare that we get a spirit-to-spirit hello that it remediates, for that moment, some of the spiritual loneliness in that person's space. People notice that.

Being neutral is key. You can create a groupie if you add any non-neutral energies into that hello. That's not as fun in real life as it is in rock-and-roll bands.

This is why you sometimes feel so good when a total stranger smiles at you. On a spiritual level, they've recognized you and said hello. They said hello to you, not your body. All loneliness leaves your space, your energy brightens, and your body sees this brightening of your energy and creates the good feelings.

TRIGGERS

If someone talks about something triggering them to behave a certain way or experience a certain feeling, it is safe to assume that they have a matching picture in play. This is true whether you are reading someone else or yourself.

If something sets someone off, triggers them, and they feel awful or behave irrationally or behave aggressively or dramatically or just shut down, asking yourself what the matching picture is that makes this trigger possible will almost always find the picture. When *that* picture gets blown, the trigger effect disappears. You're welcome!

All that "bad energy" that you experience is not the problem. It is the result of the problem, which is a picture that is lit up with enough energy that your body senses it and creates the corresponding emotions.

This is the power of blowing your pictures. It grants you neutrality (well, you grant yourself neutrality, lol). You can still dislike someone. You can still have a crush on someone. Neutrality is not the same as acceptance or letting go.

Neutrality grants you more time to think, and when you think even just a little more, you tend to make better choices and paradoxically you make them faster.

Roses

You can use the image of a rose to learn to read energy. You can use it to protect yourself, your home, your friends and family. You can use it to heal yourself and others. You can use it to discover where your aura ends, which is useful to know. You can use it to distract someone else, which is useful in confrontations. You can use it to send a message to someone. You can use a rose to create a mockup, which is a technique to get what you want, sometimes called manifesting.

In the lexicon of BPI, creating a rose and mocking up a rose are synonymous. Creating a mockup however comes with an intent of getting what you want. Mocking up a rose is just creating the image of a rose.

An image of a rose is a neutral symbol. Yes, there is some cultural heritage for this symbol. It's been used in some societies and secret societies. It's used by the Rosicrucians, which predate the Berkeley Psychic Institute in similar grounding and running energy techniques.

A rose can be used to represent the energy of anything you wish to learn about. A rose can represent the energy of an answer to any question. This could be your question or someone else's question. This makes a rose a powerful tool for reading and healing.

You can use a rose to show you where the pain is in someone else's body, or where the disease is, or where their energy blockage is. This helps you cut to the root cause or the big answer to their big question or their next step in their journey, or yours.

Learning to manipulate images for different purposes is very useful.

CREATING AND DESTROYING ROSES

Try this. Sit in a chair. Create a grounding cord, allow the cosmic and earth energies to flow through your body, and be in the center of your head. Isn't it fun how you know exactly what that long sentence all means now. Well done!

Create an image of a rose out in front of you. Notice the color of the rose, how open the bloom is, how long the stem is.

Destroy that rose.

Create another rose in front of you. Reach out with your hands and hold the stem. Feel the bloom with your fingertips. Notice the weight of the rose. Lightly touch any thorns. Smell the rose.

Destroy that rose.

Create a rose. Have this rose represent the energy of someone you know and are friendly with. What color is the rose? How open is the bloom. How long is the stem? Touch the rose with your fingers. Say hello to the rose.

Destroy that rose.

Take a deep breath. Bend over and touch the floor. Yawn and stretch.

HOW DO YOU DESTROY A ROSE?

The standard instruction when I went through the program was 'blow it up,' meaning put a bomb under it and explode it. However, after graduation, I met other graduates and they destroyed roses in other ways.

One guy told me about turning the page and described it as you're looking at the rose and it exists on a page in a book. You can see it and feel it. Then you turn the page and what you saw is gone. Destroyed. This did not work well for me, LOL.

Another man told me about his psychic etch-a-sketch for creating and destroying roses. Yet another told me he rips them up with his hands, meaning he creates an image of hands tearing apart the roses he creates.

A woman told me about her soap bubble technique. Instead of a solid rose, she imagined the rose on the surface of a soap bubble. The soap bubble worked much better for me than turning the page. I could see the energy that I collected with the rose floating around on its surface.

When it popped, it all shattered, falling down because of gravity. I found this to be effortless.

One teacher had us stand up, tuck our hands into our armpits to form chicken wings, then had us peck at stuck pictures in our auras with our noses, LOL! Embarrassing as hell!

But then everyone started getting into it and we started pecking each other's pictures, breaking them up and releasing the energy trapped inside them. Everyone was laughing and giving and receiving healings.

The lesson from this absurd exercise? It's difficult to take a stuck picture seriously when you're pecking at it like a chicken.

The "real" lesson? All you need is awareness of a picture and some way to focus your energy.

The technical lesson? This gets more nuanced because each spirit is capable of destroying a picture in a different way. There are a few patterns of destroying pictures that I've read in others and others have read in me. All of these patterns can be seen by asking this question: Where does the energy that destroys the rose come from?

For some, it comes from a healing ring of blue energy that encircles the head just above the temples. Some folks will confuse this with a halo.

Other folks fire off the energy from their crown chakra. A few used one of their kundalini channels that comes from over the top of the head and curves down in front of the forehead. This is a combat kundalini channel. If you even read someone and they had a Berserker past life, look for this bright channel. It's very interesting to read and see how it works. Someone using this in present time is probably doing martial arts. That is the other venue I've read it in.

"Seriousness" is its own energy, and it tends to reinforce something that's stuck, making it seem more difficult, more capable than you, and more than it really is. "Amusement" is its own energy, and it tends to relax all the energy around it, making life seem easier, making you seem more capable, and making problems seem less than perhaps they really are. Enough amusement overcomes stuck energies. It doesn't bring world peace to everyone else, but it can restore your faith in yourself and get you moving again.

Please notice that nothing in that last paragraph is a judgment. Being serious about something is not bad and being amused about something is not good. The two energies function in different ways, that's all. Knowing about these differences is useful, especially during a crisis. Being aware of the two energies in a hospice gives you more control over your choices. Being aware of the two energies in a bank robbery gives you more control over your choices.

Speaking of bank robberies, LOL, one of my teachers was at his bank when a crew came in to rob the bank. "Everyone down on the floor!" and all that. Real guns and masks. This teacher was standing at a long desk thingy where people filled out deposit slips and such. He didn't get down on the floor. He pulled his aura all the way inside of his body and just watched.

The robbery went off without any violence. The robbers never acknowledged my teacher's presence. The only outcome was the police questioned him at length about being an accomplice to the robbers because they ignored him on the security recordings, LOL!

Back to blowing stuff up!

Bombs or missiles destroying the roses works great for me. I switch back and forth between the bubble popping and blowing it up. Why? It keeps it fresh. I don't want my ability to destroy energy to get stale.

That's an indication that a tool has gotten out of sync with where I am, or sometimes has been programmed.

Programming. Big word! Sounds scary. It's not. Programming means any energy that works like a loop, controlling you in some way that is not useful to you now. It's an instruction that got placed in your space to get you to behave in a certain way.

Different cultures call programming different names: hexes, curses, divine intervention, motherly love, respecting your elders, etc. Programming is some energy that is an instruction to get someone to behave a certain way. That's the loop aspect. This behavior repeats itself over and over again whenever the right conditions occur.

All parents program their kids to keep them safe from running out into the street. Families program each other to keep the heritage and goals in focus. Most folks who have something to hide will program their auras so that everyone else, psychics included, only look at certain parts of their auras.

Create a rose. Destroy that rose any way you please. Create another rose and destroy it in a different way. Experiment. Play. Playing with energy is the strongest form of training. If you want to get into heaven, you have to come like a little child, and little children play with energy, imagining whole worlds and filling them with characters and invisible friends. Stretching your imagination and laughing at what you're doing makes you stronger, safer, and more adept, and does it in a shorter timespan than seriously applying yourself with great discipline and no mistakes. It's only energy. Mess it up and learn something. You already know, on some level, how to put it all back the way it was. Mess it up and have fun.

Try this. Sit in a chair, ground and run your energy, and be in the center of your head.

Create a rose in front of your face and blow it up. Create another rose in front of your face and blow it up. Create another rose in front of your face and blow it up.

Notice how your body feels when you are creating and destroying energy. This is the first step towards increasing your creativity. How does your body feel when you create and destroy a rose? Is the rose too close to your face? Is the explosion too bright? Not bright enough? What's left after the rose explodes? (Clean up your toys after your play time, lol!)

Does part of your body get happy? Does some part of your body hurt? Are you still breathing or are you holding your breath?

Create a rose and destroy it. Notice what changes. Create another rose and destroy it.

Parents say, "Don't break that!" and over the decades, this turns into "don't destroy anything." This might have been useful when you were a kid, but now it's an inappropriate constraint on your life. This is also programming.

Create a rose and let it represent the energy of "don't destroy anything," and destroy that rose. Where'd you feel that one?

Create a gold sun over your head. Fill it with your highest creative essence, your affinity for yourself, and your present time growth vibration. Bring that sun down into the top of your head.

Open your eyes. Dump out. Stand up and stretch.

In almost every class, this is the point where someone raises their hand and says this exercise gave them a headache. Not everyone gets a headache, but often enough one person will have this complaint. What's going on? You don't really know until you take a look.

A clairvoyant student would be pulled into the beginning class and asked to take a look at what energy caused this headache. They'd be paired up off to the side of class if the room was big enough, or into another room if not. I got pulled into reading beginners and most of the time got stuck in a small closet, LOL!

Almost always, no matter whose energy was in their head being a pain, what the energy said was that same: do not be a destroyer of energy. Isn't that amusing!?

Creating and destroying is a basic process of life, so, quite naturally, it's what everyone wants to control. It starts when we're quite young: Don't Touch That! You'll Break It! LOL!

If someone wants to control you, what is the easier target? your ability to create or your ability to destroy? It depends, eh? Every person is a different person, but the basic wiring is similar. Some people have cultural tendencies placed on them. Gender expectations. Social class expectations. Family expectations.

If someone thinks that destroying is evil and creating is good, then controlling their ability to destroy energy is probably easier than controlling their ability to create energy. The sad thing is we need both to survive and prosper, so having either one diminished compromises our lives.

Close your eyes. Ground and run your energy. Be in the center of your head. Do this even if you are standing up. (Yes, Dorothy, you can stand with your eyes open, not go into trance, and still ground and run your energy, even in Kansas.)

Create a rose. Have this rose collect all the energy out of your space that says "Do Not Destroy." Move this rose away from your body, closer to arm's length away, and destroy it.

Fill in. Dump out. Stand up and stretch.

Nice job!

This is one way to use a rose to heal yourself in meaningful, targeted ways. Create a rose, put all of some type of energy in it, destroy the rose.

Why does this work? It stirs the pot, so to speak. It's like pulling the bay leaves out of your energetic stew.

When you pull an energy from your space into a rose, it breaks that energy's connection to the place you pulled it from. When you destroy the rose, you neutralize the energy you placed inside it. Any residue from the destruction of the rose and energy simply grounds out of your space, guaranteeing it all gets neutralized.

Trouble with an ex's energy? Put it in a rose and destroy it. Trouble with someone at work triggering you? Put the energy of the trigger in your space in a rose and destroy it.

This doesn't mean that all of a sudden, you like that coworker much better. It might, but that's not the goal here. The goal is simply to manage your own energy better, and eliminating a trigger accomplishes that goal. You are not your coworker's keeper. They aren't your problem. The picture they light up in your space is your problem.

This doesn't mean that you should wipe out all of your reactions to everything. Nope. Someone does something to put you or your family in danger, you don't close your eyes and say, "Ground. Run your energy. Be in the…" You do whatever you need to do to keep everyone safe.

However, after you're done doing what you need to do, take the fallout in your space from that experience, put it in a rose, and destroy it. You threw a drunk friend out of your party. Don't let the energy of the drunk friend continue to spoil the party for you. Put it in a rose and blow it up. Do this for your space. Do it for the space of the party and observe how the remaining partier's energy lightens up.

When you meditate or do a reading, ground and run your energy, be in the center of your head, and create and destroy roses. Grounding accelerates your rate of spiritual change. Running energy accelerates what grounding began. Being in the center of your head accelerates your rate of change because you are neutral, which means you can let go of more old junk. Creating and destroying roses deglazes your spiritual frying pan of all those crusty bits that you don't want in your gravy. Filling in accelerates the growth of your ability to release energy. You never feel like you're running out of energy.

By the way, there is only a small distinction between meditating and doing a reading of someone else. Meditation is grounding and running energy with your focus turned inwards. Reading someone else is grounding and running energy with your focus turned outwards. Same tools. Same reading techniques. Different focus. Healing someone else is the same as reading someone else.

CREATING AND DESTROYING
ROSES EXPLAINED

Creating and destroying energy is a basic process of life. It's what we're doing when we think "I want this but not that." Decisions create and destroy energy.

Creating and destroying roses is a technique. It uses the neutral symbol of a rose to calm your mind and focus your energy and awareness.

The energy of creating and destroying is a spiritual cleansing that helps your energy to get moving and keep moving. It takes no effort to create and destroy roses although sometimes some other energy can interfere with this process. When you realize that something is interfering, that's a wonderful moment because you've probably uncovered some energy that does not serve you well. It could be your energy that is stuck in the past. It could be someone else's energy that is diddling you.

Discovering a stuck or foreign energy is always a wonderful event, because it's a strong indication that you are about to release something that's been in between you and getting what you've wanted for a long time.

The fun thing is when you discover some energy that is diddling your ability to create and destroy energy, just knowing that is happening and then creating and destroying roses is often enough to get rid of the energy that is diddling you.

Healing yourself often involves creating and destroying energy to get you from one state of energy to a better state. "Better" is subjective. Sometimes, healing is just moving things around a little, getting the flow going again. Other times, something needs to be removed or replaced before our energy can get moving again. This most often involves some form of creating and destroying energy.

BLOWING PICTURES

This is the main course, psychic diners! This is how you heal yourself and get unstuck. This is how you heal someone else who is stuck. This is one way to change the dynamic in a group from one state to a better state.

Almost every kind of stuck energy has, at its root cause, a picture. A picture can behave like a tuning fork. When it vibrates, or gets lit up, your body perceives it and creates the corresponding emotions. Blowing that picture destroys the frame and takes the charge off of it. With no charge on the picture and no frame holding it together, your body no longer perceives it and stops creating those emotions.

Try this. Create a rose. Have that rose represent the energy of the thing that really pisses you off. Notice where in your body the energy of that rose affects you the most. Notice what thoughts fly through your awareness, what images flash by.

This process of creating a rose to piss yourself off is making pictures light up in your space.

Now create another rose. Put the pictures that you've lit up into the rose and destroy the rose. This breaks the frames of the pictures, allowing the contents (memories, information, and energy) to go to where they belong. The picture no longer exists, so cannot be perceived by your body, so your body settles down. Now you can blow up the first rose that was that energy that pisses you off. You will remember everything about that energy, but it will no longer affect your emotions the same way.

You show up to a meeting at work. Before the meeting even starts, you begin to feel bad. Normally, when we feel bad, we assume these feelings are actually about us. Next time this happens, mock up a rose for the energy that is making you feel bad. Whose energy is it? Is it your problem? Do you have a matching picture in your space? If you do have a matching picture, put that picture into the rose and blow it up.

If all this discomfort is just a matching picture, you'll feel better immediately. Blow a few more roses just to clear your vision and enjoy the meeting.

You walk into your favorite eating place. You've been looking forward to eating here all day but now feel sick to your stomach. Mock up a rose and ask if this is a matching picture. If yes, then put the matching picture into the rose and blow it up. Take a deep breath. Fill in. Enjoy your meal.

You're on a sales call with a new, important customer. You've heard they are difficult to work with, always complaining about almost meaningless stuff. You've traveled to take this meeting and are sitting in your hotel room. You feel lethargic, which is unusual for you. You're the top salesperson at your company. You are always on top of your game. Feeling down just doesn't happen.

Create a rose to represent the energy that's making you feel down. Bingo! Black rose. No stem. Flower is totally closed.

You ask what black means and you get that someone was just at a funeral. Worried, you ask if it's one of your family members and get a solid "no." Is it someone in this morning's meeting? You get a firm "yes."

Put all of your matching pictures into that rose and blow it up. You feel some tension release in your crotch and notice your grounding for the first time today. Your first chakra was wide open but now is closing back down.

Create another rose for what's making you feel down. Oh! A different rose. White and green petals. What does that mean? You ask and get "opportunity." Your energy is coming back to your normal self. You are pretty sure someone died, so you Google a bit and find the obituary of the father of one of the people you are meeting with today. Hmm. Should you offer to reschedule? Create a rose and ask. You get "no" as the person in the meeting wants to take their mind off their loss and get back to normalcy. You decide to keep the schedule as is.

You show up for the meeting and three women are in the conference room. They greet you professionally and ask you to sit down. You create three roses and send a neutral hello in a rose to each of them.

At the end of the meeting, you've got the bones of a new, much larger contract with this customer. You realize that everyone that told you they were difficult to work with were just stuck in their own pictures and not really listening to the three ladies, LOL! Their loss is your win. Salespeople, right?

Last thing you do is create a rose and put all of the energy from the other salespeople into that rose and blow it up.

NEXT SCENARIO.

You're in a Zoom meeting. Everyone is tense. No one can express why, but they are really, really concerned about something.

Create a rose for the energy that's holding the meeting in this state. A nice, red rose, but full of thorns. The energy says, "We're all doomed!" Whose picture is this? LOL. Seven of the nine people in the meeting, including you, have matching pictures with "We're all doomed!"

You blow your matching picture and immediately see the picture everyone is matching on was leftover from a previous meeting. It's one person's picture and it was lit up when they binged a Netflix SciFi drama and got stuck on the world coming to an end in a terrible way.

You create a rose for that leftover picture. The rose goes to the com device in the center of the table where three of the participants are sitting. You put that leftover picture into the rose and blow it up.

Everyone's shoulders on the Zoom feed relax. A few people shrug. One shakes their head as if something is rattling around in there. The leader of the meeting asks about the next agenda item, and everyone agrees that it's not going to be a problem.

When they were all stuck on their matching pictures, they couldn't see. When you blew the picture in the room that they had matching pictures with, it allowed their matching picture to stop resonating and go dark again. Then they could see.

This is one of my understandings of the biblical phrase, "Those who have eyes to see, let them see." The phrase is about giving people permission to see energy and spirit simply by being able to see energy and spirit yourself. Two thousand years ago, that was about it. Poor old Matthew didn't have the chops or vocabulary to write down *how* to give them permission. All he knew was it was a good idea and that we shouldn't judge others for not seeing what we see.

Don't judge; give them permission and leave the rest to them.

SEPARATION ROSES

Human beings share energy. It's what we do. It's especially true when we are having sex, or intense conversations, or just catching up with a friend we haven't seen in a while.

Another way of saying this is we get into each other's spaces. Sometimes getting in someone else's space is okay and sometimes it is not. That's kinda obvious. What is not obvious is we can leave our energy in someone else's space, and this dilutes our awareness. We can leave our energy in other places, and this dilutes our awareness.

Our awareness is dependent on how much of our energy we have under our control. This is particularly true for psychic readers and healers. We can literally leave our awareness scattered across everyone we've passed by in our daily lives since we started having a daily life, LOL! We rub off on each other.

Energy left in past lives is obvious. Energy left in your work computer is more subtle. Energy left in people is usually the first to come to mind because we are more attuned to reading people's energy. Energy left in a classroom, a lab, our car, or our pets is more subtle.

Getting this energy back is super simple. Mock up a rose. Pull your energy back into this rose and blow it up. Pulling your energy back into a gold sun works. Grounding attracts some of your energy back to you as well.

But how do you stop leaving your energy everywhere?

A separation rose.

Ground and run your energy. Be in the center of your head. Create a rose and have that rose show you where the edge of your aura is right now. If the edge of your aura is not, say, eighteen inches away from your body while you're grounding and running energy, pull it closer. If you're walking around, just hanging out with friends, if your aura is not within arm's length from your body, pull it closer.

When you have a conversation with anyone, create a separation rose between you and them, and pull all of your energy onto your side of that rose. They don't need to do anything. You are, after all, grounded, so most of their energy never reaches your body anyway.

If your awareness is in your energy, and if your energy is spread out over four city blocks, you are on some level aware of every other being, human or otherwise, in that four city block area. You might uncon-sciously begin to heal some of those people and drain your energy. You might start to read some of them semi-consciously, like "Where'd this thought come from? That's strange. I'd better take a look to be sure…"

Attention is an energy. Energy can be divided. Your attention can be divided, which dilutes your awareness.

Knowing where the edge of your aura is can be a lifesaver. If your awareness is closer to your body, your signal processing in your chakras is stronger. You may hear that out-of-control car coming several blocks away and step out of harm's way well in advance, maybe saving a few others with you.

Practice. There are opportunities to practice all around you. Listening to an audio book? Put a rose up between you and the narrator. Reading online news sites? Put up a rose between you and the computer screen and between you and the talking heads.

Checking out that beautiful boy or girl walking across the street? Put up a rose, arm's length from your body, and have all of your awareness and energy on your side of that rose. You can check them out without getting in their space to do it.

The last one is really important. Beautiful people are already objecti-fied. Their lives are lonelier for this, but don't take my word for it.

Create a rose for your favorite celebrity. It doesn't matter if they are beautiful or not. They just need fame.

Now create a rose for each person's attention point within that celeb-rity's space. That's a shit-ton of roses, eh?

Now do the same for your space, one rose for you and one rose for each person that has their attention on you. Fun stuff, eh? Maybe a few too many roses?

This is one of the reasons that some advisors recommend you not talk about your creative activities before you complete them. All of that attention drawn into your space can impede some people from completing their projects, if they don't know how to manage that energy. Some folks are that sensitive to attention points.

Attention points? These are exactly what it sounds like. You can see them in your aura or someone else's aura. They look like points of light, but are not spirits. They don't twinkle like a spirit guide. They are more like a dot of static energy. And they are divisible, meaning someone can have their attention split among lots of different things.

Pulling your attention back inside of your space, behind your separation rose, makes your life easier in two ways. First, you become more focused. We shift our attention throughout our day. This is healthy and normal. However, sometimes we only shift part of our attention from one project or interest to the next because we aren't done with it yet. We leave our attention on something we aren't really doing at the moment.

Some folks think this is protecting their creativity or somehow making getting back to some task easier, but that's not true in my experience. It's just a habit that divides their focus, making all of their projects more difficult.

The second benefit of pulling your attention points back from everyone else is they pull their attention points back from you, too! How cool is that! By being on your side of your separation rose, you've even brought your wandering attention points back inside of your space, and in response, everyone pulled their attention back from you. Pulling your energy back from someone almost always gets them to reciprocate and pull their energy back from you.

Think of this like an exchange of pressure. You put your energy and attention in someone else's space and the pressure of your energy pushes their energy away from them and into your space.

Think of this from the perspective of someone who is sensitive to energy. You place your attention on them and they automatically place their attention on you to find out why you're looking at them. In some ways, this autonomic spiritual system is for protection.

Does this work for everyone? In my experience, there's often that one person, that *guy*, or that *gal* that thinks it's okay to stay in your space, and you have to remove their attention points and energy. Roses and grounding cords to the rescue!

For the rest of this book, please practice reading it with your separation rose between you and the text. The same goes for the audiobook; create a separation rose between you and the sound of my voice reading the book to you.

PROTECTION ROSES

This gets fun fast! Imagine a separation rose. Now *give it its own grounding cord* and instruct it to ground out any energy coming into your space that is not your energy.

When is this needed? In the early days of the clairvoyant training program, it was necessary all the time. Everyone that had a bone to pick with either me or the Berkeley Psychic Institute would throw energy my way, and not just my way, but at the instructors and other students. Having a tall and powerful body made me a target for smaller men and some women. If I can get one over on the big guy, then my status will go up. It's a shit game that has been in my life since middle school.

Women would throw energy. If I can control the big guy, I can probably control anyone. It feels *wonderful* being someone's practice target, LOL! Very reassuring! They'd throw a little sex energy until they could light up a big picture in my space, then leave me standing. It's just a game, and I was their pawn.

"Mongo just pawn in game of life." Google it.

It became less necessary as I recovered more of my energy and my confidence in grounding, running energy, and blowing roses increased.

Even at the end of the clairvoyant program, a protection rose was still useful in some situations, like letting another student take me to coffee so they could spill their guts about every possible problem in their world. Having a reliable protection rose makes one a better listener. You don't get caught up in the energy of what someone's telling you. If they're your friend and they have some awareness, they'll probably detect when they're getting in your space and shut down, never finishing the release of what they needed to talk about. Using a protection rose with a friend in need is a kindness. You are not pushing them away; you are giving them permission to really let go, and doing it without drugs, LOL!

In fact, one exercise we used to train our protection roses went like this:

Partner up. Sit across from one another. Choose who is the complainer for the first round.

The non-complainer just sits behind their protection rose and says, from time to time, "Not my problem."

The complainer makes up complaints in the form of losing the only job that really ever engaged their mind, finding out their significant other was cheating on them, and when he/she moved out, they took all the pets, even though the pets all predated the arrival of this SO, who was now more like an SOB!

You get the picture. Tragedy and sob stories for five full minutes and all the while, the non-complainer is sitting behind their protection rose, watching all of this negative energy hit their protection rose and disappear without a thought. That. Was. Beautiful.

Then we traded roles and repeated the exercise another five full minutes. Fun!

You should try this exercise with someone. There really is nothing quite like seeing energy come at you from the person across from you and disappear down the grounding cord of your protection rose.

All of that stuff sounds like training for some kind of psychic combat, and it can be just that.

A protection rose can be so much more than protection.

Consider that friend who is going through a tough time and just needs to talk. She's being pulled in so many different directions, she can barely walk straight. She desperately needs someone to talk to and she sees you in the coffee shop.

She's a real friend. She's been there for you in the past, even helped you move out of your ex's place. You want to help.

Invite her to join you. Put up your protection rose. Let her dump it all. This is an expression of grace on your part, and the energy never even touches you. It grounds out through your protection rose.

There is something divine about using your tools to help those in need. It displays a generosity of spirit and gives hope where before only despair or confusion existed. You didn't need to solve all their problems. In fact, you only solved one energy problem that a true friend or even a stranger was carrying around with them: too much energy in their space.

Enabling someone to heal themselves whose first reaction to being overwhelmed by life is to hold onto all that energy because they feel responsible for it and don't want to get any on the folks around them, is a divine gift from you to them. Some people need our help in the short term. They need to clear their minds and see what's real. You and your protection rose can safely enable that for them.

If it's not already obvious, protection roses are an awesome tool for therapists and massage therapists. And nurses. And, well, pretty much everyone, lol.

Oh! And patients. When you see your doctor or dentist, put up a protection rose between you and them. Can you guess who is in their space? If the dentist has their hands in your mouth and suddenly cuts loose all the other morning patients' energies, and is doing so because you are more grounded than everyone else in the building, it's just good energy management to let all that flotsam and jetsam to ground out through your protection rose and never get into your body.

PROTECTION ROSES EXPLAINED.

But it's easy. It's self explanatory. What's left to explain?

No effort goes into creating a protection rose. You create an image of a rose at the edge of your aura, or between you and someone or something else, and then you connect a grounding cord from the base of the rose's stem to the center of the planet. For psychic work, all grounding cords should lead to the center of the planet.

There's nothing left for you to do after that. Eventually, your protection rose may disappear. Energy can wear out and need renewal. It's just energy, and it can wear out if a ton of energy gets thrown at you, but if you are mindful of your protection rose, and amused at the energy that it's redirecting on your behalf, it will last as long as you need it to last.

If you put the energy of effort into its creation, the protection rose will disappear even sooner. If you clad the rose in cast iron and use a superduper grounding cord of Kevlar, you risk putting effort into the protection rose and compromising its spiritual usefulness. Effort is for bodies, and no-effort is for spirits. However, if you play video games, and imagining a cast iron rose makes you laugh uncontrollably, it's going to work. Play with the imagery and find what works best for you.

Redirection is the key. You aren't pushing on the protection rose to keep it attached to the edge of your aura. Maybe your protection rose gets overwhelmed and disappears; it happens. So what? Just create a new one with the intent that it can handle whatever this new, overwhelming energy is, and you're back in business. You learned something about a different energy in the process.

If your protection rose gets pushed back, pull your aura in behind the rose and smile. You can modify your protection rose with a thought, like "Cool! Bigger rose!"

A woman came into the trance medium healing clinic one evening. She brought her tween daughter in to get a reading. Mom was a professional psychic. She was training her daughter in the craft.

There's a line of four readers. There's a control standing behind the line. The daughter sits down in front of the line and asks, "What are all these roses about?" LOL!

Practice your protection roses enough and even non-psychics will notice that you're up to something. They may not see what, but they will notice.

DECOY ROSES

These are a personal favorite of mine because they are so much fun to watch in action.

Almost all of the time, when someone throws energy at someone else, it is energy that specifically targets someone else's vibration. Let that sink in for a minute.

It's like physical fights. A punch is not thrown randomly. It's thrown at Kenny or Beth or <fill in the name of someone you'd like to see punched>.

So you're minding your own business, reading your email in a coffee shop, and a party of people run into the shop, arguing loudly, their body language aggressive, and their energy flying all over the shop. Maybe they're mad at the shop manager. Maybe they're mad at the world.

Everyone in the shop is being hit by the energy coming off this loud party of people.

Create a rose. Have that rose represent the space in the shop. Send that rose to someplace far away but easy for you to visualize. Ground that rose through that far away spot to the center of the planet, and watch all of the rowdy party's energy get thrown and just disappear.

When we made decoy roses at BPI, we would put them out at Alcatraz Island. The park would be closed at night, so we weren't risking messing up someone else's space with our diverted energy. Plus, during the day you could make the intent that the grounding cord for that decoy rose would not pass through anyone else.

The first time I saw something like this, based on the same principles, was in Aikido, years before I found my way to BPI.

We were doing partner practice with weapons, specifically the Jo. This is a round staff about five feet long. The instructor at the seminar I was attending was Terry Dobson, a big man who was an understudy to the founder of Aikido. He'd spent ten years in Japan, immersed in the culture and traditions and the energy.

We were doing the simplest exercise, where we'd partner up, one of us attacking and the other defending. The attacker was to try to skewer us in the gut with the end of their Jo. The defense was to stand there with our Jo, one end planted lightly on the mat in front of our left foot, our left hand holding the Jo a bit below the top.

The defender's hips were square to the attacker. This presented a juicy target. The defense against the thrust to the belly was a simple parry. The defender turned their hips slightly to the right, causing the end of their

Jo to hit the side of the attacker's Jo, parrying it off target without lifting the other end of the Jo off the mat. A very small but powerful motion.

This defense depended on timing. Turn your hips too soon and you get stuck in the side. Turn your hips too late and you get stuck in the belly and torn open by your late, twisting hips. At least, that was the theory. We didn't use sticks with sharp ends. Who'd want to practice with you after getting disemboweled? lol.

After we had practiced enough to be consistent, Terry sprung the real lesson on us.

He told the story of how the Samurai would imbue their Jo's with their energy by rubbing the oil from their noses onto their thumb and then into the wood of the Jo. He had us project our energy into our Jo's, and we did. Nice shortcut to all that nose oil.

The attacker would attack. The defender would let go of his Jo, leave it standing straight up, and move onto the attacker's side to take away their weapon with another standard technique.

Here's the thing: even when the attacker knew what was coming, their Jo would hit my Jo instead of tracking my movements, every time. They couldn't change their attack once it was launched. Their eyes would track my movement, but their arms and Jo would not.

This was the kind of experience that kept me practicing Aikido. It made energy real. Back in my home dojo in Tucson, AZ, I would practice this decoy deception with lots of techniques, just imagining my energy staying where it was but moving my body off the line of attack. No Jo required.

BEING SOMEONE ELSE'S PROTECTION ROSE

When someone throws energy with the intent to disrupt, say, a classroom full of beginning psychics, who are they going to throw it at? The teacher. All the students are watching the energy, even if they don't know they are watching. All those human beings brought in their valuable bodies to get some energy management training, so their attention is on the teacher. If she or he can't manage their energy when under the same kinds of attacks that the students experience, then they're wasting their time and money.

So Hanna Jane was teaching another beginning meditation class. She was greeting her new students as they came through the door of the institute. I was in the house to do a reading, but why wait! I was reading the energy coming through the students as they entered the door. All of that energy was hitting Hanna Jane.

She looked at me, saw I was already reading the energy, and made a request. "Would you be my protection rose?" I'd never heard of such a thing, so of course I said, "Sure!"

She said to match energy with her protection rose. Never having done anything like this before, I postulated matching her protection rose and felt something like putting on a long rain coat. My space changed with a kind of mild thump, and I watched all the energy flowing at Hanna take a left turn and come at me, LOL! It was a lot of energy and it didn't phase me in the least.

Now, every new student that walked in smiled and said hello to Hanna, and the energy coming through them at Hanna took a sharp left turn and hit me instead. And then it just grounded out without affecting me in the least. Funniest thing I'd seen all week!

Hanna was laughing and talking now, without distractions. I was reading everyone that walked in, excited to see what energy might come through their space. None of the energy affected me in the least because it was not targeted at me. It was fun!

What does that mean, "not targeted at me?" It means that whatever spirit was throwing that energy had seen a picture in Hanna's space and intended to light that picture up, getting Hanna stuck and distracted. If they threw the right vibration, they could explode that targeted picture, rip her aura open, and create a whack. This could cause her physical pain. This would show her students how worthless she was to them. Yes, some spirit guides of some teachers are competitive little shits, LOL!

However, I didn't have the same pictures as Hanna Jane, LOL! The energy thrown at her and diverted to me and my grounding cord passed through me as harmless as a spring breeze.

Another way of saying this is I was completely neutral to the energy being thrown at someone else. It would be different if I was the one being targeted, but I wasn't.

If you want to try this, I suggest creating a rose to represent the person you want to protect, then match it. Become their protection rose. You can match your crown chakra to the vibration and match your aura as well. I found it a fun thing to play with at parties, picking out one stranger and becoming his or her protection rose, and just watching what happens.

Observation: some men grow up in cultures that encourage them to wrap their auras around women to protect them. This works but at a cost to the women. Over time, this protection energy can become a constraint on how much a woman can change her energy. Some women put their auras around other people to protect them as well. Same unintended effect; the protection energy turns into a constraint over time.

If this is something that you do, consider being their protection rose instead. Better yet, take a look at their energy and ask yourself just how much protection it really needs. You might be pleasantly surprised.

The Rose Reading

You can read anyone with a rose. The basic rose reading consists of an image of a rose with a sun above it. As simple as can be. You create the rose to represent someone. Here's how you read a rose.

The rose and sun represent the spirit you are reading. Could be in a human body. Could be in a non-human body. Could be without a body.

Every part of the rose represents something of interest about the person you are reading.

The color of the rose represents the dominant vibration of this particular spirit. Noting the color is a first step towards doing an aura reading.

How open or closed the blossom is can represent how open or closed this person is to hearing what you have to say during the reading. The blossom's open or closed state can also represent how much of their own information they are using in their life.

The position of the rose under its sun represents whether or not this person is on their path. The blossom looking up directly at the sun means this person is on their path.

This can also mean the person is looking at their own information. Sometimes, when you see the rose is bent to the left and their sun is off to the right, this may mean this person is lost and not on their path, or not using their information to return to their path. The meaning can vary so you have to ask yourself what it means for *this readee.*

I recall only two readings that I've done where the rose and sun were offset like this. In one case, I said, "You're not looking at your information and you're not on your path." The readee said something like, "Yep. That's why I came in for a reading."

I said the same thing to the other case, and they argued that this was a lie. They were absolutely following the path, and there was no other path but the path. They weren't even talking for themselves, but letting their guru come through them. Well la-de-da! Not much to do in that case. All the other readers saw this exchange. I was the most beginning reader in the room. We went through the mechanics of completing the reading. During the Q&A portion after the break, the readee asked no questions, and just continued to criticize us for being such poor readers.

If this happens to you, don't take it personally. I had this happen at a psychic fair once, and I smiled politely, refunded their money, and said I could not read them today. Technically speaking, I lied when I said that, but why be punished for a whole reading when there were more interesting readee's waiting in line?

Key point: you never have to read someone.

Back to our rose reading.

The blossom's open or closed state, and relationship to their sun, represents how much of their own information they are using in their life.

The length of the stem indicates how long this person has been on this planet. Roots on the bottom of the stem indicate they've been here since the planet was formed. Red energy surrounding the roots indicates they were part of the group of beings that created this planet and all its spiritual games and content. These folks are called Red Giants (not to be confused with the stars of the same name).

Don't make a hierarchy out of this information. Some spirits were around when the planet was made and helped set the energy of the planet. If they happen to incarnate and you get to read them, enjoy it. You've met someone special and you probably have some matching pictures with them, and you'll probably give them a marvelous reading. Enjoy that feeling.

Leaves on the stem represent contracts, or agreements, to have children this lifetime; two leaves mean agreements to give two spirits their bodies this lifetime. This doesn't specify with whom they will have these kids. It could be with one of your partners or two different partners. The agreement is only between you and the baby beings.

Rings around the stem represent past lives that are influencing this lifetime. This could mean information from those past lives is important to something in this life, or some business from a past life is to be completed this lifetime.

If you zoom in close to the stem, it is made up of thousands of these rings, each one representing a past life. Only the past lives pertinent to this lifetime expand to look like rings around the stem.

This is the basic rose reading that every new student in the clairvoyant training program learned. It's a simple question and answer reading, programmed to tell the reader some key things about the readee. The questions are implicit in the rose reading; they are why you're looking at the meanings of the different parts of the rose.

Each answer to each question is an opportunity for an interpretation.

Are they open to having this reading? If yes, then cool! If not, then wait and watch. This can change.

Are they on their path? If yes, then cool! If not, then make a note to yourself to ask why after the initial rose reading is done (typically takes five minutes or less). Or, ask why now.

In the training readings at the institute, the new reader would just get through the basic questions and a scribe would write down the "answers" by drawing with crayons a picture of the rose and sun, as described by the rose reader.

You're doing this on your own. Do it in the way that is easiest for you to manage. I would do full two hour readings during the clairvoyant training program by myself on days when there weren't enough read-ers. Rose, chakra, and aura readings, and controlling the energy of the room, and scribing, LOL! It was a lot of fun.

Are they creating this life with their own information? If yes, then cool! If not, then where are they pulling the information from? Whose information is it?

How long have they been here? This was always fun for me and fascinating for the readee. I always explained what I was looking at, especially those rare times when I was reading a Red Giant. Really cool energy to read.

What's the nature of their time on this planet? This is all about the roots and any red energy around the roots. It clarifies the previous question about the length of the stem. It's also a training tool to make the reader look past their comfort level and matching pictures.

Do they now have, or will they have, any kids? This can be really important to the readee. It's also a bit of proof that can establish credibility. It's a simple shortcut to common questions about marriage and family, couched in terms of spiritual agreements. It's more fun than it sounds. The first time you say, "I see two leaves on the stem, which represents two agreements to give bodies to other spirits," and the readee volunteers that they have had two miscarriages in the last few years, things begin to get real. Now you get to read those two leaves in more depth.

Did the miscarriages fulfill the agreements, or do they still have active agreements to give bodies to these two spirits?

With some more experience, the nature of the leaves will change. Fresh, green leaves for strong agreements. Dead leaves for miscarriages and abortions. These changes to the symbols are coming from you improving your reading skills. The symbols take on more nuanced meanings as your reading skills improve.

Are their significant past lives in play? A fan favorite! In a training reading, we would say, "I see two rings around the stem, one right underneath the blossom and another half way down the stem." Usually things stopped there unless the readee asked questions. Sometimes the center chair would answer these questions if the side chair reading the rose was struggling. This gave them time to blow more pictures, rematch their crown chakra to the center chair, and oftentimes see the same past lives that the center chair was describing.

That's it. That's the rose reading. Nice and simple and quite meaningful.

WHAT ABOUT THOSE THORNS AND APHIDS AND WORMS?

When you put a bunch of psychics in a room and have them read together for months, they evolve and grow. One aspect of this growth is seeing energy in finer and finer detail. As their clairvoyance is refined by practice, alone and with other readers, their tools evolve along with them. Great for them. Not so great for the brand new clairvoyant student.

Why? Because the basic rose reading is already lighting up a lot of pictures for the new reader. They are already overwhelmed sometimes. They can't see the same detail and can become invalidated when they are expected to see more detail. The new student reader already has expectations of themselves that may not be realistic, along with a lot of "I don't know wtf I'm doing" energy, lol.

So the staff would have a few cleanouts and resets of the tools during the year, especially the rose reading. The reset was as simple as, "Allow the rose reader to read only the basics." Most of the advanced readers got it right away; "OK let the new kids read the sun, rose, stem, leaves, past lives, and call it a day!"

Yeah, there was often one advanced student who didn't get it. A couple of times, I saw them in more in-depth discussions with the staff after the reading cleanout was done.

The purpose of a training reading is always twofold. It's to practice reading energy, but it's also to blow your matching pictures and clear your space. Give to someone while giving to yourself. This is what enables you to read without pain. You are blowing all of your matching pain pictures and healing yourself, while describing the exact pain that the readee has and wants to learn more about. People in general don't come get a reading because they're overjoyed with life. They have some problem in their life that they want your perspective on.

I do get readings when I'm overjoyed with life, but that's because it's fun for me and fun for the psychic reading me, and I get my bearings on stuff.

But the general public often thinks of psychic readings as solving their big problems.

I read with one clairvoyant student whose thorns were pain, aphids were spirit guides, and worms were psychic attacks. Can you see how all that might just overwhelm some newbie a teeny bit? Telling someone they are a bit off their life path is not enough? You want to go for the throat right off the bat?

A professional reader does that. A reader reading another reader does that. A reader in training doing a rose reading is almost doing that, and then the rose reading is over and they have the rest of the two hours to heal themselves and catch their breath.

More ways to read a rose

Create two roses, one for each party in the relationship. Look for lines of energy joining the two roses. These represent cords that are pertinent to their relationship. Look for leaves on the stems; baby beings can be a major influence, both pro and con, on a relationship.

It's often useful to look at a third rose that represents the partners' relationship space. This can make the energy of the relationship easier to see. Is the relationship bigger than the partners? Is the relationship dominant to the partners? Who else has energy in their relationship space? Does the relationship have its own path?

Simple and fun! Really useful answers and insights.

This technique of using two roses to represent parties in a relationship and a third rose to represent their relationship space can work for lots of relationships. Your relationship to your job, career, home, family, another group, specific rooms or places, school, the car wash. Who doesn't love their ride through the car wash? It's a relationship.

Here's a good one. You can use two roses to compare different energies, or the same energy but at different times.

Want to know how much your reading skills have grown? Mock up a rose for your grounding cord the first time you created one. Mock up another rose for your grounding cord today. Read what's changed. This is like a shortened version of an energy check and can be really validating and healing.

You can do this for yourself, and you can do it for someone else. Imagine the benefit to someone down in the dumps to read their creative energy from the last time it was flowing clear and strong, and their creative energy right now. Look what can happen when you remind someone of what they're capable of creating. Help them find that energy again and turn their life around.

Use a rose to read the dead, read pets, read the newspaper, read the energies of a path, of birth, of death, of life.

Use a rose to tell the truth from the lie. Create a rose between you and someone else who's talking, telling a story. If they lie, have the rose fall over dead. If they tell the truth, have the rose blossom open more. Make up your own variation on this that works best for you. There is no particular value in making your roses look and behave like someone else's roses. The value is in using a symbol made of energy to read other energies.

All you need is a symbol and a question. Creating the symbol yourself removes the variables inherent in using external tools like pendulums, for instance. I'm not knocking pendulums; to each their own.

Reading a symbol trains your clairvoyance because the symbol is energy. Clairvoyance is the ability to read energy and spirit.

How about reading families? Create a rose for each member of the family. Here's a really fun way to do this. Instead of asking how many people are in the immediate family, just postulate creating a rose for each member of the family agreement. How do you interpret when you do this, get five roses, but there are only four members in the immediate family? Which rose is the extra rose? Who does it represent?

Or how about creating a rose for three generations? What are the possible meanings to seventeen roses if grandma and grandpa only had two kids, and each of them had three kids? Who's missing?

The extra roses might represent miscarriages, abortions, a foster child, maybe a cousin. Spiritual agreements are not controlled by the DNA. Ask each rose what it represents and that's your answer.

Find the center of your head as you're doing this. Find some amusement. You may have just uncovered some family secrets about who had babies out of wedlock and had left town during the pregnancy, gave up the kids for adoption, and returned.

The questions you ask of a rose always show you the answers. They may be the wrong answers for someone to hear, but you are seeing the answers.

Healing and Roses

Time to play!

Create a rose. Shrink it down really small. Send this rose through the earth energy channel in your left leg and gather up any stuck energy in that channel and clean it out. Destroy that rose.

Create another rose and cover it in a spiritual polishing compound. Run this rose back and forth in that same earth energy channel in your left left until it gets all shiny inside. Blow up this rose.

Create another rose and clean out the foot chakra in your left foot. *My Left Foot* is a wonderful movie, by the way. Blow up this rose.

Now run earth energy through your left leg and notice the difference.

Do the same for all of your energy channels and all of your chakras. Play!

Do the same for the center of your head.

In your face, along the paths that the sinuses take across the brow ridge, below the eyes, and along the bottom of the jawbone, are your telepathic channels. They send and receive.

Create a rose and clean out your telepathic channels. Woot! Notice the difference? For some, this answers why they clench their jaw shut at night. To avoid this, turn down your telepathic channels before you go to bed.

If someone walks into a coffee shop and your attention is grabbed by them, totally distracting you from what you were doing, turn down your telepathic channels and see if that helps. Some people just shout telepathically all the time, LOL!

Feeling really off? Reading someone that wants to know if they have a health problem?

Create a rose and have it find the energy of the disease in that person's body. Watch it lead you to the problem.

Want to ease someone's pain? Create a rose, match it to their fourth chakra, and send that rose to neutralize their pain.

A variation: set the rose to cobalt blue and send the rose to neutralize their pain. Cobalt blue is an anesthetic vibration. You can also set your hand chakras to cobalt blue and do a little hands on healing. You can also set your body to cobalt blue and see what happens!

Create a rose and have it clean out your trance medium channels. These are two channels starting at the back of your crown chakra, running down your neck and across your shoulders. Different folks have slightly different trance medium channels, so have the rose show you where yours are located from start and end. These are the channels that we use when we are channeling another being.

Create a bunch of roses and have them clean out your creative channels. These originate in your fourth, fifth, sixth, and seventh chakras and end in your hand chakras. Clean these out every day and see what changes in your life.

Create a rose and have it find an energy problem in your space. This could be a whack in your aura or chakras, stuck energy, etc. Have the rose find the energy that is next in line for you to remove, then have at it!

Remember those golden suns that you create and fill in with? Create a rose for the energy of your amusement. Notice the color and texture of the rose. Create a gold sun and fill it with your amusement. Bring that down into your space and see what happens.

So the same thing with a rose created of your enthusiasm. Fill your sun with a matching vibration of your enthusiasm, bring it in through your crown chakra, and see what happens.

A Reading
Technique with
a Tennis Ball

By the end of the Silva Mind Control seminar, which runs for two weekends, we had learned to go to level (their description of going into a light trance to read) and our bodies had become comfortable with us doing so. This was in the early 80s, several years before I would first walk into the Berkeley Psychic Institute.

The final exercise was to pair off, sitting across from each other, with one partner in the exercise just sitting and the other partner going to level to read the one just sitting.

When my turn came to read, I followed the instructions and created an image of a tennis ball. Mine was lime green, just like the ones my high school tennis team used. The image was of a brand new tennis ball, fresh out of the vacuum packed can. I loved those fresh tennis balls. Too bad they didn't make me play any better, LOL!

On this day, we asked our tennis balls to show us some energy problem in the space of the person we were reading. Immediately, my tennis ball went to the center of the person's chest. I began describing what I was seeing. It played out just like a movie.

The tennis ball is right in front of your chest. Now it's moving over your heart. I see a man in the cardiac ward of a hospital. He's hooked up to IV's and monitors. His heart looks like a big, red heart with a break down the middle, tearing the heart in half.

Inside the crack in his heart is a young boy, maybe fourteen or fifteen. He has long brown hair, down past his shoulders. He's skinny. He's sitting on a beach on his knees, pulling sand with his hands towards his knees.

The person I'm reading asks, "Which beach?"

My perspective widens a little bit and I see the lifeguard towers on Huntington Beach, California. He's sitting near lifeguard tower nineteen. It's a weekday and he's alone.

The next question comes: "Is he happy?"

It's interesting. He's a young teen. He's still figuring out what makes him happy. He seems safe and that seems to make him content for now.

A hand touches my shoulder gently, and the teacher says, "That's enough."

I do some little ritual that I no longer remember and come out of trance. I open my eyes, grinning ear to ear, and see my partner crying his eyes out.

His son disappeared a year before. His son was his grandfather's favorite grandchild and granddad had a massive heart attack a few months after the boy went missing. Kidnapping was assumed, and I was asked if I could see who took him.

I went back to level and was instantly looking at a station wagon with a young family, mom, dad, two kids younger than the boy in question. The boy was hitchhiking and the family stopped to check that he was OK. He got in their car and they gave him a ride all the way from Tucson, Arizona to California near the coast.

I lost the trail after that.

I came out of trance again. Everyone else was finished with the exercise. Everyone was looking at me like I had three heads. This was at the height of my martial arts career; I had lots of energy, some awareness of my energy, and no lack of confidence in my energy. I smiled politely and ignored their stares.

The teacher did a short ending meditation, then thanked all of us for a wonderful seminar. Hands were clapped. People were excited and chatting with each other. Everyone but me. I was left alone. I nodded to the teacher, which got his attention. I shook his hand, thanking him for the experience, and left before everyone else.

This was my first reading of someone's energy.

I was sorry for that dad's loss. I was really excited by what I saw, how clear it all was, and how alive it all was.

I didn't really get to read like that again. I did, however, get to incorporate a different healing technique into my martial arts healings. The seminar had us ask for a spirit guide to help us with anything we wanted. I asked for a guide to help with healing people, and I got a very small dragon. I named him Draco.

My first evening teaching Aikido again, one of my friends said he was having trouble with his shoulder. Bad fall. Landed wrong. Might have dislocated his shoulder but it popped back in on its own. (His words. I didn't know what that 'popping' bit meant, and wasn't sure I wanted to.)

We talked about the seminar that had finished two days before. I mentioned my new friend, Draco, and asked if he'd like a healing. As soon as he said yes, Draco began icing his shoulder with a freezing flame.

Best part for me right then was my friend describing how cold his shoulder was getting. Not his body, just his injured shoulder.

When Draco said he was done, he smiled before flying away. I asked my friend to move his arm all around and the pain was gone. Things still felt a little weak but more like he'd overtrained a bit than injured.

While this wasn't my first healing, it was my first time using a spirit guide to heal someone.

At least, it was the first time I was *aware* of using a spirit guide to heal someone, LOL!

Bubbles

Sometimes you're in a hurry. Who wants to keep track of all those roses? Plus your grounding cord? Plus your energy channels? That's a lot of roses in the air.

You can use one image that combines all the benefits of your awareness that you would usually focus on one tool at a time. This image can turn them all on at once.

Be in your bubble. Imagine a bubble all around, above, and below your body, about arm's length away.

This image puts you into the center of your head, grounds you, lets your energy run lightly, defines the edges of your aura, just like a separation and protection rose, and connects the edges of your aura to your grounding cord well under your feet. Whatever energy hits your bubble grounds out. The energy coming out of your crown chakra splashes off the top of your bubble and down all through your aura.

Be in your bubble.

A Basic Healing

Everyone that walked into the Berkeley Psychic Institute received a five minute healing. Staff, clairvoyant students, beginning students, people there to get a reading. Everyone.

Let's do a five minute healing! Let's assume that you've never done a healing of any kind before.

Pro Tip: You can have matching pictures that light up with the person you are healing. You can also have matching pictures with your healing guides. What this means is whenever I say, during this basic healing, to blow your matching pictures, I mean blowing your matching pictures with the healee and your healing guides and the healee's guides.

Stand next to a partner sitting in a chair. Bend your elbows to raise your hands, palms towards the healee in the chair.

Ask them if they'd like a healing. After they say yes, you may proceed.

Check your grounding. Be in your bubble.

Create a rose and have it match their crown chakra. Match your crown chakra to the color of the rose. Put all of your matching pictures with this person into the rose and blow it up. Now you can see their energy more clearly. Fill in with a gold sun. This takes less than one minute.

Match your hand chakras to the healee's vibration.

Notice if the healee has a grounding cord. If so, clean out their grounding cord with a rose. If not, create a new grounding cord for them and connect their first chakra to the center of the planet.

I like to place a large bell at the center of the planet, and then drop a rose down their grounding cord. If the rose rings the bell, I know they're connected to the center of the planet. I apologize in advance for any clutter of bells you may find at the center of the planet.

Use your hands to create a gold sun over their head and call back all their energy through your hand chakras and into their sun. When it's full, bring that sun down into their body and aura.

If your hands are matched to their energy, it won't feel like much is happening with the energy and your hands, maybe nothing at all. The match is for their benefit.

Conversely, if you are not matched to their energy and give them your energy, they will feel like something is off. Their energy in their space feels right to them. How it feels to you doesn't matter.

Move your hands in an uplifting motion through their aura. So palms up, lifting handfuls of their aura up a little in a circular motion, and letting it go. This is fluffing their aura. It's similar to fluffing someone's long hair with your palms or fingers.

Move all around them and give them an aura fluff for a minute. This gets their energy moving in their aura. Smooth out the edges of their aura with your hands. End of minute number two.

Now stand to one side of them, one hand in front of their torso and one hand behind. You're going to clean out their seven main chakras. Move your hands in a circular motion to stir the first chakra. Move on to the next chakra.

Or, create a rose, hold the stem, and spin the blossom in the first chakra. Blow up that rose, create another, and do the second chakra, etc.

Conversely, you can pull a rope of gold energy back and forth through each chakra: AKA chakra floss!

Or, you can bounce the rose back and forth from one hand to the other, through their chakras, like a ping pong ball. You get the idea. Play with the energy to get the energy moving.

Continue on until you've done the sixth chakra. At the seventh chakra, since it faces up instead of forward, you can curve the rose or the rope through the seventh, back and forth, or just swish the crown chakra with one hand to spin it and clean it out. End of minute three.

All this back and forth, flossing motion, spinning, stirs up and cleans out foreign energy from the chakras. This enables the chakras to move with more ease.

Create roses to clean out each leg channel, the four back channels and two front channels. Destroy those roses.

Now, hold your palms over their head again. Double check that your hands are still matching their energy. Create a gold sun. Fill it with their highest creative essence, their present time growth vibration, and their affinity for themselves, and bring it down into the top of their head and throughout their aura, filling them up.

This should take no more than five minutes.

We fill them up at the beginning because that makes their energy easier for us to feel. Having more of their own energy also makes it easier for them to heal themselves. Aura, chakras, energy channels, everything, easier to feel. Feeling energy leads to seeing energy, because all the abilities in the seven main chakras are mirrored in the hand chakras.

We fill them up at the end because they've been grounding and releasing energy as we fluff their aura and clean out their chakras. They'll be at least a quart low, LOL!

Last bit: unmatch your hand chakras from the healee's energy. Pull any of your energy or attention that was left in the healee's space back to you. Match your crown chakra to their crown chakra, create a rose, put any more of your matching pictures into that rose, and blow it up. Check your grounding cord. Fill in your space.

Matching pictures can come in layers. Don't assume you got them all with the first rose at the start of the healing. You may have removed enough energy from their space during the healing that you've uncovered a new layer of matching pictures.

Notice the cycle: Ask permission. Blow your matching pictures. Give them a five minute healing. Blow your matching pictures. Fill in. Make your separations from the healee and your healing guides.

This is the same pattern we use in readings. Give to yourself. Give to them. Give to yourself.

In a beginning healing class in the 80s, the first class would be learning to ground and fluff an aura. The second class would be grounding and running energy, grounding the healee, doing the aura fluff, and filling them in. The third week would introduce healing the chakras. The fourth week would introduce the students to their healing masters which are spirit guides with a lot of healing information that agree to help the students learn. That's a lot of fun in a six week class!

After the students received their healing masters, they were invited to attend all the healing clinics and do basic healings on whoever showed up. Big Fun! Lots of improv at the healing clinics, depending on who showed up. Usually, a reading and healing would cap off the evening, where a clairvoyant student would do the reading and healing with the healing students sitting side chair or controlling.

There were two beginning series of healing classes. In the second series, the students got another guide called a psychic surgeon. No chicken guts were pulled from the healees. Where the healing masters focused on the aura, chakras, and energy channels, the psychic surgeons focused on body parts, removing foreign energies from organs and the nervous system, repairing a cell's DNA, that sort of thing.

I mention the classes and the healing guides so you have an idea of what questions to ask of your spirit guides. If healing is not their thing, you can ask for a healing master and/or psychic surgeon from your group of guides. You've read about the classes. This gives you the vibration that you can match to find the help you want.

Yes. You can find healing guides just by going into a light trance and asking for some healing guides. You can hold tryouts, like your very own healing master pro sports combine! OK that might be overkill, lol. Just have in mind what kinds of healings you want some help with and guides will show up.

There is some gatekeeping that goes on with any school. It's part of the responsibilities of running a school. If you don't have access to a school or don't want to attend one, I see no reason why you shouldn't have healing guides.

If you can match the energy of the healing masters, you can make agreements with them, too. Ground and run your energy. Blow some roses for any pictures that get lit up. Create a rose for the energy for each of your desired healing guides. Match your crown chakra to the color of that rose, and say hello to whoever shows up.

There is no shortage of healing guides. Once you've had some practice working with them, you'll understand why.

It's useful to create a grounding cord on the floor or ground just behind your aura and have the guides show up and stand on that grounding cord. I see this as a circle on the ground or floor behind me, big enough for two people to stand on, and just outside of my aura. When they show up, I see them in my mind's eye standing there. This helps you learn how to maintain separation with them. They don't want to get stuck in your space, either.

Some instructors would teach us to make that circle on the floor ten feet behind us. This would sometimes make this space outside of the room we were in. This was never a problem. The lesson was we were no longer playing in a strictly physical space.

Start here: Have your healing guides create cords into the backs of your hand chakras. It works like this. First, have them match your energy and blow their pictures. Next, have them put cords into the backs of your hands. If you are healing someone else, have your guides match the healee's energy and blow their matching pictures. Then the healing begins.

Note: some people channel healing beings and reading beings through their bodies. This looks like a silvery energy in their aura behind their throats or the same silvery energy coming down through the back of their seventh chakra, where the trance medium channels are.

You've blown your matching pictures. Have your guides blow their matching pictures as well. Have them match the energy of your hands before they connect to the backs of your hand chakras. Then have them match the energy of the healee, if it's not you, before they begin working on them, and blow their matching pictures with the healee. This is to guarantee neutrality.

The same process applies when working with healing guides. Give to yourself. Give to your guides. Give to the healee. Give to your guides. Give to yourself. Giving to the healing guides is you allowing them to work through your hands, match and unmatch energy with you, the healee, you again, and reminding them to blow their matching pictures, and to stay on their grounding cord behind you. The only incursions into your space are the chords that your healing guides connect to the backs of your hands.

If you wish, you can have your guides blow your matching pictures for you as they light up during the healing. This is useful for saving time. It's not as useful if you wish to read your matching pictures, like when you're getting a healing from your guides and are curious. Let them know you want to take a look before they blow any pictures in your space. You can always create a rose for the pictures they blew while healing you after the fact and read them that way.

One more comment on how to use healing guides. You can use them for more than just healings. Send them ahead of you to your next job interview and have them prepare the energy for your interview. Have them help you create mockups. Have them bring you people to read and heal. These kinds of guides have a lot of information, and you can get help in all kinds of areas of your life.

If you are controlling in a room full of healers and see someone call in their healing guides onto that grounded space behind their aura, it can appear as a fuzzy energy on the back of their aura, kinda like a parachute shape, conforming to the curve of their aura, but just outside of it. This is one way to tell if someone is NOT using healing guides to do a healing; you won't see any distortion. Nothing in their aura changes because no other spiritual energies arrived either behind them or in their aura or in their body.

Energy checks.

An energy check is a technical reading of the condition of the tools taught in this book: grounding, running energy, blowing roses, protection roses, being in your bubble, being in the center of your head, etc.

It can also be about any other kind of reading technique. When you do an energy check, you are asking what is causing someone's energy to not run. This could be your energy or someone else's energy. You can give yourself an energy check.

You can give yourself an energy check at any time. If someone asks you for an energy check, you can give them one at any time. All you need is to get into a light trance and you know how to match that vibration.

Remember: you don't have to ground or run your energy or anything else in order to read energy. The benefit of grounding and running energy while doing readings is it removes all the pain energy that you run into. This means you can give an energy check to yourself even when your grounding stinks.

To do an energy check for someone else, just sit down, find your space, and ask where their energy is stuck. Maybe they are grounding OK but their energy is not running. Maybe they're running energy or look like they are running some kind of energy, but their grounding isn't working.

Finding your space is another shorthand from BPI. It means ground and run your energy, be in the center of your head, blow roses for any pictures that are lit up, and fill in. Finding your space also means just getting into a reading space, which is a light trance.

By the third or fourth week of the beginning meditation or healing class, students in those classes received an energy check on their grounding cord from a clairvoyant student. Very basic: Does the cord connect to the bottom of the first chakra? Does the cord connect to the center of the planet? Does the cord carry energy away to the center of the planet? Maybe looking at what's stopping their grounding cord from, well, grounding. Really basic.

Once you've done a few energy checks, it becomes automatic. Your attention is drawn to the root cause of whatever energy problem this person is facing *with their tools.* Energy checks are focused on the tools and don't sway too far towards personal issues in their life, unless there is, for instance, a picture from an uncle in their first chakra that limits how much energy their grounding cord may release and take away. You read that picture and watch the readee blow it up, if they can. In the case of a beginner, you might blow the picture for them, but once they know how to create and destroy roses, let them take care of the pictures themselves. Some healers take a bit longer to learn to read someone's tools and let them fix things for themselves, LOL!

Giving yourself energy checks is easy. For example, you sit down, start finding your space, and notice that no energy is running down your left arm. You see static energy in your aura in front of your first chakra.

Your grounding cord is not at full volume. Wow! You can notice a lot of stuff in a few seconds.

So then you ask why your energy is not running, and immediately see a small picture near your first chakra of a dead body. It's a past-life death picture, and it's frozen your first chakra.

Wonderful! Just blow some roses for that picture and watch what changes. Your energy starts to ground out. Your left arm cools off as energy starts to run down it again. Eventually, your fountain clears out that static in front of your first chakra, too, and you're back in business.

Death picture? That sounds like a really big problem.

Nope. It's just a picture and when you blow it up, it loses its resonance and can no longer affect your space.

But why wasn't the energy running down my left arm? Why just my left arm? This is an example of swaying away from focusing on your tools. Is it too far? That depends more on when you ask it. In this example, you noticed three things right away. No energy running down your left arm, some static in front of your first chakra, and your grounding cord not flowing freely. These are symptoms of an energy problem.

Then you asked why your energy is not running and the answer took you to that death picture in your first chakra. This *is* the energy problem. Deal with this first, and your energy flow smooths out. Then you can read more about why you only noticed your energy wasn't running in your left arm.

You don't have to keep a problem around in order to read the problem and build your understanding of it. This is especially true when the problem is so fresh in your mind, but even days or weeks later, you still have the information available to you that answers this question. You will remember exactly what the symptoms looked like and can do a rose reading on each symptom; i.e. create a rose for the energy not flowing down your left arm and create another rose for why it wasn't flowing. Do the same for the static energy in front of your first chakra and the constraint on your grounding cord. When you create these roses, also blow any matching pictures that get lit up.

Key Point: every time you do a reading, blow your matching pictures at the start of the reading. You may need to repeat this during the reading, if the images you are reading get fuzzy. You should repeat this after the reading is done. Pictures can come in layers, just like energy.

Notice that two things are happening here at the same time. One is solving an intellectual problem and the other is solving an energy problem. The intellectual problem is, "Oh this is connected here and causing that thing that isn't supposed to be purple over there to…" and the energy problem is, "I have a death picture lit up in my first chakra and need to blow it up." Solving both puzzles gives you intellectual validation and spiritual validation. You can skip the intellectual puzzle, but you cannot skip the energy puzzle.

Sometimes, during the after-reading cleanouts at BPI, when we were sharing some neat things that we saw during our readings, a reader would say, "I blew a big death picture," or something similar, and say nothing else. What's a big picture? It's just a picture with more energy on it or anchoring it more than other pictures. No explanation was necessary; the other readers were already taking a look at the energy of the picture that reader blew, and were busy blowing their matching pictures.

When do you need an energy check?

Suppose you've been grounding and running energy for some time. You really get a lot out of it. Life seems a little easier.

All of a sudden, for no apparent reason, nothing seems to work quite right. Life seems off. Work seems more difficult. Relationships seem a little flat. You rationalize this as just having a bad week; maybe you're catching a cold, but then the same thing carries over into the next week.

Obviously, the "right" thing to do is to find whatever energy is behind all of these symptoms and ground it out of your space, blow any pictures that are anchoring it to you, and get back to your new and improved life, and so you up your game by doubling how long you ground and run energy each day. This is a good approach and is what happens over the course of six months of taking the beginning courses at the Berkeley Psychic Institute. You go from struggling to ground ten minutes a day to grounding and running energy and creating and destroying roses for sixty minutes with ease.

But what if nothing in your life gets back to that new and improved state? You're meditating twice a day, morning and night, for twenty minutes each, but meditating is beginning to feel like work, and you don't get the kind of healing you were getting only a few days ago.

What happened?

Nothing particularly bad happened. In fact, just the opposite.

You've uncovered some energy or a picture or both that has been in your space and hiding for a long time. Your awareness has grown enough that you're aware of the energy or picture, and it's now affecting you.

Congratulations! You've uncovered something in your space and you are ready to heal this and take your next step in your spiritual growth, awareness, and understanding. Well done!

So how come reading that last paragraph doesn't make you feel any better? Simple. You haven't blown the picture yet. This is a bigger picture than the ones you create and destroy all day long, and it's probably anchored into some energy that's stuck underneath it.

It could be a core picture, meaning it's bound to many other pictures. When you uncover and blow a core picture, it causes a cascading release of more pictures and stuck energies. This can be like an avalanche and managing it usually means running your energy a bit longer each day for a few days. The goal of running energy longer is not to overcome the avalanche; that's not possible and would probably just cause parts of the avalanche to get stuck together again.

The goal of running your energy longer during an avalanche of energy and pictures being released is to accelerate the avalanche and get through it faster.

This would be a good time to create some amusement. Fake a laugh until you can laugh at faking a laugh.

You've uncovered some repelling energy in your space that freezes you and makes you want to puke.

How do you fix this? You fix it with an energy check. Sit down. Find your space for a few minutes. Take a quick look around, and ask what's up. What caused your energy to stop?

An energy check is a reading of your tools. You might be thinking this means a reading of your grounding cord and running energy. That is almost correct. You are asking what caused your energy to stop running. This question leads you to the energy that is affecting your tools.

The tools you have learned and are practicing actually have many components, and each component is a potential area where energy can get stuck. I'm giving you this list not as a checklist that you must work through during every energy check, but more like reading prompts. The list is useful to prime you with things to look at, not all during the same energy check, but as they are needed.

Energy checks last five minutes, sometimes fifteen minutes if you're really having fun. Go back to that first example in this section on giving yourself an energy check, where the first things you see are no energy running down your left arm, static energy in front of your first chakra, and your grounding is choked off a little. These are symptoms. You asked what's causing all this and went directly to a past life death picture in your first chakra.

From the time you noticed the symptoms to the time you saw the root cause took less than a minute. It feels longer when you're in the middle of it, but it really took less than a minute. Then you have plenty of time left in that five minutes to blow that picture and observe what happens next.

Sometimes, sometimes, you blow a picture and what happens next is a cascade of pictures and energies that get released, and your only option is enjoying the ride! That's a fun fifteen minutes! Or more. Or maybe less. It's going to happen whether you're watching it or not.

Take a look at one or two of these each week as a practice energy check. It will begin to teach you a vocabulary of energies that you become more aware of in yourself and in others. This can teach you more about the workings of your energy. This is studying. You're reading your own book.

Here's the list of components of your tools.

- Creating a grounding cord
- Attaching it to the bottom of your first chakra
- Attaching it to the center of the planet
- Being in the center of your head
- Finding your neutrality
- Creating a protection and separation rose
- Creating and destroying roses
- Running cosmic energy down the back channels
- Running earth energy up the leg channels
- Mixing cosmic energy with earth energy in the first chakra
- Running the mixture up the front channels through the remaining six chakras
- Creating a fountain of earth and cosmic energy out of your crown chakra and up to the top of your aura
- Having some of the mixture flow down your arm channels
- Creating small fountains out of your palms with your hand chakras
- Allowing the mixture and any energies released by the mixture to flow down to your grounding cord and into the center of the planet
- Grounding your aura
- Grounding a room or vehicle
- Creating a gold sun over your head
- Filling the gold sun with your highest creative essence, present time growth vibration, and affinity for yourself
- Bringing the gold sun down into your aura and crown chakra, allowing it to fill up the empty spaces created when you released energy or blew pictures

This is more tools than you thought, eh? This is what grounding, running energy, blowing roses, and filling in are made up of. The benefits of looking at these discrete pieces of your meditation space during an energy check are many. In fact, it's fair to think of any skill you have with energy work to be a tool that you can practice and improve by looking at all of its components. By doing so, you are practicing reading in more detail.

Each tool is a potential inflection point in your personal growth. In the same way that running energy accelerates your grounding, which accelerates your healing of yourself, each of these tools, when focused on for a bit, enable your process to improve. Your awareness grows to include more details in your space, and this enhances your ability to see details in other people's spaces. In short, you become a more capable reader and healer.

Let's take a look at two of these tools: attaching your grounding cord to the bottom of your first chakra and creating the fountain out of your seventh chakra. These example scenarios will give you the basic idea of what questions to ask when you read each tool. I'll give a more comprehensive list for all the tools and things to look at after this. You'll more easily see the patterns of questions develop and better understand how and why they work.

Example: You've called me and asked me for an energy check. In preparation before you get here, I've meditated for at least ten minutes, cleared my space of any matching pictures that got lit up when you called, completed my communication with anyone else, and filled in completely. We're both psychic and a simple call of twenty seconds is plenty of time to light me up if I have matching pictures with any of the energy you're dealing with. In fact, your intention to call me will begin to light up my pictures, so receiving the actual call just tells me why they're lit up.

You arrive and sit down in a chair directly in front of me. I'm sitting in my chair. There's nothing else in between us, unless one of my cats takes an interest in your energy and comes to see for themselves.

I close my eyes and check that my grounding is working and my energy is moving. I close down my lower three chakras and slip into a light trance. Closing down the lower three chakras brings more of my energy up to my head. This makes seeing and reading energy easier. I double check that I'm comfortably in the center of my head.

You just sit there with your eyes open. I'll ask you to say your name and when you do, I'll see you light up as a sparkle, a small point of light somewhere in your space or nearby, typically somewhere around or in your head. I'll ask you to do something and then watch you do that.

I see you already have your grounding cord. I ask you to drop it and create a new one. When you do this, I see a gap between your first chakra and your grounding cord and tell you I see a gap and that your grounding cord is not connected to your first chakra. Then I watch what you do about it.

Let's say nothing changes. I ask myself why and see some energy from a close family member between your first chakra and your grounding cord. The energy is from a male.

I ask myself what kind of energy it is.

It's from a childhood picture of you playing with a male family member and you getting hurt. He felt responsible for your injury and put his protection energy around your first chakra to make sure you were safe. He also hoped this would hide his role in you getting injured from your parents. Ah. Same parents. He's your sibling.

So that's the when and what of this energy. It's in past time. It's a male protection energy that your sibling learned by copying what your father did when protecting mom and the kids. Neither of you are kids anymore.

Next, I ask what this energy is saying. Every energy has a message. Asking what it says is an easy way to see its intent or effect. Notice this might yield a different answer from when the energy was first created. Originally, it was to protect a female sibling and make them feel safe. What does it say to the adult sibling now carrying it around?

In the present, this energy says you can't take care of yourself. It's an invalidation of your adult survival information and impacts both your relationships and career. It limits how well you can ground. I tell you all this.

If you aren't already, I ask you to blow some roses. I blow roses at the same time. This creates more permission for you to blow roses. It might also put my attention on how you create and destroy roses, and if that tool appears to have a problem, that's what I'll look at next.

But you blow roses just fine and the energy from your childhood has cleared out of your space.

Your space looks different now. Your energy is moving more. I ask you to drop that grounding cord and create a new one. This one attaches solidly to the bottom of your first chakra and your energy starts running.

We could stop right here and call it a success. An energy check should last no more than fifteen minutes. At least, that was the standard at the Institute. You aren't trying to answer all the questions about every tool, or everything else, including the meaning of life. Your intent is to get the person's energy you're reading moving again, even if you're reading yourself. It's a health check on your tools that enables you to take a look at any energy for yourself and take your next step.

That said, if you see a picture and their energy begins to go wild just because you saw that picture, follow that rabbit down that hole! Those are some of the best readings. That person has uncovered something deeply meaningful to their life and sticking to the rules serves neither them nor you very well. Go for it! Read that picture!

Every energy check usually begins with looking at their grounding cord but it doesn't have to. You can sit down and just take a general look to assess if their energy is running. Sometimes it ends with looking at the grounding cord.

Sometimes, just taking a look at the overall energy is enough to get their energy moving again. Like, "Wow! None of your energy is moving at all!" This may be the very picture they need to hear about in order to validate what they've been experiencing, blow the picture, and move on.

I had a great energy check from a staff member named Richard Lawrence. We had just finished a class in basic male energy (he was teaching it), and I asked him if he'd take a look at my energy.

I sat. He sat. He laughed. "You're running your cosmic energy in your legs and your earth energy in your cosmic energy channels."

I sat still, kinda dumbfounded for a moment, then felt my space turn over. Everything started flowing in that familiar way and the energy check was over.

"Cosmic on top, Earth on the bottom, big guy," and he laughed some more. That was it.

It is a fun practice and very educational to take a look at the connection of the cord to the first chakra. Look at the connection of the cord to the center of the planet. Look for breaks in the cord. Look for the cord being in present time. Look for blockages in the cord. If all looks well, move along to the next tool.

But I'm having a bad day. Now what?

Example: I'm having a terrible day. I feel awful. My energy is not moving at all. And I can't see a thing. When I try to ground, I just want to cry and go back to bed.

Can't see? No worries. Use your hands instead. Rub your palms together lightly and that will brush off any energy that's mucking up your hand chakras. Take both palms and feel the energy around your left foot, then your right foot. Feel the energy around your throat and face. Your hands don't need to touch your body. They don't need to be close to a body part to sense the energy there.

Scan with your hands all around your aura and energy channels.

My hand will stop on the biggest issue, and I'll begin to read it.

If I see that I cannot create a new grounding cord at all, I ask myself why. The times I've been giving an energy check to someone or have been getting an energy check from someone, if there was trouble creating a grounding cord, the person creating it was often not in the center of their head. They were in their third or fourth chakra and some picture or energy there was blocking them from creating a cord. What this means is they were not creating the cord with their clairvoyance. This isn't necessarily a bad thing, but I've noticed some people have more difficulty creating images from their lower chakras. It's worth asking the question, and you'll learn something about how you use your chakras.

Back in the beginning days, I just felt around until I found the energy that says, "Don't ground and run energy." Then it was time to blow some roses, break up that energy, create a new grounding cord, and run my energy. And nowadays? Yeah, pretty much the same, LOL!

Can an energy be in present time and mess with your grounding cord? Yes! That's called present time energy. (I am sometimes a smartass. My apologies.)

Some assume this must mean it's an active attack. Calling it an attack *might* be accurate, but that doesn't do you any favors. The more neutral "present time energy" label makes it easier to laugh at, and that's an advantage.

You can read it using the same basic pattern of questions: Whose energy is it? What does it say?

Or, you can create and destroy roses until the energy breaks up without ever reading it. Your choice. Sometimes you don't want to go down the rabbit hole, and that's okay.

Let's look at my beloved fountain tool.

I'd been doing energy checks for two years, every week on several other people, every day on myself. I got energy checks from the staff every month, sometimes more often. I looked for something new to learn in every energy check. I would read at different institutes and get energy checks from new people while I was there. (Note: in the 80s there were nine institutes, mostly in the Bay Area. Traveling to a different one was not a big deal.)

Looking at grounding cords, the patterns of the energy started to repeat. Yep, that energy is your grandpa's best hopes and dreams for his granddaughter. Too bad you don't really have a use for the energy of a VHS video player, so that energy now says get married to someone well off enough to own one of those new fangled video playing thingies. Not useful today. Let that energy go.

Grounding, running energy through the channels in the body, not in front of or behind the body, being in the center of the head, blowing roses, protection roses. All the big guns.

I asked a really good question one day: what are we not looking at?

Up until then, I'd looked at breaks in the energy channels, death pictures in the chakras, stuck spirit guides in the creative channels in their arms. My energy checking chops had gotten pretty specific, lol!

What were we missing? More accurately, what was I missing? We never looked at the fountain as its own tool. We looked at the energy coming out of the crown chakra and down through the aura, but only as a small part of running energy up the front channels of our bodies. This kinda sold our auras short because the fountain wasn't keeping up with spiritual growth. As you blow more pictures, you get more energy in your aura.

No one looked at my fountain at any length and I never looked at anyone else's in any depth. This is always a risk in a group of people. The group does something and is successful in that effort, and then standardizes so they can repeat that same success again and again. Basically, the group programs itself to not look at anything else or look at something in a different way. Repeatable processes provide predictability in life, and by definition suppress innovation. Fun, eh? Lots of cliches come to mind: we've always done it that way; if it ain't broke, don't fix it; respect tradition; keep it simple. Blah, blah, blah. This is how rules are born. Rules come from the desire to repeat our success.

Standardizing only works when the system is stable. When you are grounding, running energy, and blowing roses, your system is evolving. Updating your tools to be in affinity with where you are in present time solves this.

So I asked "what am I not looking at?" and I got "the fountain." I took a look at my fountain and discovered it was not doing at all what I thought it was doing. Since I'd only read it as part of checking if my energy channels were working, I didn't look at what the fountain did all on its own. It was there and that was enough. My energy came up through seven chakras and left my head. Mission accomplished. Move along.

When I looked at my fountain, it didn't reach the top of my aura. It didn't clean out the back of my aura either. It looked like a veil, weakly drizzling energy down across my face and not all the way to the edges of my aura. And that was it. The energy stopped at my neck.

I knew that in class, everyone's fountain flowed high and strong. We were all matching the teacher. But alone, my fountain reverted to a wimpy thing. Isn't that interesting?

The fix was embarrassingly simple and easy: destroy the old fountain and create a new one. Destroying the old one was simply taking it off my head and sending it down the grounding cord. This is called grounding it out (my apologies, lol). The new one I created looked far more powerful than the original one. This is because of all the energy and information I had gained since I created that first fountain. It had been two full years since I created that first fountain. I graduated from the clairvoyant training program for Pete's sake LOL! Creating a new fountain was far overdue.

Key Point: look at all of your tools. Recreate them from time to time and update them to take advantage of your new energy and new information.

All of my tools evolved and got stronger, but my fountain remained unchanged, stuck at the energy of where my abilities were *in my very first meditation class.* Embarrassing.

What sealed the deal for me about asking "what am I not looking at," and fountains specifically, happened this way.

I took my newfound enthusiasm for reading fountains up to Calistoga, California, to a small cabin on some heavily wooded acreage north of town. This was Lewis and Susan Bostwick's home and it was my first day on the job as Susan's bishop's assistant.

I'd graduated from the clairvoyant training program five or six weeks before. Two of us in my graduating class, myself and a wonderful woman named Nancy, had the most readings every month by a large margin. The program required us to do at least two, three hour training readings per week. Nancy and I did double that most weeks, sometimes doing six in a week while taking classes and holding down full time jobs. We were the freaks among the freaks, LOL!

Every reading released another chunk of energy, increasing our space and our own energy. This happened because we were blowing our matching pictures. I read often enough to be invited to join the missionary healers, which got me into readings of haunted houses, readings in hospitals and hospices, and fun stuff like that.

In short, I read a lot and had some certainty about how I handled my energy. It's interesting to note that while Nancy and I were aware of each other due to checking the Dot Board (each clairvoyant student got a little dot stuck by their name for each reading they did during a month), and we shared some classes, as best I can recall we never read together.

I pulled up to the cabin in my beater car. I grounded myself for a few minutes before leaving the car. I wasn't nervous. I was scared. What did I just volunteer for? The energy around the cabin was not intense. The pictures that lit up in my space were almost overwhelming. I hadn't felt like this in almost a year.

I looked at the cabin, grounded myself, and blew my matching pictures. I did the same with the barn and other buildings, and the redwoods. It was winter, and I had a light jacket. Getting my body calmed down took ten minutes. Brrr.

I filled in and approached the porch. The door opened, and Susan called out to me by name. That surprised me. We hadn't really talked much before then. I had asked Lewis if I could work for him and he assigned me to be Susan's assistant. I got a call telling me when and where to be from one of her assistants, and that was how I ended up knocking on their door.

Susan told me to sit down and ground and run my energy, and "get here." "Getting your energy here" was a common practice before readings and classes, which meant grounding and running your energy for thirty minutes to retrieve your energy from your work day, your commute, your arguments with roommates, whatever. It also meant matching the energy of the place you were in.

So I looked around for a chair, and picked the one next to Lewis, who was already grounding and running his energy.

We sat like that for an hour. I matched and unmatched Lewis several times. Where he would go with his energy I could not always follow, but I'd learned to keep up with him in his clairvoyant class for the most part. I went unconscious a few times. Running energy with him one-on-one at the cabin was more intense than in his class, but also more fun!

When that was done, I was assigned to give energy checks to Susan's staff, who consisted of other graduates of the clairvoyant program. I could use the front porch for this, I was told. Brrr!

There were five staff members. I gave each one a fifteen minute energy check and took five to ten minutes in between to meditate and make separations.

In all honesty, I struggled. I had one arm crossed over my third chakra to keep it from opening wide and blasting the person I was trying to read. It felt like a knot in my solar plexus. I had to use my other hand to read the energy of the staff member because I couldn't blow roses fast enough to see clearly without that hand. I was getting lit up so fast that I couldn't glance at my own pictures. I just trusted myself and blew roses as fast as I could, filling in every minute. Yes, a fresh gold sun every minute. My energy was churning.

When I was done with everyone, Susan came out with this unreadable look on her face, and I was sure I'd royally fucked up. Then she yelled in an excited voice that her staff got more done in their first two hours today than they usually get done in a full day. What did I do to them?

That's when I noticed Lewis standing behind her in the doorway, smiling. I found my courage in his smile, and told her I read their fountains. I looked at what energy was preventing their fountain from reaching the top of their aura and healing their whole aura. She was surprised. I guess everyone was programmed to skip over that. (Note: my editor on this book said she attended some of the classes at BPI in the 90s and checking that your fountain reached the top of your aura was standard in all the classes. Hmm. That might have been because of me.)

I told Susan that in every person's space was the same energy of their family's expectations for them, hovering six inches over their crown chakras like a thin cloud, preventing their fountains from reaching the tops of their auras and flushing out their auras like a sprinkler under a clear plastic dome. After pointing that out to them, I described their changes in their fountains: halfway there now; blow some more expectation pictures; 80% there now; okay your fountain is at the top and flowing part way down your aura; now halfway; good! Everything is now grounding out of your aura.

I impressed my new boss 😛

There is power in asking questions. There is healing in finding your own answers. Rinse and repeat.

Pro Tip: If your fountain is not flushing the whole aura, simply yawning, stretching your arms up over the top of your head, and then bringing them out wide to the sides of your body with your palms out and fingertips running along the edges of your aura is usually enough to clear out the energy blocking the way. Blow some roses as well. Yawning and tilting your head back also blows pictures that accumulate in the center of your head while reading or meditating. It's fast and easy.

If you yawn when reading someone else and they get a little of-fended, like thinking you are bored by reading them, explaining to them that it's just releasing energy settles things down. In fact, the readee will usually start yawning as well, lol. You just gave them permission to release more energy.

Similarly, if your grounding is not feeling strong, simply lower-ing your arms with your palms facing your grounding cord, fin-gers pointing down, will refresh your grounding cord and its at-tachments to your first chakra and the center of the planet. Hand chakras are wonderful! Use them liberally.

PRO TIP: When you read someone's traumatic experience that's been blocking them from moving forward with their life for a long time,

there will be a lot of bottled up energy in their space. When they begin to realize just how much time they've lost, the tears start to flow.

At BPI, we always handled this the same way. We gently explained that they should not be embarrassed, that crying is just another form of energy release. As soon as they looked up to hear this, we'd say, "Besides, the more you cry, the less you pee!"

The readee would laugh, releasing a ton of energy, leaving a grateful smile on their face. And then the reading would carry on.

When you sit down to do an energy check on your energy or someone else's energy, the first question is this: is their energy moving? (From here on, I'll talk in terms of reading someone else, but the same steps apply to reading yourself.)

If it is moving smoothly and the flow looks complete, tell them so, congratulate them and ask them, "Do you have a question?"

This is a good question to ask when things are going well. Sometimes, they want you to look at some energy from the near past, like, "Whenever I'm with <some person or pet or something else>, I feel really off and my energy stops flowing. What is causing that?"

This sounds more like your typical reading, and it might turn into that, but your attention and intent is on what happens to their grounding and running energy, and their other tools. So your answer will be couched in terms like, "When you're with your brother-in-law, your energy stops running. The reason it stops is <some past life as a pokemon, or a monster, or just your mother-in-law in your BIL's space being critical of you>."

Then you observe what they do with this communication. Do they heal themself? Do they get even more lit up? Sometimes just waiting it out for a few minutes is a good strategy. Don't say anything and be like a cat; wait and watch.

If their energy is not moving, just relax, ground yourself, let the cosmic and earth energies flow through your body, and see what energy is getting between them and running their energy. Grounding, running your energy, and blowing pictures creates permission for them to do the same. They see your energy moving and can match it.

This is the essence of any energy check. You see their energy is not moving. Almost always, your attention will go to the exact place in their space where some energy is mucking everything up. It could be some energy that they picked up during their commute. It very likely could be a picture that's lit up. It could be an energy that they've just uncovered by grounding and running energy.

Sometimes, all you do is describe the energy that's blocking them and wait for them to heal themselves. Wait and watch. Cats really do understand this kind of energy work. I've had cats sit side chair with me during readings and energy checks. One big fella would touch my leg with his paw if he thought I was missing something. I'd look at him. He'd look at something in the space of the person I was reading. I'd look there and see something new, LOL! He'd look up at the ceiling and there would be a big spirit guide for the readee, jumping up and down, pointing at some picture in the readee's space. I'd read that picture and watch the spirit guide and the readee heal themselves. Big fun!

Sometimes, they may ask you for a healing, or you may offer a healing. Always ask them first before you heal them.

The reason permission to heal is asked for is not just good manners or any ethical concerns. Those are valid reasons. The larger reason is they may want to learn how to deal with this energy themselves. Don't take away their learning opportunity by jumping in and solving their energy problem. Ask first.

One of the best validations I got as a beginning clairvoyant student was exactly this. I was getting my first student reading. Everyone else had gotten a student reading *before* joining the clairvoyant training program. I was special and just jumped in the deep end without looking, right into the clairvoyant training program without ever experiencing what I was there to learn to do.

Hanna Jane found out I hadn't received a student reading, gave me a business card for a free reading, and told me to get one that week. So, that's what I did. Getting a reading was the fastest way to learn what all the roles were in a two hour student reading.

The reading was fascinating. The past lives, the descriptions of my adventures this lifetime. It was exciting. I was enthused. We were having a ball.

The readers asked me if I'd like a healing. I said sure. I assumed this is what I was supposed to say. And then the room kinda froze.

Everything looked like the white haze you see on the glass of fluorescent tube lights. The room got brighter, but opaque. The readers, all women, looked uncomfortable, but had their hands up, palms facing me, and as best as I could tell, they were trying to give me a healing.

Hanna Jane was the house control that day. She saw our room's energy freeze. She came upstairs and entered our room. She smiled big at me and asked, "Do you feel that static energy?" I said that I did. She asked the same of the line of readers and they said yes.

She chuckled and said, "Stop healing him. He wants to do it himself."

This rang all kinds of bells for me, and I just sat there grinning ear to ear.

Hanna left. The reading ended fifteen minutes later. The ladies learned to recognize the energy of someone complying with an offer of healing, rather than wanting a healing. I got validated in wanting to heal myself. Later on, I learned about the programming of females to nurture males because all males needed to be fixed in some way and females were just better equipped to do the job, LOL! Cultural programming can be very funny!

Here are some useful questions to ask about each tool. This is not meant to be a checklist that you must work through during every energy check. With a little practice, you'll sit down and immediately see that whoever you're looking at isn't grounding, or they are grounding but their energy isn't moving in their legs, or they left their aura in Walmart.

The list is meant to give you some ideas of things I've seen during all the energy checks I've done, and give you some references in case you get stuck looking at something during an energy check. Maybe you'll recall something from this list and jump right to the energy or picture that's causing the fuss. Please don't memorize the list, LOL! Just let it remind you of things you already know. Let it help you stay curious, a kind of "what about *this*" kind of prompt. Just read what you see. None of what you see is your problem, and may not be a problem for the one you're reading.

OK. I know you're probably going to look at every single question at least once, LOL. That's actually a good idea. You'll blow more pictures and learn to see in more detail. Just don't try it all at once.

- Creating a grounding cord:
  - Which chakra are you in when you're creating your grounding cord? It could be any, or none, if you're creating a grounding cord while out of your body.
  - Can you easily destroy your old grounding cord? If not, what energy gets in between you and destroying your creation?
  - Whose energy gets in between you and creating a new grounding cord?
- Attaching the grounding cord to the bottom of your first chakra:
  - Does it attach to the bottom of the first chakra?
  - If not, why?
  - If an energy is in the way, whose energy is it? When was it created? Why was it created? What does it say now?
- Attaching the grounding cord to the center of the planet:
  - Does the cord attach to the center of the planet?
  - If not, why not?
  - If an energy is in the way, whose energy is it? When was it created? Why was it created? What does it say now?
- Being in the center of your head:
  - Are you in the center of your head?
  - If so, can you see 360 degrees around your space?
  - If so, can you focus down to a single degree and go back to 360 degrees?
  - If not, what gets between you and being in the center of your head?
    - Whose energy is it? When was it created? Why was it created? What does it say now?

- Creating a protection and separation rose:
  - Can you create a rose?
  - Is the rose in front of your face?
  - If not, where is the rose?
  - Can you adjust the position of the rose to be in front of your face? If not, why? Whose energy gets in between you and having your protection rose protect your ability to see energy? When was this energy created? Why was it created? What does it say now?
  - Can you create a protection rose and ground it?
  - Does your protection rose protect 100% of your space?
  - If not, what energy gets in between you and protecting all of your space?
  - Can you create a separation rose?
  - Can you create a decoy rose?
    - This is a rose that matches your energy, and you stick it someplace far away from your physical body. People who try to put their attention on you or throw energy at you auto-magically get diverted to your decoy rose. At BPI, we routinely stuck our decoy roses out on Alcatraz! It's a simple way of quickly creating more space for yourself so you can focus more on yourself.
    - Just for fun: you can become someone else's decoy rose. Just ground yourself and match the outer layer of your aura to that other person, and all the attention and energy misses them, comes to you, and harmlessly grounds out. I used to do this for some of the female staff members when they were greeting a crowd of strangers coming in to get readings and healings, or at psychic fairs. It's easier and more efficient than wrapping

your aura around someone to protect them. The energy bullets curve away and miss. Very cool, in a Matrix kind of way, lol.

- Creating and destroying roses:
  - Can you create and destroy roses?
  - Can you destroy 100% of the energy used to create your rose?
  - If not, why not?
  - Where does the energy come from that destroys the rose?
  - Does the rose get destroyed if you include a picture in it from your space?
  - Does the energy ground out after the rose is destroyed?
  - If not, why not?
- Running cosmic energy down the back channels:
  - Do you have two back channels or four?
  - Do you use all the channels you have?
  - Are there any tears or breaks or blockages in the channels?
  - Do the channels connect to the crown chakra and to the first chakra?
  - Do the back channels connect to the small channels into the backs of chakras two through six? (These are like drainage channels that vent energies released in these chakras to be carried out and down to the first chakra and grounded out.)
  - Does the cosmic energy flow all the way from the top of the aura to the back of the crown chakra, down to the first chakra?
  - Where are you getting your cosmic energy from?
- Running earth energy up the leg channels:
  - Where are you getting your earth energy from?

- Does the earth energy fill up and clean out the feet chakras?
- Does the earth energy flow all the way up to and into the first chakra?
- Are there any breaks, tears, or blockages in the leg channels?
- If so, whose energy caused them? When was this energy created? Why was it created? What does it say now?
- Does the earth energy flow into the first chakra and down your grounding cord?

- Mixing cosmic energy with earth energy in the first chakra:
  - Does the mixture spin in the first chakra?
  - If not, what stops it from spinning? Whose energy is it? When was this energy created? Why was it created? What does it say now?
  - Does the mixture clarify the images you are looking at? If not, can you add more earth energy to the mix to see if it clears up?
  - If you cannot add more, what energy gets in the way of adding more? Whose energy is it? When was this energy created? Why was it created? What does it say now?

- Running the mixture up the front channels through the remaining six chakras:
  - Does the energy clean out each chakra?
  - Are the front two channels connected to the tops and bottoms of each chakra? If not, what gets in the way?
  - Are there any breaks, tears, or blockages in the front channels?
  - If so, whose energy caused it? When was this energy created? Why was it created? What does it say now?

- Creating a fountain of earth and cosmic energy out of your crown chakra and up to the top of your aura:
  - Does it reach the top of your aura?

- - Does it use all the energy coming up through the crown chakra?
  - Does it flush your whole aura?
  - Does it ground out of your space?
- Having some of the mixture flow down your arm channels:
  - Does the mixture reach your hand chakras?
  - If not, why not? Are there any breaks, tears, or blockages in your arm channels?
  - How many channels do you see in your arms?
    - This is a fun question. Some people have one larger channel that changes purpose. Sometimes it's the creative channel. Sometimes a healing channel. Sometimes a reading channel. Sometimes the channel for the mixture.
    - Other people see multiple channels, one for each kind of energy.
    - However you see your arms is correct. It may change over time, and that's okay too. We're not so much concerned with spiritual anatomy as with the functional health of the channels, however many there may be.
- Allowing the mixture and any energies released by the mixture to flow down to your grounding cord and into the center of the planet:
  - How far down the edges of the aura does the fountain go?
  - If it doesn't reach your grounding cord, why not?
  - What areas of your aura does the fountain miss?
- Creating a gold sun over your head
  - Where are you when you create your gold sun? In a specific chakra, above your head, on your left shoulder? Where?

- Some of us like to watch the sun come into our space from outside of our bodies. This is not a problem.
- There is no rule saying where you must be in order to bring in a gold sun of your own energy.
 - Is all of the energy in your gold sun your energy? If not, whose energy is in there with yours? How did it get there?
   - You may have some programming in a chakra or your aura that says "this energy belongs with your energy forever," or "pay no attention to this energy," or some other attempt at hiding the intent of the energy. It may say something about ethics and proper behavior. Ask yourself if that's really true in the present. Take a look at when that energy first entered your space. Maybe it was true back then, but is no longer useful now, even if it was given to you with a positive intent. Maybe it's a crap piece of energy that you've been seeking for a long time and now that you've found it you can get rid of it.
   - Ask good questions. Figure out who, what, where, when, and why, and ask what that energy says today.
- Filling the gold sun with your highest creative essence, present time growth vibration, and affinity for yourself:
 - What are the ratios of the three energies? There's no one right answer; this is just an interesting question that can lead to other interesting questions.
 - Are there any energies in your gold sun that are not your energies? This may not be a problem. For instance, you could be given some supreme being

energy to help you out. Over time, the SB energy turns into your energy.

- If it's not a neutral energy, you most likely want to get rid of it. Aunt Sally's gift to you from five years ago, might keep on giving, but most likely has run its course and needs to be grounded and recycled. It's no longer an appropriate energy for you.

- Does the present time growth vibration match your body's needs? This is never an idealized energy, like your highest creative essence. This is the energy of an immediate need in your body and is used to sustain your body while your energy changes.

- Is your affinity for yourself in present time? Yeah, you used to recognize your own energy with ease, but you've been changing and growing. Your affinity for your energy has to evolve, too.

- Is your affinity for yourself in future time? Yeah, don't get ahead of yourself, LOL! The goal is learning to manage your spiritual energy in your physical body. Stay here now.

- Bringing the gold sun down into your aura and crown chakra, allowing it to fill up the spaces created where you released energy or pictures:

  - Does it fill you up? If not, then your gold sun may be too small. A good compromise until you can create a larger sun is bringing in multiple suns until your energy meter reads full again.

  - Does it leak out of your aura? Bringing in a gold sun is a great way to look for rips, tears, and holes in your aura.

  - If you find damage in your aura, whose energy caused it? When did it happen? Was energy thrown at your aura? Did your aura tear because of the thrown energy, or because the energy hit a picture in your aura and exploded it?

- Make repairs to your aura by imagining a magic glue that heals the damage. Use your hands to apply it and feel the damage until it smoothes over again and your energy flows through the same area without leaks.

Cool healing tip: If you're healing your aura with your hands, you will run into a challenge with the backside of your aura. You can't reach it. The easy solution is to stand up, detach your body from your aura and turn around. Feel and fix whatever you find in the back of your aura, then turn back to the front and re-attach your aura. Alternatively, you can stand up, detach your aura, and rotate the back of your aura around to the front. I've done this while in line at the coffee shop and it always gets curious stares, LOL! They don't know what I did to warrant their attention, but they looked.

Spirit Guides

Have you ever wondered what's in it for a spirit who guides someone?

Some traditions assert that everyone has one ancestor that guides them through this life. Other traditions assert that everyone has five guides, each a specific kind of guide. I've read different people, some with one guide, some with several, a few with no guides. I don't see a hard rule here. I do see cultural filters and cultural group agreements.

What's in it for the guides? What could they possibly get out of hanging out with us? From hanging out with me, LOL?

Our behavior is mediocre, sometimes awful. We can destroy everything we set our minds to and anything we aren't aware of. I take that back; we especially destroy things we're afraid of. Why would spirit guides want to hang out with us, especially if they're "enlightened"?

There must be better things to do, right? How engaging can it be to watch us make the same mistakes over and over again? Unless, of course, we are the spiritual sitcom of the universe, lol. We are kind of a spiritual rerun, LOL!

I asked a spirit guide, "What's in it for you?" They replied, "I get to experience Time."

Imagine that. It wasn't getting a hit off of my sexy time with my girlfriend. It wasn't fast cars. It wasn't the drone of a bored-out-of-his-skull lecturer in college. It was Time. Some spirit guides really do get a kick out of cars because of the novelty, but Time is the thing. Time enables experiences on a physical level.

"The past is history. The future is a mystery. Today is a gift. That's why they call it the present." – Eleanor Roosevelt

Time is the observation of change. This is close to the definition used in physics, which says that time is the interval over which change occurs. I prefer the shorter version. This is one case where I prefer the poetic verse over the technical explanation. Time is the observation of change.

Spiritual growth is change. Time is the observation of change. What a spirit guide gets from being our spirit guide is growth for themselves.

BUT WAIT. WHAT IS A SPIRIT?

In my understanding, a spirit is energy organized around awareness. There are examples of organized energies that have no awareness in them. Nuclear reactions are highly organized energies, but are not aware. Gravity is an organized energy but is not aware. Punishment energy thrown by one person at another is organized energy, but is not aware. Group agreements have a specific spiritual energy or vibration, but the agreement is not aware. Yes, there can be spirit guides in a spiritual agreement that monitor compliance with the agreement, but the agreement itself is not aware.

A spirit is energy organized around awareness. Those little twinkling lights you catch out of the corner of your eye? It might be a condition of your retina, or it might be a spirit saying hello to you.

It is useful to introduce the idea of two types of energy: spiritual energies and electromagnetic energies. EM energies we can measure with external devices. Spiritual energies we can measure with our chakras and bodies. We have no physical tool by which to measure spiritual energy. We have no spiritual tricorder that can read a spirit's energy. For that function, we have us.

This is why when I look at someone's Kirlian Photograph of their "aura," I don't see the energy of their aura at all. Mammal bodies have EM fields *and* auras. Kirlian tech is just capturing the EM field and calling it an aura. It's a coincidence that our EM field overlaps with our auras.

Auras are more sophisticated than just one color. I've never read an aura that had only one color. Dominant themes? Sure. One color? Never. I once saw someone come into the institute for a reading and his aura and hands were black. I'm not talking about dark energy: jet black. I wasn't in his reading, but the women that read him said he reminded them of a serial killer. Once they got into reading his aura, though, he had multiple colors, only the outer layer was black.

So are Kirlian photos useful? Yes. I think they are. I didn't used to think this. In fact, I was a bit of an asshole about it, but now I've changed my mind.

If the photographer doing the interpretations of the photos has been practicing long enough, they will learn to read the person's aura, even though that's not what's depicted in the photo. They will look at an individual's Kirlian photo, which looks very much like every Kirlian photo ever taken, and interpret this fuzzy red haze for this individual in a unique way. This makes it a gateway experience for very new seekers, and I think that's useful. I didn't used to think this way. I thought it was total crap, but then I asked more questions and saw more youngsters at psychic fairs walking away from the photo booth with big grins on their faces and validation in their auras, and I corrected myself.

Something can be true. Something can be useful. Sometimes it can be both. Faith is useful without proof. Experience is useful even when the interpretation of the experience is a lie: "I ran into another spirit, face to face, and it scared the shit out of me." Some priest: "Demonic attack!" Some evangelical: "Satanic spawn!" Some psychiatrist: "Delusion!"

Notice how none of those "experts" that were so quick to judge asked me what happened next. Their responses to my little story are good examples of reading by rote. In other words, what I described triggered their dogmatic response; they never even glanced at the energy I described.

Don't read by rote, even with the Tarot cards. Read the energy that's in front of you when you're reading someone. Orange energy does not mean healing energy unless that's what it means to the person you are reading. Headbutting a spirit guide does not mean anything negative until you have read that it means that. It could be a past life picture of how you and that spirit used to play. Vikings do have a weird sense of what constitutes play, after all.

If spirit is energy organized around awareness, what does it look like?

At its most basic level, it looks like a point of light with a glow around it. No body type. No cultural shapes or coloring or gender. Just a purely energetic little ball of awareness with a soft glow of energy organized around it, twinkling at you to acknowledge you seeing it and it seeing you.

All spirit looks like a small ball of light with a glow around it. It looks like one sparkle from a sparkler firework when they say hello to you. When the dementors in the Harry Potter movies suck the soul out of someone, the movie paints a pretty accurate image of a spirit.

Just to be clear, "soul" is another word for spirit. Our language allows us to talk about our spirit and our soul as if they were two different things, as if they were somehow separate from, what? From us? Conforming to the grammatical rules of a language does not make something real or possible. What's real is we are a point of light. We are energy organized around awareness, and we look like a ball of light until we create an image in front of us for the world to see.

The same is true of the dementors. They are little balls of light. The dementors create a spooky image to go along with the role they are playing.

The same is true for all spirits. Angels and demons: balls of light.

So what's the difference between the reader of this book and a spirit guide? You, dear reader, have a physical body. This has more value to you than you may realize. It also has more value to your spirit guides than you probably used to think. Having a body means having time.

Key Point number one: I do not follow the more popular and positive or negative traditions in my labeling of spirits. If it has a body, it's a spirit in a body of some kind. If it doesn't have a body, I call it a spirit guide to begin with, even if it gives shit for advice. I know this is sometimes misleading and causes confusion, but even if a spirit is giving you shit advice, or punishing you, or lying to you, it's still a guide without a body. It does influence your direction, which might be a somewhat twisted interpretation of guidance, but it's useful. It's just not as useful to you as you might like it to be.

The reason I find it useful is that it's more neutral. This allows me to look at anyone without judgment, without losing my grounding and space, but mostly, it's a safe assumption that keeps me more neutral.

That archangel? Spirit guide. That demon? Spirit guide. That entity attachment? Spirit guide. That being from your astral? Spirit guide. Lucifer? Spirit guide (he doesn't have a body in real life). Your personal good luck spirit guide? Spirit guide. The Luck Dragon from *The Never Ending Story"* Cool spirit acting as a guide. Granny Goodwitch? Fun spirit guide.

Why is being more neutral to your spirit guides useful? If you decide that one of your guides is really having a negative impact on your life, you can end your agreement with that spirit and it goes away. No drama. No magic rituals. Just ending the energy of your spiritual agreement.

Agreements are energy and you can change energy. It's what psychics and healers do, eh?

There are some rough and tumble players in the inventory of spirit guides, and they can challenge you in ways that will make you and your body uncomfortable. As long as you're in your body, you are senior to all spirits.

You? You are in charge of a body. Sometimes you can be a spirit guide with a body. That's usually called being a parent or friend or teacher or mentor. Sometimes you are neck deep in the energy of life, struggling to figure something out and grow. That's usually you realizing again that you are more than just your body. You are a spirit with a body.

Key point number two: You don't have to use my simple system if you prefer a hierarchy or some other cultural system. My system comes from how I read. It is useful to find the little ball of light that owns the body in front of me, and read just them. This sometimes aggravates some spirit guides who want the reading to be about them, but hey! They didn't necessarily bring in the body in front of me and pay for a reading. The priority almost always goes to the spirit that owns the body.

It's worth mentioning that some readees who come into the Berkeley Psychic Institute only find their way there because of their spirit guides. This was a case of a spirit actually guiding someone. All due respect was paid to those guides. Sometimes they were part of that reading, but most often they were not the central issue. We gave them their props and returned our focus on the readee with the body.

We humans love our hierarchies. However you see beings-without-bodies is how you see them. I don't find it useful to tell people they must see things the way I do before they can grow their understanding. I didn't start out seeing everyone as little balls of light, so it would be rude to expect that of everyone else.

I have exceptions as well: healing masters and psychic surgeons, two specialist roles that I've heard others call healing guides. I find it useful to teach about psychic surgeons separately since they deal with changing things in the physical body, while healing masters stick to working on the aura, chakras, and energy channels. I only allow these players to plug into the backs of my hand chakras, but other styles of healing do things differently with their guides.

Another exception I make is for Akashic Record Keepers. Very specialized role. Still just spirits without bodies, but in a very specific role. However you see your Akashic Record Keeper is perfectly fine. Not much use in trying to standardize the appearances of everything. That kind of defeats the goal of having as little dogma as possible and getting you to look at things for yourself.

Sometimes my Akashic Record Keeper looks like the little duck that fell down from the ceiling on Groucho Marx's *You Bet Your Life* game show from the 1950s. At the beginning of each show, Groucho would tell the audience a secret word by having this duck that was dressed up to look like Groucho drop down with a note in its bill with the secret word printed on it by hand, and if the contestants said the secret word, they'd take home an extra twenty dollars! (In the 60s, this was increased to one hundred dollars.) Groucho would try his best to feed them questions that would pull the secret word from their mouths and it was often hysterical how close the contestants would get and still miss.

When the word was said, down came the duck with a card in its beak, and cheers and laughter rang out.

I figure that's a good energy for retrieving a vital piece of information that I've lost through the turmoils of this life. "Viaduct? Vi not a chicken?"

Basically, when I'm reading, everything is just a spirit guide until I see otherwise and understand their role and why they're with the person I'm reading. There probably is an Archangel Michael. There are imposters pretending to be the Archangel Michael and manipulating people for their own gain. If you take the first image you see, it's easier to miss important things. Trust, but verify. This is respectful and a real archangel, if that's even a thing, will not mind in the least. The very few angels I've seen were amused by me. I took that as a good sign, lol.

If you see a spirit guide, and then suddenly can't see it because some energy is right in your face, blocking you, blow your matching pictures and read it all anyway.

We were talking about time.

It ain't easy to get a body. You have to make agreements with someone to give you a body. Bodies don't just materialize out of thin air like the images of bodies that spirit guides make. And then you have to create all of your chakras in your shiny new body. That takes a lot of information and know-how. Not all spirits can pull this off. And you have to lower your vibration enough to get into the physical body and create your anchor points. A spirit with a body can come and go from their body, visit someone else's body, play on the astral, and settle deeply into their body. Some spirit guides that get too close to your body just turn off and get trapped. They don't know how to match the vibration of a body yet.

There are more spirits than there are bodies. When the demand is higher than the supply, competition ensues. There is a state that spirits go through when they want a body. I learned to call this state a "baby being." Baby beings are really capable spirits and make plans for what they want to experience. This was you and me, right before we incarnated this lifetime. They are often close to human bodies and are aware of Time. This can be wonderful to read. This can also create a lot of spiritual competition between multiple baby beings and the single body they are vying for.

This energy of competition can make the bodies of the adult humans involved get sick. It can strain or destroy relationships. It can damage the energy of those spirits who already have a child body with these parental humans (siblings). Competition energy is not nice.

Here's an example of spiritual competition from one of the clairvoyant classes about baby beings.

We had a guest teacher in my advanced clairvoyant class. She was an RN. She taught a class on baby beings.

She was wonderfully pragmatic in her style of teaching. She said, "We're going to learn about baby beings!"

She didn't explain about baby beings to us at all. She opened the class bubble up to baby beings and let us experience them ourselves. It was like being in a maternity ward ten times over.

Some were friendly and open. Some were mean and whacked the teacher and students. The teacher let this go on for fifteen minutes, these intense points of light zooming around, in and out of the room like fireflies.

Note: a whack is an energy thrown at someone with the intent to damage their aura or chakras.

When a whack is successful, the damage in the aura looks like either a tear, like the aura was slashed with a knife, or many tiny holes, like the aura was shot with a shotgun, or one large hole. It's useful to ask where the whack came from. Sometimes a pattern emerges. At BPI, I saw whacks from women almost always looked like shotgun blasts, and rips or tears almost always came from men. Whacks from spirit guides could look like either. Don't prejudge; look and ask.

Whacks can be subtle, just something to distract you and manipulate your choices.

Whacks can come through you and hit someone else. My mother once came through me and whacked the breasts of Hanna Jane, lighting up some cheesy sex picture.

Hanna was showing off a new silk blouse to some other ladies. I was admiring the blouse from across the room. I had been grounding and running my energy before class and came out of trance to see what all the excited energy was about. I felt and saw something dark whiz past my right temple, shoot across the room, and hit Hanna in the bosom.

Hanna yelled at me, "Watch your sex pictures, Wayne!" and left the room really angry. I felt guilty as hell for spoiling the joy that the ladies were having.

Then Hanna comes back in the room a few minutes later and says, "Don't worry, Wayne. It was your mother coming through you. Seems like she doesn't like me."

She had blown the picture, healed herself, and was all smiles again. It took me a while longer to find my space again, but little by little I felt better.

Whacks can cause breaks in cords, like your grounding cord or your first chakra cord to your small children. Basically, anything made of spiritual energy can be whacked.

The damage that whacks create is often caused by the whack hitting a picture already in your space and lighting it up strongly or even blowing it up. This is not a controlled explosion like when you create and destroy roses. This means the damage can be inside of your aura, not just at the edges. Just something else for you to look at, LOL!

Back to the class on baby beings!

After sitting in the soup of a bunch of baby beings for some time, we read each other. The teacher closed the class bubble, moving all of the baby beings out. We paired up and looked at what lit up for each of us by just being around baby beings. We were lit up like a fireworks show. Lots of prenatal pictures. Lots of postpartum pictures. Sibling competition. Divorce. Circumcision. A ton of core pictures!

Core picture: the picture at the bottom of the pile. Life leaves layers of energy. Some of this energy turns to pictures. Some of these pictures stack up like the interdependent layers of energy. When you find a matching picture during a reading or meditation, if it's a core picture, it feels stronger than usual. If you blow a core picture, it tends to blow some of the pictures stacked on top of it.

Not only does blowing a core picture release a ton of energy, it causes the pictures that were connected to it to be rearranged, releasing more energy. This rearranging tends to last longer than just blowing a picture does. This is one cause of a big growth period. Be amused.

Back to baby beings.

Divorce was fascinating to read. Example: The baby being wanted the father's DNA but didn't want him hanging around. That was a really capable baby being. The baby being's agreement was with the mother only. There was no agreement with the father. The baby being picked the daddy and set things in motion, eliminating all other suitors, then dismissed him like the wrapper from a candy bar once it had its body.

In addition to the pictures that were lit up by the baby beings in the class, there was lots of damage. Our auras were ripped in some cases. Our grounding cords were cut in some cases. It was a violent and graphic spiritual demonstration.

We took a short break, then she let them do it all over again! This time, we were not lit up as badly. We'd blown most of our pictures while reading each other. Now we could read the baby beings more clearly.

Some of the baby beings were amazing healers, keeping mom healthy, dad healthy, and making strong agreements with their siblings. Some gave us healings in gratitude for us reading them.

The poopy ones we read a little, and helped a few blow their competition pictures, but a couple we were told to leave alone by the supreme being. Sometimes things have to play out on their own terms. It's not for us to judge or automatically change. Just because we can read the agreements between a spirit guide and someone with a body, and we can bring those agreements into present time and end the agreements on behalf of the person with the body, we don't automatically do this. Sometimes the very thing the person with the body needs to learn is how to manage their relationships with their spirit guides.

It's usually obvious. The person says, "Get rid of this spirit guide for me!" and you hear the lie in their voice, or you look at their energy and see a strong, if misunderstood, agreement to keep this being around. Or, the spirit guide says, "Uh-uh! I need to be here and it's not time for me to leave. I'm supposed to act like a jerk."

Or, sometimes the supreme being sticks its energy in the room and says, "Stop." I don't know how this sounds to you, but it always made me grin. Imagine reading someone or something important enough that it gets the attention of the old SB!

Key point: This is hard for some people to hear, especially some healers. Sometimes the right thing to do is nothing at all. Sometimes we leave a spirit guide with bad manners as they are and let whatever their role is in other people's lives play out on its own. If you aren't sure, ask the supreme being for a recommendation. Think of it like the referees on the field asking for a play to be reviewed by the booth.

WHAT ABOUT MOMS?

For many moms, once they are pregnant, their energy expands to blow the competing baby beings away and keep the embryo and the baby being they have agreements with safe. To use the Harry Potter movies again, a pregnant mom's energy reminds me of the Patronus Charm from *The Prisoner of Azkaban*. I'm not saying that energy deer jump out of mom's uterus. I'm saying the *effect* is like the way the Patronus Charm banishes the Dementors from the area. Pregnant women, when they are spiritually healthy, are amazingly powerful. Really fun to read. Wonderful to be around.

Back to spirits being guides.

A baby being can be a spirit guide. They can help keep someone safe, guide them through parts of their life, and become their child.

A dead relative can be a spirit guide. A friend from a past life can be a spirit guide. Who you keep as spirit guides depends on your agreements with them, nothing more. I know this is the case because I've seen so many people in readings and healings end their agreements with their spirit guides. I've changed healing masters more than once. The idea that you get assigned one or more spirit guides for life is only partially true.

Yes, in special cases, you can be assigned guides. One of these guides, the cosmic cop, can restrict your life experiences. Think of someone with a cosmic cop as a spirit that's been paroled. Paroled from what? I have no idea. What did they do to deserve a CC? No idea. I was not allowed to look the few times I've read someone who had a cosmic cop.

Who gives someone a cosmic cop? This gets very cultural very fast! I'm not going to go there. I'll share only what I've read. I've only seen two sources that give someone a CC. The first, and most obvious, is a group of beings that monitor the state of the games on this planet with an eye towards preserving the games. Not preserving us. Preserving the games.

The second is secret government agencies. Sometimes that top secret clearance comes complete with a CC to enforce your compliance with all articles of your agency agreement. Isn't that sneaky?

When you have a body, you are senior to all spirits while in your body. You can change your spirit guides, updating your workforce, so to speak, lol.

In some cultures, there is no acknowledgement of spirit guides having agreements with us. I see this as a blind spot for them. I can't say that they are wrong, however. How would I know that? I've not read everybody, LOL!

You can make agreements and end agreements. If your only question is "Do I have spirit guides?" the answer is most likely going to be yes, yes you do. This is because spirits want, and in some cases need, to experience time.

Time is where you can resolve your karma, complete spiritual cycles, end or create new agreements, experience something new. All of those are available when you have a body, and all of those are more or less available if you're near a body. Spirit guides get some life experience by hanging around you.

Proximity matters. If you bring more of your energy inside of your body, your awareness increases. If you allow another spirit to come into your body, if it's capable enough, its awareness increases. If you agree to let a spirit hang out with you, just near your body, its awareness increases.

This awareness that increases, what does that mean? It means spirit becomes more aware of time, the physical world, and the spiritual worlds. The Astral is one such spiritual world. We visit the astral when we dream those real dreams.

You can see energy. You may say that you meditate and only see black. It's likely this is the energy in your head or aura, and it truly is dark and unconscious.

Your expectation is that energy will be wonderful and inspiring and beautiful and fascinating, so seeing black can't possibly be the same as seeing energy, but it is. It's just dark, unconscious energy. You can be blinded by darkness as easily as you can be blinded by bright, white light.

Grounding and running energy and blowing pictures is spiritual housekeeping. It's one effective way to clean off your abilities and bring light to your personal darkness.

IF SPIRITS ARE SMALL BALLS OF LIGHT, WHY DO SO MANY PEOPLE SEE ANGELS, BOOGEYMEN, MONSTERS, GRANDPARENTS, AND SUCH? WHY DO WE SEE A HUMAN FORM WHEN WE SEE A SPIRIT GUIDE? WHY DO WE SEE MONSTER FORMS?

This is such a great question. This comes back to having a physical body.

After you've lived in your body long enough, it can come to dominate your view of everything, so much so that seeing a small ball of light that you realize just talked to you can be, shall we say, unsettling, lol. Spirits without bodies are quite often aware of this, and the basic workaround is to create an image of a body that elicits the desired emotional response from *our* bodies.

When a spirit guide wants to convey that they are on your side, they can make an image of something you are familiar with and reassured by.

When a spirit guide wants to manipulate you to do something, they can make an image of something you are afraid of, which causes your body to create the emotion of fear, which makes you behave the way they desire. Got your ears plugged, listening to music, staring at your phone? How does your spirit guide get your attention to stop you from stepping in front of a bus? It either throws a picture at your body, causing an emotional response that pulls you out of your musical trance, or it shocks you with some energy, or it whispers to you.

Or! Or! It yells at the spirit guides of the person near you and that person intervenes. Yeah, spirit guides talk behind our backs, lol! Bunch of gossipy faeries. I guess it's OK since they saved you from getting squashed by the bus.

This same act can be played out with a positive image. A spirit guide can show you the image of a kind grandmother, knowing that is someone that you trust. It's a gentle comfort that makes it easier for you to talk to them, and to listen.

Key point: A spirit without a body creates an image to aid in communicating with you in your body.

You can take a look for yourself at your experiences with spirit guides, and see how you responded to the images they created.

Spirits communicate through pictures. Bodies can interpret pictures and create the corresponding emotions. Bodies communicate to spirit through emotions. This is the derivation of the phrase, "Do you get the picture?"

SO DO ALL SPIRIT GUIDES LOOK THE SAME, LIKE THE STARS IN THE NIGHT SKY?

Actually, yes, from a certain point of view. But when you go into your light trance, grounding and running energy and blowing roses, you learn to focus in finer resolution and you'll see spirits of all different colors. You can identify your healing master from your psychic surgeon solely based on their unique vibrations. Or you can tell them to give you the same picture of themselves.

Game time! Everyone in my clairvoyant class had a party in the park. Burgers and hot dogs, sodas and chips. And a raucous game of capture the flag. I volunteered to captain one team. We won hands down. And we cheated like crazy!

First, I selected all of the big-energy females in the class, the crafty and clever ones, while my opponent chose the big brute, athletic males. We had a brief team meeting and picked a vibration for our team that meant "winner." We matched our crown chakras to the color of the winning team *after* the game was completed. This set the future. Then we laid our flag on the ground in the open, visible to all.

This may have looked like a loser move, but we weren't finished.

Then I asked everyone to have their healing masters and psychic surgeons to hide our flag. Our guides hung out in the trees above our flag. We could always see our flag, but the enemy could not.

We played for an hour. We'd get captured but always escaped. We'd capture them and have our healing masters hide them as well. It was so amusing to watch our opponents run across the grass, stepping on our flag, run right by our captives and off down some random hill at top speed, LOL!

After the game, my team met briefly again. We gathered up all our energies from the park and each other, ended our agreement for the game, released our healing guides and gave them a vacation in the Bahamas, blew our matching pictures and filled in.

Are spirit guides good or bad? Wrong question. Is my spirit guide useful to me right now? Good question.

Why? Because our agreements with our spirit guides can be specific, which means the conditions of our agreements can be fulfilled, but the agreement is still binding on our spirit guides. In essence, our relationship and agreement with our spirit guide goes into past time. The only agreements that can benefit us right now are usually agreements that are in present time.

Remember that you have the body, which makes you senior to all other spirits. This is the fundamental implementation of free will. This means you can end, modify, or create a new agreement with any of your spirit guides. You don't need their permission. If you were not senior to all spirits while you're in your body, you would never have free will.

Be careful. You have a brain in your body that wants to react and do shit. Your brain is not always aware of your spiritual agreements. This means you may read something in your agreement with a spirit guide, judge what you read as bad, and destroy an agreement from a place of ignorance. Your ignorance. Be curious, not judgmental.

The good news is this is easy to manage. Just read the agreement, watch how you respond, watch how they respond, and take a breath. Sit back in the center of your head, ground and run energy for a bit, blow some roses, and take a second look with more neutrality.

Sometimes, all that's needed is to ground the agreement, however you see it. Some see parchment scrolls, and others see a simple piece of paper with one word, and still others see some symbol from nature like a stick. Grounding anything brings it into present time. Just create a grounding cord from the agreement to the center of the planet and this takes any foreign energy that might distort it off the agreement and brings it into present time.

Grounding an agreement that is no longer useful or is confusing or sounds terrible to you oftentimes ends the agreement automatically and sends that spirit guide on its way to its next step. You can then ask for another guide and create a new agreement with it.

Ask who? Ask, and it shall be given. Ask yourself. You might be astonished if you take a look at all of the spirit guides in the waiting room next to your space, just waiting to be called up to be on your team. You have choices. There's a lot of good spirit guides waiting for their turn.

Some cultures believe spirit guides are always assigned. This is partially true. Some guides are assigned, but not all guides. Even the assigned guides have agreements with you. You can find out why they were assigned to you in the agreements.

Who exactly do you ask to get another guide? Most of the time, you have a waiting list of spirits that you know from past lives that would be happy to work with you again. Some cultures say, "Ask the universe," and others say, "Ask your ancestors," and some say, "Ask God."

In my experience, when you put your attention on finding a new guide, more than one can show up, lol. Put some time into determining what you want from your new guide. Not much, just a little time. Remember; you've got the body so if the next one isn't working out, place another spiritual want ad asking for help.

Fun little fact time! During psychic classes, the bodies show up and sit down. All of their spirit guides show up as well. It can get a little crowded, lol. So we, meaning the teacher and the students, even if the students are brand new beginners, create some bleachers off to the side of the class and have all our guides sit there to observe the class. This is usually the time that one or more of the students notices that the temperature in the room drops a little. It's less crowded.

WHAT KINDS OF AGREEMENTS CAN BE MADE WITH SPIRIT GUIDES?

Anything you can think of! The most common agreements are protection, insight, and healing, but you can create an agreement to help you find a job or someone to date or find an adventure.

These agreements can be implemented any way you want. The only limits are the capabilities of the guide and your imagination. You can get information from the guide about a new job, or you can have them walk you into the reception area of a company and bump into the hiring manager that just so happens to want to meet you.

Why do they want to meet you? Your guides talked to their guides. The groundwork has been laid. The decisions and the follow through are still up to the hiring manager and you. It's that free will implementation by seniority thing again, but things can move your way quickly when your guides are given the task.

This kind of job search is not unethical. You aren't manipulating, you're networking! You just happen to have more help than your computer and your smartphone.

When you assign a task to your guide(s), it's really useful to ground them and show them what the world looks like now. If they haven't had a body for several centuries, their idea of what a job is may be very inappropriate for you today, lol! Bringing your agreement into present time and bringing the guides into present time helps everyone perform better. Yes, that means grounding your agreements and grounding your guides. Teach them to ground to the center of the planet and make this a requirement for them to hang out with you, unless there's an emergency. You can put this into your agreement with them.

When you are creating something using your guides, it's useful to ensure they understand what's in affinity with you. Remember when you created the energy of affinity for yourself in your gold sun? Create a handful of affinity for yourself and share it with them. They will know exactly what will resonate with you.

Mockup: it's a picture of what you want. It can be specific, like the exact image of a car you want to own, or more general, like just the image of a rose with the energy of the next type of car you want to own.

The more specific the mockup, the more trade offs that might be implemented to get it. The more general the mockup, the more surprises that might fall into your lap.

You can use a spirit guide of some kind to help manifest your mockup, or you can use an image of what you want and send it off for the universe to manifest your mockup.

I like to create more general mockups and leave myself open to being surprised with something I might not have otherwise considered. This is fun for me.

I've also created very specific mockups to the point I was invited to interview for a job that I had no real world qualifications for. I showed my mockup to my healing master and sent him off to set things up.

The interview went extremely well, with the interviewer telling me several times that she knew me from somewhere. I didn't get the job, but I shouldn't have gotten that job. She was disappointed that she couldn't hire me. I was delighted that my mockup worked out so well, and would go on to refine how I mocked things up. The person who interviewed after me was the ideal candidate for that job, and he got it.

When using your guides to do healings on someone else, there's a key step that makes everything work better, and that is having your guides match your energy before talking with you, and then having your guides match the energy of who you want them to heal. This makes the contact between the guides and the healee non-jarring. The healee may notice their energy changing but there isn't a big, upfront shock that makes them resist what's happening.

In some Japanese traditions, there is the notion of using Universal Ki to do healings instead of using your own ki. The reality is often the teachers are not using Universal Ki, but spirit guides, and the students learn to use those same spirit guides to do healings. They match energy with the teachers and make agreements with the spirit guides. It's not spoken of so the students aren't aware of it, but it's what's happening. Fun!

There was a wonderful Kiatsu master named BJ Carlyle. I took classes from him at several Aikido seminars. He always talked in terms of Universal Ki. He didn't want us using our own energy to heal other people. His explanation was we would run out of our own energy and damage ourselves, while Universal Ki was infinite. It made sense. It presented a coherent model of the spiritual world. It was simple and I liked it, but it was not entirely correct.

I was in a boat wreck and injured my back. The muscle spasms were so bad that Flexeril, a really strong muscle relaxant, wouldn't release them. I couldn't walk or sleep. Friends drove me from Tucson to San Diego and carried me into BJ's home, and put me on a massage table.

Ten minutes later, I was jumping up and down, feeling several inches taller. BJ had decompressed a vertebrae in the middle of my back and released a ton of energy. He asked me what had happened when I was thirteen. Sneaky psychic! All these memories of middle school came rushing back, where on the last day of school, a play day for everyone, I happened to piss off the girl athlete of the year (it's a talent of mine, lol) and she snuck up and hit me with her fist in the middle of my back.

I laid on a heating pad in bed for three days and missed the graduation ceremony and graduation dance. BJ released all that trauma from my back in just a few minutes, leaving me whole and pain free. The man was magic. He trained with Japanese and Hawaiian traditions.

A decade later, after I had graduated from the clairvoyant training program, I met up with him again for lunch. I wanted to work with him, trade techniques. I told him what I had learned. At the end of the lunch, he commented that he used his ability to see energy, too. We seemed to be getting on quite well.

Then, to impress me, he held up his hand and said, "Sometimes I use five different energies, one in each finger!" and each of his fingertips turned a different color, but that wasn't the only thing I saw.

Standing behind him was a group of five spirit guides in long robes, with Hawaiian and Japanese features. His hand trick with the different colors wasn't interesting; I'd already matched the energies with my hand to experience what he was showing, but his healing guides were fascinating. Their robes roughly matched the colors on his fingertips. I said hello to them, but they disappeared. Then he looked a little upset and said he needed to leave for an appointment. We never met again.

Those guides didn't want to work with me. There was no other option.

Amusing what some folks will do to preserve their model of the world. In a way, I was not allowed to work with him because I saw the five spirit guides that made up his "universal ki." In order to preserve the idea of universal ki, the guides had to remain hidden.

Or perhaps the opposite is true, and the guides were hiding behind the idea of universal ki.

Guides all plug into you in some way. For healings, I prefer they plug into the backs of my hand chakras. This gives them access to all of my abilities without disturbing the rest of my body. It also helps them not get their energy stuck in the gravity well of my physical body.

Other styles of communication plug into the fifth chakra or the seventh chakra. Some come down the back of the head and channel energy down the arms to the hand chakras. It's possible to find these cords in the front, back, or sides of chakras.

Key point: Have your healing guides match your energy first and then plug into the backs of your hands. Then have them match energy with the person you want to heal.

What this matching energy does is eliminate any dissonance between the vibration of the healing guides and the physical bodies they are working through and on. It makes healings go smoother and faster, with less distractions.

Bonus: If you are giving someone a massage, match your hands to their fourth chakra. Just hold your hands over the middle of their back and ask your hands to match their energy. Don't overthink it. You'll feel your hands change. Then, your hands can touch anywhere they are needed on their body without causing their body to reject your touch, because your hands feel like their hands.

At the Berkeley Psychic Institute, I was taught to create a grounding cord on the floor ten feet behind me, and have my healing masters stand there. Then, I had them match the energy of my hands and plug in through cords (same idea as a grounding cord: a line of energy). Then, I had them match energy with the person I was about to heal. They guided my hands, beginning with grounding the healee. This maintained separation between the guides and my space. It made the healings super easy for me and when the healing was done, the "cleanup" was fast. We healed ourselves, unplugged the cords, and separated our energies completely.

In the beginning, I had my healing masters blow my matching pictures with the healee before the healing began, as well as having my healing masters blow their matching pictures with me and the healee.

This became automatic in short order. We did the same at the end of the healings as well.

You don't have to ground someone before you heal them, but it does give the energy you may be removing from their space a safe place to go. It's like a laundry chute for energy. It also calms their body, which builds trust. Grounding them also enhances their awareness of energy, which can help with the healing.

But the main reason for grounding them before the healing is it brings their energy closer to their body, making it easier for you to see what's going on in their aura and chakras and physical body. Again, it's not required but it's so useful and easy there really isn't a good argument for not grounding them.

All of this takes place after receiving permission from them to do the healing. If they don't want you to heal them, and you go ahead and heal them, you may have destroyed some part of their life experience and set them back in some way. Never just assume that someone's trauma is okay for you to fix. Ask first and don't argue. It's their decision.

Key Point: Not every healer is a good fit for every kind of healing or every person that needs a healing. Advanced practitioners of any style of healing still have their individual points of view and information, pulled from all different kinds of past lives. Don't feel bad if you cannot make someone feel better. Instead, take a look at what's between you and giving them a healing. They may have verbally granted you permission but denied access on an energy level. You may have karma with them. You may not have the information to heal what ails them. Or they have a spirit guide that prevents you from changing their energy. Take a look for yourself, don't assume. You can learn some really neat things this way.

This is, again, one of those things where we tend to impose a hierarchy where there is none. "Advanced" healers are still individuals, and no individual has all the answers to everything, even though sometimes it sure appears like they do.

LET'S ASK AGAIN: WHAT'S IN IT FOR THE SPIRIT GUIDES?

My first answer was that they get to experience Time. Notice how that's a little bit mysterious and true. Some traditions may stop here, or may have a different explanation altogether. Some folks really like the feel of a mystery and stay with it like a favorite poem.

Then my guides and I got more specific with what they could experience, especially the idea of being in present time, versus being in past time. This is a big deal for spirit guides.

Think of everything in the human experience on this planet that a spirit guide has missed if their last incarnation ended in 1900. Think of what they'd miss if they died just before the internet. How could they understand the International Space Station or titanium hip replacements or televising the NBA playoffs or social media? They've missed so much. What a great way to play catch up. Getting to hang out with you and willingly lending you some good luck is more than a fair trade; it's a blessing for each of you.

Key Point: Whenever two spirits say hello, healing occurs.

When you say hello to a spirit guide, and it gives you a hello back, you are both validated and your energy changes slightly for the better. Sometimes one of you changes in a huge way.

I once read a woman who was having trouble communicating with her spirit guide and wanted to know why. I asked the woman to say her name out loud. When she did, she lit up as a little sparkle of light just above and a little behind her head. This was not the spirit guide; this was the spirit of the woman requesting the reading. I said hello to that sparkle and it flashed a hello back.

I had seen no spirit guides around her at first. I created an image of a rose to represent the energy of the spirit guide she was talking about and it was obvious what had happened.

The rose was reddish gray and dried out. I could see that someone was home, meaning the spirit guide existed, but the lights were off. Her spirit guide was unconscious.

I had the rose show me where the spirit guide was right now, and the rose went directly to the woman's right shoulder. Somehow, the guide had gotten too close to the woman's physical body while neither it nor the woman was prepared, and the guide simply went unconscious and got stuck in the body's gravity well, right next to her shoulder.

Neat-o stating the obvious: Bodies vibrate lower than spirits, LOL!

I said hello to the guide and nothing happened.

I told the woman what I was seeing and her energy dropped even more. I told her a joke and she laughed, raising her body's energy. We started telling each other funny quips, puns, and jokes, and her energy kept rising. We were goofing off like a couple of middle schoolers, not a woman in despair over her lost guide and a serious psychic man, lol.

Then I said hello to her guide and it blinked back at me. It was waking up. I continued saying hello, over and over. I described what was happening with the guide to the woman, and she got excited, raising her energy more.

We got into a virtuous spiral of rising vibrations, and the spirit guide moved away from the shoulder, said hello to both of us, and stood outside of the woman's aura.

What happened? The woman raised her energy enough that it reached the vibration that bridges a physical body and a bodiless spirit. That's all that was necessary to get her guide unstuck.

Something else seemed off, so I hooked the spirit guide up to the supreme being. The SB spun the spirit guide, getting rid of all of the energy that didn't belong to the spirit guide. The SB gave the woman some information from her Akashic Records. I didn't bother to read why that info got lost; we were on a roll and I didn't want to distract from the healing. I could always replay the reading later and pick up the thread for that question.

Fun fact: if you imagine you are recording your readings, you are recording your readings. You can play them back at your convenience to see what you missed or didn't understand, or just to match the energy of a really good reading and heal yourself again.

The woman was now in her head and body. Her aura was bright and dense, easily seen with the naked eye and third eye. The spirit guide was bright and twinkling, saying hello to everyone in the background that it had not been communicating with since it got stuck and went unconscious.

They left in a really happy, fun space. I did this reading in the Berkeley Psychic Institute. There is always a reading cleanout where all the readers get together in a room with the house control. There's a brief guided meditation on grounding and running energy, symbolically completing the communication of the reading, and then it's time for show and tell.

When it was my turn to show and tell, I related the spirit guide story, so naturally, right after the reading cleanout, several clairvoyant students asked me to check out their spirit guides, LOL! When you're on a roll, let it roll! We got kicked out of the institute just before midnight.

Key point: A lot of attachments are nothing more than a spirit that got stuck in someone's body's vibration. They got too close and their energy matched the energy of the body, and trapped them in time and space. This puts them into a kind of hibernation. The fix is to simply raise the body's energy back up to where the being that is stuck starts to wake up. This is not a possession, even though it may feel like one. This is not a spiritual attack, even though it feels like the remnants of an attack. So take a look and see what's going on for yourself.

The image of a gravity well, while not accurate because gravity has little to do with a spirit getting stuck near or in your body, is very useful. It clearly describes the process, both the capture and the release.

BASIC SPIRIT GUIDE READING.

Let's say we see a glob of white energy in someone's aura. It's just sitting there, taking up space, not moving. What is this?

Two different readers could see this same energy in the same person's aura, and give very different interpretations. One says it's a being attachment. This is true. It's a being and it's immobile just like it would be if it were attached.

The other says it's a being that's stuck. This is true. It's a being, and it cannot move away of its own volition. In fact, it appears asleep.

In neither reading was there any mention of something being misaligned. That's because alignment issues present a very different picture than a being in your space does. Saying someone's energy is misaligned tends to stop you from continuing to read the energy. Problem solved! Your tires need an alignment!

So who's right? I think that's the wrong question. The right question is, "What do they look at next?" What questions will the readers ask next?

They both see the being in the readee's space. Both interpretations can be useful in removing the being. If the being is seen as a negative energy, this tends to make the removal more difficult. The difficulty is a cultural thing. Demons and sprites and other nasty entities! These are negative energies! Booo!

Cultural perspectives aside, if the being is seen as just a being that's attached or stuck, that's an easy fix on an energy level. If it's asleep, wake it up! This is the classic example where raising the vibration is the real answer.

Beings get stuck in the gravity wells of our bodies. If we raise the body's vibration, this raises the being's vibration, waking it up and enabling it to escape from the body's spiritual gravity.

All energy that is not your energy and is in your space can have negative effects on your well being. If you express the problem in terms of too much energy, that's an easier problem to solve than if you express the problem in terms of thirty-two past lives running in twisted threads through your chakras and aura, freezing your ability to create new energy and living your life.

Everyone fits the second description of the problem, by the way. Everyone has a ton of foreign energy in their space, and for the most part, it doesn't matter to them at all. They get on with their lives just fine.

So the real focus of a reading is only on what matters to the readee right now. That may be as simple as taking a deep breath and releasing a small amount of energy from your space. Just because you can see it does not mean it's a problem for the readee.

A HEALING AT THE TRANCE MEDIUM HEALING CLINIC.

At one point during the clairvoyant training program, I got a huge cyst on the back of my neck, right at the base between C-7 and T-1. It grew to the size of a giant marble and was solid. It hurt.

I showed up at the trance medium healing clinic and asked for help. Other students had tried to read the energy of the cyst but hadn't gotten to the core picture. A staff member suggested the trance medium clinic, so I went for the first time.

There was a line of five psychics, all seated in folding chairs, and a single chair in front of them for me. The control stood behind the line, helping them raise the energy of their crown chakras and bodies up to a high white. None of them were grounding. I found out later that the energy level, or vibration, they needed to be at didn't work with grounding.

I saw two of the psychics' energies change dramatically. The other three were simmering along at the same color but their energy stayed the same. The control asked the two on the end that had changed their energy their names. They answered with names that were not the same as the names they used when I met them at the start.

Okay, I'm playing nice, keeping my poker face and not saying anything, but I'm getting a sense that there was some bullshit going on. Were these two bringing in beings? What about the other three? The energy in the room was ungrounded but crisp. I didn't dislike it. It was kind of familiar, but I couldn't place it.

The control asks, "What's your question?" I described the cyst, how no one had really been able to read the energy of it, how I could not see what was going on when I meditated on it.

The being named Joseph laughed and said the energy was like the energy of a generational curse from my maternal grandfather. It was meant to limit what I was able to say, but with a special condition that limited what I could ask.

I'm like, whatever. Sounds like psychic boilerplate to me.

Then the control asks the being in the body at the end of the line if it would walk this female body over to me and give me a healing. That person hadn't said anything during the reading. I'm still like, whatever.

She nods and stands up. She walks over (just fine, by the way) and stands behind me. I'm thinking this has been a big waste of time.

She isn't touching me, just standing behind me.

I got hit with a blast of energy that felt like someone hitting me hard on the back of my neck with a ping pong paddle. It knocked me forward and knocked the wind out of me as well (weird). I almost fell off my chair.

All this energy was running through my neck and shoulders. My eyes were wide as can be, and I was struggling to breathe. I stared at the control behind the line and he said, "Welcome to the trance medium healing clinic, Wayne!" and laughed his ass off. My face must have looked spectacular. The control was Paul Ohmart. He's a dear friend now.

The next day, I feel different, calmer. The tension in the back of my neck is different. The pain is gone. In the evening, I ask my girlfriend to look at the cyst. She touches it lightly with her fingertip and it bursts open, spewing out blood, pale fluid, and what looked like shards of bone, all white, hard, and shiny. She debrided the wound and put a large bandaid on it.

It sealed up and completely healed in a few days. There's almost no scar.

Everyone told me the trance mediums were scary. Even the staff at the institute were not comfortable with the trance mediums. So, I did what I usually do and started hanging out at the trance medium healing clinics to see what all the fuss was about. I just might learn something by watching the energy and blowing my matching pictures.

HOW DO SPIRITS KNOW WE ARE LOOKING AT THEM?

We each have a set of senses for physical energy: touch, vision, hearing, taste. None of these are initially involved in the answer to this question.

We each have another set of senses for spiritual energy. The ones pertinent to the answer to this question are clairaudience, clairvoyance, clairsentience, and claircognizance. These abilities sense spiritual energies.

All spirits have these spiritual abilities. Only spirits with physical bodies have the additional physical senses.

There are two kinds of energy. The first type is physical energy and the other type is spiritual energy.

You raise your eyes away from your cell phone and look up to lock eyes with someone on a passing bus because you picked up on their spiritual energy. A spirit without a body puts their attention on you because they picked up on your spiritual energy. In both of these scenarios, the spiritual energy involved is an attention point.

When you give your attention to someone, you create a focal point with your awareness. This is an attention point. It focuses those spiritual senses mentioned above so that they may receive as much information as needed in that moment.

That's how you know when someone is looking at you, which feels different than someone staring at you. The energy of the attention point is different.

That's how a spirit without a body knows you are looking at it.

ARE THERE SCARY BEINGS OUT THERE?

Everyone has something that scares *them*.

What scares us can be found in pictures in our auras. Spirits without bodies can see these pictures and learn what scares you. If you are from certain forms of religion, demons are real for you and will scare you when you see the image of a demon, or throw you into some kind of hyper defense mode.

If demons aren't part of your pantheon of spirits, that image is not going to work on you.

That's one part of the game.

The other part is this: what is it in your space that scares spirits without bodies?

You have a body. That can be scary because having a body enables you to use many of your powers. Your body is "home base," meaning it's your safe zone in a game of spiritual tag.

Fortunately for the spirits that are devious little shits, most folks don't know this about themselves, lol.

There is some part of you that spirits can see that makes them not play their "let's scare the shit out of <insert your name here> and see what happens!" The beginnings of your awareness that you are more than just your body is often enough to scare away most of the pranksters.

Criminals are lazy. They don't want to break into a modern safe with state of the art defense systems. That's too much work. They want to find out who's on vacation out in the suburbs and stroll in the back door without worry. Make a coffee. Steal some jewelry, stuff that's easy to sell on the black market.

Devious spirits are just like criminals. Once you begin to become aware of your own energy, you quickly begin to be not worth it to them. When you are grounding and running energy, you're too hard to touch. There are plenty of easy targets for them to pester, usually just across the hallway or on the street.

Just saying hello to a spirit dressed up like one of Dante's real nightmares can be enough to bust the game. Dante's *Inferno* is total crap, but then so are most Hollywood movies that deal with demons and possession and poltergeists and such. Why write it? It sells, baby! It sells!

Before I got some training for my clairvoyance, spirits would show up looking like Darth Vader, or T-Rex, or those aliens that tried to eat Sigourney Weaver. After I trained up my clairvoyance, I could see that those images were just that: images created by some spirit, meant to manipulate my emotions.

Once I saw the game, the pranksters just stopped coming around. Perhaps they see something in you that affects them in a similar way. My guess is it's your psychic abilities. You can tell the truth from the lie, which breaks up a lot of games that spirits play.

Even nice spirits, like our spirit guides, create images, but do it to facilitate communication with us. Which would be easier to understand: an image of a sweet grandma that smiles a lot or a small ball of light with no face and no other context? The latter is what all spirits look like, including you and me.

Cords

You've learned to make a grounding cord. You've likely heard of cutting cords to end relationships. Let's talk about cords.

Cords are lines of energy that carry information, communication, and energy. Cords are really useful and we use them unconsciously all the time.

Parents will almost always have a cord from their first chakra to the first chakra of their children. This cord carries survival information which helps keep the kids safe. After all, the last time they had a body, there may not have been a reason to look both ways before crossing a road, or a reason to stop, look, and listen when approaching a railroad track. Cars and trains may not have existed, so these represent new life experiences for the kids.

You know how to ground from your first chakra to the center of the planet. That was the first page of this book. You can adjust your grounding cord to change your body's energy, to make you appear differently to strangers, or set an energy for yourself when you're with a group at a party or gathering. You can make these adjustments by changing the color of the grounding cord. You can also make them just by creating a specific intent: "I want to ground like Arnold Schwarzeneger."

A fun game is to ground yourself like someone else's mother and watch their behavior change when around you. Fun! If you add in matching your crown chakra to their mother's crown chakra, the effects are even more dramatic and fun.

To be clear: you are not putting a cord from your crown chakra to someone else's crown chakra. That's rude and invasive. You are matching the primary color of your crown chakra to the primary color of someone else's crown chakra. This is polite and allows you to see the world almost the same as whoever you're matching sees the world. This is really useful during readings. But it's also fun to punk someone with!

Do be careful in your choices when playing. Someone I dated hated her mother, and with good reason, so matching her mother's energy would probably be an unforgivable prank.

The value of matching your grounding cord and crown chakra to someone else is learning what your energy is like when you unmatch. Matching and unmatching energy with someone else helps light up your matching pictures with them, which makes them easier to blow and get your energy back from them. The repetition of matching, blowing your pictures, and unmatching serves to refine your awareness of your own energy. Knowing your own vibration enables raising your vibration; i.e. growing your awareness and understanding. Being at your own vibration is how people will find you. Play with matching others, but pay attention to what happens to your energy when you unmatch.

The first chakra cord from a parent to a child goes both ways, so as the child releases energy, it grounds out through the parents most of the time. Imagine a parent that isn't grounding their body. Where does all that energy from the kid go? It grounds into the parent. Ew! Ever wonder why some parents get so overwhelmed? This is one possible cause.

If parents are grounded, then the kids' released energies come to the parents and immediately ground out. Nice and safe.

Cords also carry communication. This cord is how parents suddenly know that their kid is in danger or is about to break something valuable. This is a good thing.

As kids age, they often rely less and less on grounding through their parents. This is enhanced and accelerated if you teach the kids to ground for themselves. There is no age before which a spirit cannot ground their body.

But kids are kids, eh? They don't get all excited about a "line of energy," but they do get thrilled and engaged with animals and nature. You can teach your kids how to ground.

My wife and I volunteered to babysit for my friends who hadn't had any adult time together since their first child was born. Three years. Ugh.

I taught the two year old and three year old to ground. I created a tree branch at the center of the planet. I asked them to take a look at the tree branch that I just created. They both laughed and pointed at me. Then I asked them to create a huge monkey tail on their tail bone, curling up between their butt cheeks. This got the giggles flowing.

Then I asked them to grab the branch at the center of the planet with their monkey tail. They both did without hesitation. I pushed on their sternums with one finger so they could feel their body being grounded.

I took away the tree branch and their eyes got big. I pushed on their sternums with one finger again so they could feel the difference in their balance. I asked them to make their own tree branch at the center of the planet and wrap their monkey tails around those branches.

They did so and both came down into their bodies and behind their eyes and stared at me for a few seconds.

I clapped and congratulated them and pushed on their shoulders and sternum. They were solid. I had them walk in a circle while grounding, continuing to test them by pushing with one finger on their shoulders and sternum.

Then we sat down to play a game. I held out my hand and created the image of a banana cream pie. They had eaten this kind of pie before. I asked them if they could see it and they grinned and nodded their heads. Then I pushed the pie into the face of the older child. He started laughing and licking his lips.

I threw a pie at the younger child and she laughed. Then they looked at each other, then looked at me, then back at each other, and attacked me with invisible pies!

The really cool part? They noticed when I changed the flavor of my pies to chocolate cream!

Key point: To get into heaven, just come as a little child. What do little children do? They play with energy and have fun. Make believe, and what you make can become real. This is also how mockups work.

WHAT ABOUT CORDS AND RELATIONSHIPS?

So you know you can create a cord from your first chakra to the center of the planet. Why does this work so easily? The first chakra of the planet is at the center of the planet, so the energies are similar. First chakra to first chakra. Your body is part of this planet. We created our first chakras to work well on this planet.

You know about the first chakra cords between parents and their children. First chakras, especially within families, have similar energy. Do you see a pattern here?

People in sexual relationships usually have a second chakra cord connecting them. Your second chakra holds sex energy, but also your ability to feel someone else's energy, including emotions. This is called clairsentience. It's the psychic ability you are using when you are making love or having sport-sex and want to know if you're giving your partner the good time that they need and deserve.

People in loving relationships usually have a fourth chakra cord connecting them. Your fourth chakra holds your affinity for yourself. This is how you recognize your own energy. It's also how you recognize other energies that are in affinity with you.

It's also how sometimes, as a reader or healer, you recognize that there is something off and you no longer want to read or heal some person.

Your fourth chakra also has its own healing abilities, so sometimes a fourth chakra cord is used to heal someone else. I remember as a small boy being hugged by one of my aunts and always feeling great for a few minutes until one of the "other" aunts hugged me and took those good feelings away. There are healers in this world that give great hugs, and these are often the fourth chakra healers.

When someone would come into the institute and request a long distance healing for someone they knew, we would get into a reading space, create a fourth chakra cord to the remote person, and have the cord sync the person's energy in front of us with the remote person's energy. Then we would read and heal the person in front of us. It was exactly like having the remote person sitting in the chair in front of us: chakras, aura, channels, and diseases in their physical body. All the energies! It was really fun to do this!

As soon as the healing was complete and the cord disconnected, the person in front of us returned to their own energy with no residual energies from the remote person in their space. It was always amazing to me how this worked so cleanly, and I made a point of checking the person in the chair for residual energies every time.

Artists in close collaborations may have fifth chakra cords. Your fifth chakra holds part of your creativity, your telepathy (both broadband and narrow band), your clairaudience (hearing energy and spirit), and your inner voice. There are creative channels from your fourth, sixth, and seventh chakras into your fifth chakra, and larger creative channels from your fifth chakra down your arms and into your hand chakras. This also has something to do with your mockups, getting what you want, and healing.

A cord in someone's fifth chakra can distort what they're trying to create. Don't assume such a cord is causing them harm, just take a look and see what it does. If you're reading it and it's causing them harm and you tell them what you see, the person will often end their agreement to use this cord themselves and it disappears.

This raises an interesting question: does a cord always indicate there's an agreement? No. However, there is always a picture on the end of a cord that matches with a picture in your chakra. If you gently remove a cord, you can read the picture on its end, blow your matching picture, tie off the end of the cord and remove it all the way out of your aura to heal yourself of this cord.

Tying off the end of the cord is good manners; whoever is on the other end of the cord will not leak energy out of this cord. Moving it all the way out of your space and healing your aura smoothes out your energy flow again. Blowing the matching picture means that whoever stuck the cord into your chakra will have to find another way of controlling you.

This is amusing, is it not? Someone's been controlling you with a cord that you didn't agree to. You ground and run your energy for a short while and become aware of some cords. You remove them and blow your matching pictures. Guess who you might get a call from out of the blue? They may find other pictures to attach their cords to, but you'll just smile and blow those pictures, too. That's amusing. They can't keep up with someone who has a little awareness of cords. Eventually, you will only have the cords you're in agreement with.

Now be patient. Energy comes out of your space in layers. The same applies to cords. A cord may be hidden in an energy from the first few days of your life. It doesn't matter. Be patient. Be well. Do good work. And have fun!

Every minor improvement you make to your space gives you more energy. More energy enables your creativity and your ability to destroy. The more you create and destroy energy, the more energy you have. More energy enables your creativity and your ability to destroy. It's a virtuous cycle. Embrace the cycle and have more and more fun.

Cords can control you.

Some preachers, for example, will try to put a sixth chakra cord into your sixth chakra. I've seen no benefit to this kind of cord. It's always been a way to manipulate someone's view of the world, their view of spirit, and filter what they are able to see. I haven't read a toxic narcissist, but when I look at them in the news, ranting in front of their followers, I see them putting sixth chakra cords into their followers.

Something similar happens with third chakra cords. I've never seen a positive use of third chakra cords, only a manipulative use.

Seventh chakra cords are not as simple. Yes, some gurus control their followers with seventh chakra cords. This is even nastier than the sixth chakra cord. A seventh chakra cord limits what you can know. Even if you already know something, a seventh chakra cord can prevent you from realizing you know it, such that you ignore your own wisdom.

However, some teachers use a seventh chakra cord to protect themselves from their students. A class of psychics can get stuck on a picture together, making them all blast the same energy outward. One teacher I had this lifetime could see this coming, hold it at bay with a seventh chakra cord, and talk the class through that matching picture that they all got stuck on at the same time.

But that's the only positive use I've seen made of a seventh chakra cord.

WHAT DO CORDS ATTACH TO?

The high level answer is generally chakras. However, in the chakra, there always seems to be a specific picture that the cord connects to.

This is somewhat repetitive with the last subsection, but it's worth repeating, and there are some more details shared here.

If you detach a cord from the chakra and look at the end of the cord, you will see the matching picture on the end of the cord. If you want to never see this specific cord again in your space, you have to blow the matching picture in the chakra that goes with the picture at the end of the cord. Just removing the cord is insufficient most times. This is, I believe, one of the failure modes of cord cutting; you cut them and they keep coming back because you haven't blown the matching pictures.

Let's talk about energy manners again. A cord carries information, communication, and energy. This sounds like a pipe, eh? And what happens when you cut a pipe? Whatever is still flowing through that pipe leaks all over creation.

When you are healing someone, including yourself, the polite way to remove a cord goes like this:

1. Using your fingers, push the cord lightly into the chakra and give a soft twist. The cord is not threaded like a pipe, but it is intended to hold on, so pushing it in a tiny bit loosens up the energy that holds onto the chakra, and the twist breaks up the tight alignment with the matching picture in the chakra, making the cord very easy to remove. All cords connect into a matching picture.
    a. Note: I can imagine a scenario where a cord does not have a picture it connects to. Imagine two layers of energy, both containing cords to the same picture. Your daily energy hygiene practice of grounding, running energy, and blowing roses uncovers the first layer and you remove the cord and blow your

matching picture. The other cord is now untethered from the picture but still contained in the other layer of energy, so it remains. When you uncover it, you'll still see the picture on the end of the cord, but you won't see its matching picture because you already destroyed it.

2. Create a rose. Put the matching picture from the chakra into the rose. Explode them both to destroy the matching picture. If you're curious what the picture was, read the picture on the end of the cord that you're still holding in your fingers. Destroying the matching picture in your chakra frees up your energy and prevents another cord from connecting in the same way.

3. Tie a knot in the end of the cord so it doesn't leak. Good manners. No judgment. Why allow someone's energy to leak until they feel drained? Besides, everyone is psychic so they'll figure it out and fix it eventually. What's important is not slipping into combat mode over a simple cord. Rejoice in freeing up your energy. Manners work to your advantage.

4. Move the cord all the way out of the aura, fill in the space that the cord took up with that person's own energy, or your energy if you're removing the cord from your space, and seal the hole in the edge of the aura. Smooth everything out.

5. Done.

I imagine that some cord cutting rituals have a subconscious portion that deals with the matching pictures. These matching pictures act like refrigerator magnets and once they line up, they stick to each other. That's why the little twist helps break the alignment of the two pictures and free the cord.

I've never done any other kind of cord removal. I invite you to take a look at your own cord cutting rituals and see what they do on an energy level, not just on the level of the written instructions. For that matter, take a look at the energy of what I just described and see how the process works. You have your own information about cords, even if you aren't aware of it yet.

RELATIONSHIP READINGS AND HEALINGS

A really cool thing to do is read a couple's relationship with both of them in front of you. If they aren't sharing or showing their fourth chakra cord, you can ask them if it's OK for you to create one for them. The usefulness of seeing a cord between the two parties to the relationship's fourth chakras is it makes it easier to read the kind of communication, information, and energy that flows back and forth between them. These three things are what the couple are sharing. It's useful to look at them deliberately.

The fourth chakra cord also makes it easier to see what gets in the way of their relationship, which is often the reason they wanted a reading in the first place.

The fourth chakra cord, when you create one for them, is a tool to assist you in your reading of the relationship. Destroy this cord when you're done with the reading.

I've almost never needed to create a fourth chakra cord for a couple that asked for a relationship reading. When my wife and I get relationship readings, the readers didn't need to make one for us either, lol. I only mention that it's possible to make one because sometimes the relationship isn't what you expect it to be and this fourth chakra cord makes it easier to read.

This technique is super useful if one party to the relationship is not physically present. Same reasons, see what they are sharing in their long distance relationship and what energy gets in the way. It's slightly different from the long distance healing experience in that the person in front of you does not become the energy of the remote person. They just appear next to one another.

WHAT KINDS OF THINGS GET IN BETWEEN TWO PEOPLE IN A RELATIONSHIP?

In some relationships, it's a very long list, LOL! Inlaws and potential inlaws. Baby beings. Any of their friends. All of their friends. Grandparents and ancestors. Spirit guides. Ex's. Past time expectations (those mockups you made of finding the perfect mate when you were six years old). Judgments made on you by your exes. Judgments made by anyone about your relationship, or your *lack of a relationship*. Past lives. Past time agreements between the two people. And resistance from the two in the relationship to any and all of everything else in between them, LOL!

Notice none of this really answers the question, "Is he/she the one?" That's on purpose. It's not a useful question, even though it's the most common relationship question, especially when the partner is not present.

I find it more useful to help them see and make separations from the dominant energy in between the two that's influencing or controlling their relationship. Once that dominant energy is separated out of the relationship, both parties almost always remember why they first got together and the question about being the one just goes away.

When they find their space from the energies controlling their energy, communication, and information exchange, they learn how to recognize when it comes back into their relationship space, which makes the whole experience of getting a relationship reading more valuable over the longer term.

Alternatively to using a cord, you can create two roses to represent the couple, create a cord between the two roses representing their fourth chakra cord, and do the whole reading just based on these symbols. With a little practice, you'll learn to see everything you need to do a great reading.

If you are reading someone remotely, you can create two roses, one for each partner in the relationship, and connect the two roses with a fourth chakra cord. Read this the same as you would if they were sitting in the room with you. If you can see the energy of the two people and the cords connecting them to each other, you don't really need the roses, but it's nice to know you can always fall back on the roses to read the same stuff. This is really useful in spaces where you may not have sufficient control over the energy of the space, e.g. psychic fairs, hospitals, on public transit, reading at a table in a nightclub.

BTW, once you've been reading long enough to be barely comfortable, please go read in a noisy nightclub, lol. You'll blow a lot of pictures. You'll see more of the games that go on in clubs. You'll grow your confidence in using your tools (grounding, roses, etc). You'll really appreciate creating bubbles!

For healings, just to review, creating a fourth chakra cord does several things. In a long distance healing, where you are reading someone in front of you who is asking for a healing for a friend that is not present, you can find the friend by creating the fourth chakra cord. This makes seeing the friend's energy much easier and tends to make the image of them more stable. That all adds up to an easier and better reading and healing.

There is a cool thing that happens when you're doing a remote healing with a fourth chakra cord like this. The energy of the person sitting in front of you appears to change to the energy of the remote person you wish to heal. Now you read and heal the person in front of you and it does the energy work on the remote person at the same time. As soon as you're done and disconnect that cord, the energy of the person in front of you returns to their patterns of energy.

The person in front of you is not taking on someone else's illness. They will not feel any different or experience any of the pain from the remote person. They may be aware that something is happening, but they know it's not happening to them. In this healing technique, they are like an exact copy of the person you are healing, an avatar, that is at once here and at the remote location. It's really cool and exciting to experience! You can see that remote person vividly.

HEALINGS AND CORDS

Sometimes you will find remnants of cords in someone's aura. These may or may not have a matching picture in their ends. Sometimes a cord is shattered in an accident or energetic event, and these little bits of cords are like splinters in the aura, disturbing its flow.

Clean those out however it occurs to you. Sometimes I melt them and ground them out. Other times I pick them out with psychic tweezers. Trust your healing instincts and your curiosity, and you'll figure it out.

Oftentimes you will come across a whole, functioning cord stuck in someone's chakra. Do you remove it? This is a good question.

How do you determine if a cord is causing problems and should be removed? Notice the built in bias in that question. It assumes the cord should be removed and is looking for a reason (a problem we can associate with the cord) to remove it.

Let's step back. What's a cord? It's a line of energy that carries communication, information, and energy. In this definition are your diagnostic questions. What does the cord say? Which direction is that communication going? Who's on the other end? What information, if any, is passing through the cord and in which direction? And finally, what energy is passing through the cord and in which direction?

Remember the question in an energy check: is this tool in present time? This applies to cords, because they are a spiritual tool of sorts between two participants who on some level agree to having the cord. If the cord is in the past, bring it into present time and then ask those more detailed questions in the previous paragraph.

You can describe the cord to the healee and ask them as spirit if they'd like it removed. Here's a fun pickle. If you describe the cord out loud, on an energy level you are also highlighting the cord for the spirit who owns that body to see. Sometimes their mind invokes a bias against all cords and shouts, "Remove it!" At the same time, they are saying to leave it alone as a spirit, because it means something more to them than they understand in their body.

Your choices then are 1) ask the supreme being for a ruling on the field, or 2) tell the healee that the cord is not ready to be removed yet, or 3) remove it. They can replace it if they really want to.

If you ask the SB, be prepared for a fast, complete answer. You will understand why it needs to stay or go. You will have no doubts. The same applies to troublesome spirit guides that are diddling a healee or a readee or you. Asking the SB about a spirit guide generally hooks up the spirit guide to the SB, where it goes through a quick spin cycle to get everyone out of its space, and then takes its next step, whatever that is: stay or leave.

By the way, you can hook yourself up to the SB anytime you wish. It's a nice healing. You can hook up anyone that does not refuse. People are still senior to the SB in their bodies. It's that "implementation of free will": thing again.

Not sure how to dial up the old Supreme Being? The easiest way to remember how it's done is to be in a group of people that are doing it, i.e. having communication with the SB.

Don't fret if you don't have a group handy this lifetime. Imagine your-self with your peers from all the lifetimes where you were a psychic or healer. In the same way you say hello to the center of the planet when you ground, say hello upwards to the SB.

CORDS REVIEWED

Cords, like matching pictures, are a big deal. These two things are often at the root of your energy problems.

"Cutting" as an image works for some people, but not all. It suits the emotions of breaking away from someone, so that's cathartic. That's using the symbol of a cord to represent your agreements with the ex and end those agreements. When the cord is real, cutting it has risks.

There are a few aspects to the idea of cutting something that are not positive. At the top of the list is it's poor spiritual manners. Cutting a cord in two leaves the cord open. This creates a leak. Depending on what you do next, that leak may be in your aura and/or one of your chakras. The other party now has a leak, too. This is not good.

Communication is one function of cords. In healthy relationships, it's the primary function of the cord. This keeps both parties to the cord literally in the loop, lol. There's a constant flow of communication, back and forth, not unlike texting each other constantly throughout the day. Cords also go into past time and stop functioning correctly, which is another way of saying they no longer serve their intended purpose and can mess things up.

Cords also carry information and energy.

What information? Background noise. Intent. Programming. It can be the context for the communication, or it can be subversive, a kind of control over the other person that rides along on communication that hides its intent. "Wow, I miss you!" can get coupled with information sent to you or pulled from you to monitor your movements, mood, who else you're with.

To pull information from someone requires either taking over part of one of their chakras or installing tracking programs. Not so nice at first glance, and that's usually a useful perspective, but in the context of raising children, it's how an adult's cord between their first chakra and the child's first chakra keeps the child safe. In the context of adult relationships, there is rarely a need for a first chakra cord between two adults. If you see one, it's sometimes the energy component of infidelity and lying. One partner is cheating and doesn't want the other partner to find out. They create a cord to distract the other partner to focus on survival issues at the first chakra level.

Some children who habitually lie will use their first chakra cord with their parents (or parent) to gain support for their lie. "My son would never do that!" Mom believes that because the boy has sent some energy through the first chakra cord that manipulates mom into believing it. This manipulation from kids can also be found in the other chakras. Look for the child's energy and ask what it says. A really common answer to this question of what an energy says is, "I don't lie." That's often the first thing a liar says, lol. It's often the first thing politicians say, LOL!

Don't judge the child or the parent. It's a game. Kids play games and some of those games they see adults playing and so they try them out. Adolescents are often the worst because, in addition to all the hormones, they have more life experience from which to model their behaviors. Their repertoire is larger. Isn't that comforting?

Remember, it's a game to them. Teach them better games.

What energy comes through cords? Emotions mostly. Second chakra cords can make for some great sex as long as the only things in the cord belong to the two people having sex. Having an ex in your second chakra cord tends to spoil things for you and/or your present partner. Not always, but still, cleaning this up is good spiritual hygiene. Use a rose to clean out your cords between you and your loved ones, SOs, and anyone else you share a cord with on purpose.

The simplest way to check if a cord is healthy or not is to ask if it is in present time. Past time cords take up space and disturb your energies, filtering what you can see and create.

Cutting a cord might destroy the cord, or it may just break the spiritual plumbing, causing other energy problems over time. Destroying a cord without healing the chakra it attached to and the path it followed through the aura creates its own energy leakage.

Removing a cord is safer and more considerate on all counts. Feel for cords coming into the front of the six major chakras and the top of the seventh chakra on the top of the head. Use your finger tips; the cord can be subtle, or buried underneath other energies, or matched up with your energy in your aura so that it doesn't feel any different at all. In the latter case, most people end up seeing an image of the cord. We're more aware than we think. You know (claircognizance) if you have a gaggle of cords coming out of your chakras like a porcupine. You feel (clairsentience) where the energy changes in your aura when your fingertips pass through them. You see (clairvoyance) cords, their color, the energy they're set at, the main message they carry, and what chakra they attach to as a result of knowing and feeling them.

By the way, you will very likely begin seeing images when you use your hands to feel for cords. This is because all of your psychic abilities found in your major chakras are mirrored in your hand chakras. Isn't that cool!

What about the cords coming into the sides or the back of the seven major chakras? (Sneaky bastards!) Once you can feel them with your physical hands, you can create an energy hand to do the same thing in the spaces that you can't physically reach. Cool beans!

So that's the basics of finding and diagnosing cords. Removing them is simpler.

Let's say you find a second chakra cord by touching it with your fingertips. With the same fingertips, lightly take hold of the cord and push it gently towards the chakra a little. This loosens the anchor point of the cord. Giving the cord a slight twist dissolves the attachment. A quarter turn is sufficient. Then pull your end of the cord out of your body. Tie a simple knot in the end of the cord. Move the cord all the way out of your aura, filling in the path where the cord used to be with your own energy, and finally patching the hole in the edge of your aura where the cord used to be. Smooth out any roughness that your fingertip feels where the cord attached to your chakra. That's it.

There is no need to follow the cord to its other end and do anything with it. You sealed the end with a knot. You're done. Trying to heal an ex or anyone else without their express permission is a bit dodgy and rude.

Doing it this way ensures your chakra heals better. Again, you can check by pointing one finger at the spot where the cord was attached and slowly move that fingertip back and forth over that spot. If it feels rough, smooth it out, and you're done healing your chakra.

Now your aura is free of a highly focused line of communication that was in past time, so not functioning as intended, or was in present time but functioning in a way you didn't want. That part of your aura will flow with more ease and clarity. That part of the chakra will flow with more ease and clarity.

The first few times you remove a cord this way, it can be a miraculous healing, like a major change to your world view. Most of the time after that, it will just be you learning how to maintain your spiritual hygiene and the releases of energy will be less dramatic. These later releases still increase your energy, feeding the virtuous cycle, so don't poo-poo them.

You can bring a cord into present time by grounding it and observing what happens. (The same applies to any energy or picture in your space; ground it to bring it into present time.) This is useful when you want to decide if you're keeping the cord or not. Bringing your cord into present time, and it is as much your cord as it is the person's on the other end of the cord, enables you to see it in your present context.

This is important because all of our lives, we are changing and evolving. That's life.

A grounding cord is a great example of a cord with a purpose and positive outcomes. Still *just* a cord, like the ones between you and your ex, but where you attach the ends of a grounding cord can make a huge difference in your life. It's also a one way cord; energy goes down a grounding cord.

A useful psychic
vocabulary

Many of the names for things can be ambiguous and confusing. I think some of the labels are combinations of abilities, like "intuitive" and "empath" and "medium." "ESP" could mean anything, LOL! Hollywood and fiction writers haven't helped either. I've never read someone with a pyrokinetic ability, which is the firestarter ability. I've read about it in fantasy novels and seen it in fantasy movies. I can't say whether it exists or not, but it's not central to my reading skills so I don't include it in this vocabulary list. I've only included the abilities I've read a lot; these are the ones I can speak to without making stuff up.

I try to use names and definitions that are less romantic but more discreet. You can call yourself by any term that resonates with you. You can be a psychic. You can be a medium. You can be a student that just dabbles with tarot cards.

You certainly can use different labels in different groups. For many folks, having a psychic ability is a deeply intimate thing, and sometimes in the company of some groups this intimate knowledge needs to remain private.

Being a beginning psychic can be frightening. You barely believe what you're experiencing yourself, and at the same time you know beyond any doubt that what you're experiencing is real. This is not a comfortable state of being, lol.

Do I like that other psychics may hide it from others? Who am I to judge someone else's choices? I recall the reactions I got from my co-workers when I mentioned I wanted to take meditation classes. I left off the bit about them being psychic meditation classes. I received disdain, indifference, an in-depth explanation of Buddhism and why it's the only true meditation. I was mocked, but since I was willing to work every Saturday and Sunday to guarantee my two weeknights off for classes, I was left alone. I was just that weird guy.

Just an odd aside: my only friend from that job in the 80s is an atheist and is still my friend to this day. If nothing else, this was a lesson for me in not judging others.

Some healers are more comfortable calling themselves energy workers. Some people avoid the baggage that comes with being a healer but maintain a spiritual context by calling themselves light workers.

Healing means changing someone's energy from one state to a better one. This isn't necessarily a higher state, just a better one. You can label this process in whatever way works best for you.

If empath and intuitive are general descriptions that may include more than one ability, one should probably ask what those abilities might be. This is a good question for those who identify as empaths and intuitives. What discreet abilities underlie my experience of this world?

A chakra is an energy center. It looks like a ball of light most of the time. Sometimes it looks like a disk. Chakra is a Sanskrit word that means wheel. If you are looking at a chakra from the front or back of the body, and the chakra is spinning in a healthy way, it does look like a wheel. If you then walk around to the side of the body and look at a chakra, it may look nothing like a wheel; more like a trumpet sometimes, and other times like a searchlight.

Spirit means energy organized around awareness. Chakras are a part of the organization.

Psychic abilities are spiritual abilities. Psychic comes from the Greek word *psychikos*, which means "of the mind," or "mental," but also means "soul." In Japanese, *Ki* means both "energy" and "spirit." Different traditions see the same thing in different ways and describe them in different ways.

I'd like you to notice that the derivation of the word psychic has nothing to do with anything paranormal. Just sayin'.

Here's a brief summary of the spiritual abilities in each chakra, from the perspective of a clairvoyant reader. I stick to referring to them by the numbers for the most part, rather than the cultural nicknames, like root chakra, sacral chakra. It's less confusing. Numbers also carry less cultural baggage, so are more neutral. Some folks online have scolded me for saying the fourth chakra has a healing ability. In their view, the only purpose of the fourth chakra is connecting to the divine. Can you see how that statement filters out everything else you might see in someone's fourth chakra? That "picture" sounds like a good way to prevent someone from discovering one of their basic healing abilities. I've heard some gurus say similar things and their followers were subservient and loyal to a flaw, unquestioning to the point of losing their curiosity.

This list may not be exhaustive, but it is complete enough to understand and read pretty much every question you or someone else will ask in a reading or healing. For those questions that don't fit, you can ask, "What am I not looking at?"

This gives you a starting place for taking a look at things for yourself, but no limits on what you can or cannot discover for yourself. This is important because it does not limit what you can see, and most importantly does not limit what you can heal.

All the chakras look like balls of light. Their appearance changes depending on you opening or closing them, or how well they're spinning, or how many cords are stuck into them, or how much energy is flowing out of them, or lots of other influences. Some books depict the chakras as trumpet shaped. This is illustrated in a side view. Other books depict them more like wheels, or mandalas; chakra is the sanskrit word meaning wheel, and from dead on in front of a chakra, they look like a multicolored wheel. Some of you may have read in a book that "this chakra is violet and means such-and-such." Take a look for yourself. Teachers simplify things for beginners. It's a useful, if not entirely accurate, pedagogical technique.

The crown chakra is different. It looks like a small disk laying flat on the top of the head. The sides may flare out, making the energy above the seventh chakra look like a funnel. The sides may be parallel, making the energy above the seventh chakra look like a cylinder. The shape of the crown chakra changes for lots of reasons, which you can discover by taking a look at the energy and asking basic questions.

1st chakra: in front of the base of the spine, holds survival information for the body.

2nd chakra: in front of the spine just below the level of the navel, holds clairsentience ability. This is how you feel your emotions and the emotions of others. It's also how you feel lots of different energies. It's also how you connect to sexual partners.

3rd chakra: in front of the spine at the level of the solar plexus, power distribution! This is your spiritual utility company! Also holds telekinesis. And holds your out of body experience ability and out of body memory. This is where your silver cord attaches to your physical body to your astral body.

By the way, astral bodies are not a big deal. They are an energy-only version of your physical body, with all the same chakras and energy channels. If your astral body gets damaged or is in past time, you can ground it out and create a new one, just like that. You'll want to create new ones if you're doing a lot of energy work and upgrading your space. This will keep your information in your astral body in sync with your physical body, specifically the chakras. Your astral body has the same chakras as your physical body.

Just sit down, ground and run your energy to get into your reading space, then dump out. Stand up. Pull your astral body out of your physical body and stand it in front of you. Put your hands on the head of your astral body and push it into the center of the planet. (Notice how cool it is that you didn't need to create a grounding cord when you did this!)

Then create a brand new astral body and silver cord, with all the latest bells and whistles you've discovered in your travels, and tuck it back into your physical body, ready for the next time you go to sleep.

4th chakra: in front of the spine at the level of the sternum (center of the chest), affinity for yourself. Affinity for yourself is how you recognize your own energy as distinct from the energy of others. Also holds your fourth chakra healing abilities. When people are healing you with love, this is the chakra where that's coming from. Also acts as an intermediary between your lower three chakras and your upper three chakras.

5th chakra: in front of the spine at the bottom of the neck, narrow band telepathy (individuals) and broad band telepathy (groups), creativity, direct voice trance mediumship (channeling voices). Clairaudience! Your ability to hear spirit. And, your inner voice. This is how you hear you.

6th chakra: in the center of the head, roughly between the tops of the ears - clairvoyance. Your ability to see energy and spirit.

7th chakra: on the top of the head. knowingness, or claircognizance. Your ability to know things off the top of your head, to connect the first and last steps to something without going through all the intermediate steps. Also trance mediumship, your ability to allow another spirit to come into your body. Also precognition, your ability to know the future, or at least several versions of the future.

Hand chakras: in the palms of each hand. ALL of the abilities of the seven major chakras are mirrored in the hand chakras. If you can't see the energy very well, holding your hand up, palm facing the energy in question, will cut through the fog. This is also why hands-on healings can be so powerful. The hands can focus all of your abilities on the energy you wish to heal.

Feet chakras: in the souls of your feet, near the top of the arch. Your ability to bring Earth energy into your body. This is more important than it sounds, LOL!

Just for fun: There are 12 chakras, but the other five are outside of and above your body. I don't pretend to fully understand those five, and it hasn't made one bit of difference in my physical or spiritual life.

I did consider bringing my eighth chakra down into my body, but I got over it. Tom Prussing, my clairvoyant teacher and healing teacher, did see me contemplating doing this during an energy check, and told me that while it looked like it was possible for me to do that, it would likely disrupt my energy in my body and my life in "undesirable" ways. I took that to heart and stopped messing around.

A couple of useful exercises:

1. Find your feet chakras and massage them with your thumbs to clean them up.
2. Feel your hand chakras. Turn your healing energy on and off and notice the difference when feeling your hand chakras.
3. Find how many chakras a dog or cat has. Feel for where their clairvoyance is held.
4. Teach your dog or cat how to ground and create a protection rose.

HOW COULD A NAME LIMIT WHAT YOU CAN SEE?

The fourth chakra is a good example.

As I said before, some people are fourth chakra healers. These folks like to hug, a lot. Healing others is often their only tool to keep themselves safe.

Imagine going to work with your healing energy on all the time. Everyone you interact with gets a little healing. You aren't sure if you're doing a good job or not, but healing everyone else gives you, at least in your mind, more time to learn your job.

Imagine your family life as a child was a bit rough. Older siblings were merciless. Dad was aggressive. Mom would betray you just to see how you'd react. Keeping all these players somewhat neutralized by healing them all the time was how you stayed safe, and most of the time it worked. So, as an adult, you find yourself still doing this but you don't know why.

Neat-o, eh? Cool game! Not really. It's draining and very difficult to sustain. These are behaviors I've seen and experienced myself. The good news is it's super easy to correct. Just ground to the center of the planet and turn off your healing energy. Presto! You're still safe but no longer giving your energy away.

One person argued that I should call it the heart chakra, and I sometimes do, but I asked why. They said because it's where the energy of the Divine comes into the body to be distributed up and down to the other chakras. I've never seen anyone use their fourth chakra this way. Maybe we just run in different circles.

The same person told me there is no healing ability in the heart chakra, that the great tradition they followed explained this all very clearly. I've read many fourth chakra healers, so I can't agree with his claim, despite it coming from a great tradition.

One time in a New Age bookstore, I picked up a book about chakras, flipped it open to a random page, and found a diagram of a Chinese man with all of his chakras diagrammed over his body. The fourth chakra was pushed to the left to line it up with the physical heart. Of the thousands of people whose chakras I have read or healed, I've never seen a dislocated fourth chakra like that. The question is, if I had been trained to "see" the world through that tradition, would I have been able to see the fourth chakra at all? Or would I see only what I expected to see?

If you're seeing a ball of energy in someone's chest, and you're not sure what it is, just ask. You know more about how energy works than you can remember. Well, more than you can remember until you ask. The phrase, "ask, and you shall receive" is not just about getting what you want, as is commonly explained. It's about getting answers.

Yoda took Luke to a cave. Luke said, "Something's not right. I feel cold."

Yoda: "That place is strong with the dark side of the Force. A domain of evil it is. In you must go."

Luke: "What's in there?"

Yoda: "Only what you take with you."

What a beautiful and terrifying way to explain to someone that can't yet see energy for themselves how pictures work.

Do some people use their fourth chakra to heal others? In my experience, yes. I have seen it happen in real time. I saw a woman heal a room full of people from her fourth chakra. I was in that room and it felt great!

Could I convince the person who told me there is no healing ability in the heart chakra the error or their ways? Probably not. He likely didn't arrive at that conclusion from personal experience. Could I show them? Maybe, but at some risk to myself. Long, ancient, storied traditions do not give up without a fight. Would I show them? LOL, it depends on how frisky I felt about them at the moment. Young me would have said "Fuck it" and gave him the experience of a fourth chakra healing, pretty much without asking permission. Now? I don't think I'd bother. His path is not mine. I'm taking swing dance classes, and he's not my problem.

Some use their fourth chakra for less nice things, like manipulating what you can like and dislike, or putting cords from their fourth chakra into the fourth chakras of others to keep their awareness tied well below their sixth and seventh chakras to make them easier to control. "There's nothing wrong to see here because we all love one another," said every cult leader ever. "Love is never wrong," said every cult leader ever. Cords are not the problem. It is the intent with which they were created that counts. When you find a cord, ask what it says.

One of the people on Reddit that taught me about the effectiveness my writing could have is a school teacher in an underserved neighborhood. She posted, asking for help. I saw her energy in her post and knew I could and would help her.

She uses her fourth chakra to provide the only safe space her children have in their lives. Reading and helping her was one of the most rewarding experiences of my life. She is the definition of generosity of spirit. She was one of the first people on Reddit that I taught to ground, to give to herself while giving to others so she wouldn't exhaust her spiritual resources.

Meeting her online warmed my heart and guided me towards the writing of this book. I should add that she is also a seventh chakra healer, meaning she automatically knows what you need on an energy level and she gives it to you. As I was writing my comment to her, I felt her crown chakra healing energy pour over me. I mentioned that to her in my comment and thanked her for the healing. Several weeks later, after she processed what I had said, she got back to me.

She knew exactly what I was describing in her life, just not from the perspective of a healer and chakras. She had tried the grounding and felt how it helped her immediately. She was seeing her pupils in a different way. I wrote some words and reminded her of who she was. I really like doing that.

I can heal someone's crown chakra by reading them and doing energy work, but it's not automatic like a crown chakra healer. I hope you run into a crown chakra healer sometime.

Healing yourself
and others

**"You can't wait until life isn't hard anymore to decide to be happy."
– Nightbirde, a 30 year old singer on America's Got Talent, with cancer and a 2% chance of survival: "Two percent is not zero percent."**

Can you choose to be happy? Maybe. You can certainly change your energy from one state to a better state. That's what healing means.

There are lots of healing traditions and tons of books that share an individual's experiences and interpretations of those traditions. One of my favorite books is *Soul Retrieval* by Sandra Ingermann. What made Sandra's book special to me is it filled in a blank in my healing repertoire. I had learned some Japanese techniques, similar to Reiki, and some Chinese techniques similar to acupressure, and some clairvoyant techniques from Silva Mind Control, and all of the extensive list of healing techniques taught in the clairvoyant training program at the Berkeley Psychic Institute.

I had good results working on women's menstrual cramps, back spasms in dancers, shoulder injuries in martial artists, headaches, energy problems in chakras and the aura, missing information that I fetched for them from the Akashic Records, and knees. Especially knees. I had poor results with endometriosis and cancer.

There have been a few instances where the results were miraculous. Miraculous as in changed their life in a few minutes of time.

Some of those miracles came from doing a soul retrieval for someone whose soul had been split during some trauma. Not all trauma causes damage to the soul, and a trauma that caused a split soul in one person did nothing of that magnitude in someone else.

Once you learn to recognize a missing piece in someone's soul, it's hard to miss it the next time you encounter it. It sticks out like a missing thumb.

Part of the reason this kind of damage is so obvious is that on some level, the damaged person found you.

It has been a consistent experience for me that as soon as I learn a new healing skill, someone shows up in need of that skill. Part of this is I'm excited to practice! This creates a mockup on my part. Another part of this is that the new skill seems to be obvious in my aura or chakras and people who need that skill see it in me. Every spirit is psychic, even if they don't know it in their body. So a newly acquired skill ends up shining brightly in my aura like a billboard, and people in need of it show up.

Read *Soul Retrieval*. I don't use the Shamanic ritual. It's not necessary. It's mostly about protecting the practitioner, and I've got that covered. The book taught me to recognize the energy of a missing piece in someone's soul, and my clairvoyant tools made it easy to implement. My wife does a combination of using her clairvoyant tools to find and fetch the missing piece, talking to it, spirit to spirit, to bring it into present time, then uses the shamanic practice of blowing the soul piece into the top of their head.

While she has no problem doing this bit, and neither do the folks she heals, I'm a 6'4" big man with a lot of energy, and women and men get a little nervous when I lean down over them, close to their face but just out of sight. I use my hand instead to guide the piece back through the crown chakra to rejoin the rest of itself. Your hand chakras mirror all of the abilities in your seven main chakras. You'll figure out what works for you.

So is happiness a result or an energy? Maybe it's both. Maybe that's why sometimes you can choose to be happy and other times not. Amusement is an energy and we can create it to help move ourselves along in a difficult situation. Is happiness the same way?

Notice your grounding cord. Bring it into present time. Bring in a gold sun or two; check your gauges to make sure you're full.

Run your energy. Blow some roses. Fill in again. Be in the center of your head.

Create a rose and let it vibrate at your energy of happiness. Notice the color, the shape, and the texture. Hold the stem in your fingers and notice every detail. Does it have a smell? Rotate the rose in your fingers. Does it have roots? Does it have leaves? Notice the color again. This is your happiness.

If it has anyone else's energy in it, drain that foreign energy out of the rose. Notice what changes.

Now match your crown chakra to the color of the rose.

How does this vibration feel? What does it remind you of? What thoughts come into your awareness? What memories are restimulated?

Blow some roses for any energy that does not want you to look at your energy of happiness for yourself. You can read that energy later if you like. For now, just break it up and ground it out of your space.

Notice your happiness rose.

Create a gold sun and fill it with one thing: your vibration of happiness. Bring that down into your space and let it flow throughout it, filling in the gaps from blowing those roses for energy that didn't want you to look at your happiness.

Bend over, touch the floor, open your eyes and kick back!

I always wanted to be a dancer. As a young boy watching Fred and Ginger on TV, dancing looked like more fun than humanly possible. I didn't get to pursue that growing up.

Then healing and martial arts came into focus for me. I tried a few styles of karate, but it was Aikido that captured my attention. It was somewhat dance-like, though I didn't see that at the time.

My fifth year in Aikido, I felt I needed to learn some different pedagogical techniques to improve myself as a teacher and better help my students. So, I did what any rational man would do and talked my way into a senior level modern dance class at the University of Arizona to experience first hand from a wonderful teacher named Dr. John Wilson a different way to teach movement.

Wow! I went from being a shining example in our dojo for how to move well to someone on the dance floor who looked like he was trying to hop on lava. It was humbling. Embarrassing. There was some animosity from the dance students. After all, they had a decade or more of dance behind them to allow them to be in this class, and I was just taking up space. And taking up space in clumsy ways.

However, by the end of the year, there was more acceptance, more conversations after class, more practicing together, and some healings. Once your hand takes the pain out of an overstretched hamstring, word gets around, LOL! Once your hand eases the pain in someone's lower back just in time for their big audition with the San Francisco Ballet, word gets around. I barely touched that young man; it was all energy work. It scared him a little, but it solved his problem. Of that he was sure.

I loved it.

Then everything I thought I had a handle on in Tucson collapsed in a treacherous way, and I left the desert for the San Francisco Bay Area. We had a 500 year flood in Tucson just before I left, damaging nine of eleven bridges over the Santa Cruz River.

Now, forty years later, what am I doing? I am finally taking swing dance lessons! It's my Fred and Ginger mockup from my boyhood, and I couldn't be happier. One evening a week on Mondays for class, and a class and social dance every other Friday evening. All those neurons that have not been firing during my IT career are glowing again. I'm losing weight. I'm gaining stamina. I'm walking better and moving with more smoothness and less pain. I'm dancing and I'm delighted!

When you know you want to do something, do it. It doesn't have to be your life's work. Hobbies are a wonderful and effective source of joy and happiness.

Ground yourself. Be in the center of your head. Run your energy and blow some roses.

Look at a rose for your happiness. Let that rose vibrate at your next step towards your happiness. Notice all the details of that rose. Notice what ideas pop into your head.

Stand by the deep end of your happiness pool, put your feet together, and jump in. That's what I'd do. You can always step out of the pool.

Be a Body of Glass

Picture this: you just finished a beautiful conversation with a dear friend that you have not seen in years. You've planned to meet up again next weekend with another friend you've lost touch with. You're really excited to be back in touch with these wonderful people.

You leave the coffee shop where you've been talking and walk into the middle of a protest about something. A line of police in riot gear are moving towards you. Protesters are shouting and gesturing at the police, trying to hold their ground. You hear the door of the coffee shop being locked behind you.

What do you do?

It's useful to know how to protect yourself. We've talked about roses for maintaining separation and protecting our aura. We've talked a lot about the many benefits of grounding. We've talked about blowing pictures when they get lit up by some random energy. We've talked about being in the center of our head so that we are neutral to whatever energy or picture is coming our way.

That's quite an arsenal, eh? As a teaching technique, look at all the details you dig into by practicing these techniques. Different energies. Different concepts. Different responses to threats or big energies.

Quite an inventory of things to remember. And that's a problem.

In a situation where seconds matter, do you create a rose, pull in your aura, be in the center of your head, open your sixth chakra, and take a look? Probably not, eh? In fact, you may have already decided what you need to do before you realize what is happening. Most likely, as soon as you stood up from your meeting with your friend, part of you became aware of the energy outside the shop.

Remember how we simplified controlling our aura by using the super simple image of a bubble around us: "be in your bubble" replaced checking where your energy was in every direction. Just be in your bubble.

The idea of the bubble came from the Yin Yang preschool at the Church of Divine Man. This is where psychic moms could drop off their little ones and know their kids would have permission to be psychic. The idea was to not turn off the kids' abilities as often happens in normal schools.

If your space can quickly be defined by one image of a bubble, what other image of a general nature might be useful?

Your bubble is clear. You can see out and everyone else can see in.

Can our physical bodies be clear?

We run into energy in our daily lives, some of it very strong energy. What if, instead of defending ourselves against all these energies, we allowed them to pass through us.

This is the idea behind being a body of glass. This was taught in the advanced clairvoyant class back in the 80s. Back then, it was believed that training in the other protection tools was required first, but that isn't really true. Those other tools might be perceived to require less energy to create and use than becoming a body of glass, but that's just someone's perception. This is also me acknowledging that you are probably more capable than me. I needed to spend three weeks grounding before I learned about running energy.

Like grounding by standing your feet on the center of the planet, some of you can skip most of the protective tools and be a clear body of glass.

Most of the energy in your daily life is not critical to keep out of your space. Most of the pictures that get lit up in your space are not terrible, debilitating pictures. In fact, many of your pictures might be enjoyable, and you don't want to blow them up.

When you go to your favorite restaurant, you are lighting up pleasurable pictures in your space. When you are intimate with another, you are lighting up pleasurable pictures in your space. Pictures are not necessarily bad.

But what if the pictures aren't pleasurable? What if, instead of the mass of energies flying around the room of a social dance like distractions or a source of pain and fatigue, they just passed on through you without any effect on your space at all. When a picture lights up in your space, you can blow it without reading it, and return to being a clear body of glass.

This is the desired effect of being a body of glass. Be a clear, neutral body of glass.

You aren't taking foreign energies in. You aren't keeping them out, either. You're not resisting them in any way. Practicing to be in the center of your head has taught you how to find the vibration of neutrality, so you can match that vibration from anywhere. Neutrality is the only requirement for implementing being a body of glass.

Amusement makes being a body of glass easier and more effective. Enthusiasm does it automatically.

Find the vibration in your past where you created enthusiasm about something, anything. Take a look at the energy of your enthusiasm. Then match it. You don't have to behave like you did then; you just need the vibration.

Do a rose reading on your enthusiasm.

So what would you look like, standing between that line of cops and the protestors? You would look like nothing at all.

Two psychics
and a Funeral

Fun story time!

I was in a class with a bunch of other psychics. This was a "ministers in training" class for new graduates of the clairvoyant training program. It was held in Pleasanton, CA, in an old hall that once belonged to some men's organization like Freemasons or Odd Fellows. It had twenty foot high ceilings with wonderful plaster coving and moldings, which volunteers at the church had painted and highlighted with gold. Very fancy and beautiful.

I got word earlier that day that my mother had passed. This was expected. I'd said my goodbyes six months before that when she could still recognize me.

I showed up to class that evening with two bottles of champagne and hid them in the back of the fridge. (Never trust psychics around your alcohol! The bottles grow legs and wander off.)

At the end of class, I asked the teacher and class for a favor. They waited while I ran to fetch the bottles. On returning, I explained that my mom had passed, I wanted to celebrate her memory, and that my poopie relatives would not participate in a wake or celebration of any kind. Everyone agreed to share some champagne with me and toast this major event in my life.

Plastic cups were passed all around, and I handed one bottle to someone else and began twisting the wire off the other one. Once that was off, I started pressing my thumbs against the cork and just as the corked popped, my mom, in a very loud voice, shouted my name in her mommy-scolding tone from high in the corner of the tall ceiling, "Wayne!"

I looked up towards my mom's voice, just as the cork bounced off the crown molding, and spun down to hit me square in the center of my forehead, LOL! Nice disrespect for my sixth chakra, Mom!

The next day, having no car of my own, my girlfriend Christine drove us from San Francisco to Los Angeles for the funeral. We stayed the night with a friend of mine near Huntington Beach, then showed up the next morning at the cemetery in the San Gabriel Valley.

The extended family had the same energy as those scavenger birds that slowly circle in the air over roadkill.

No one was happy to see me, especially with my beautiful girlfriend. Some tried to separate us. Some tried to demean me to my face. Same old family! Christine and I just laughed and smiled at each other, pointed at each other's grounding cords and protection roses, and matched our crown chakras to the vibration we wanted.

Christine sat with me on the front line of chairs for immediate family. It's my dad, older brother, older sister, me, and Christine. Dad's in his

80's. Bro and sis were ten and eight years older than me. Mom and dad were 47 when I was born. Surprise baby!

After too long of a sermon by a stranger, my older brother had the job of passing out roses to each family member so each of us could place a red rose on Mom's coffin. My brother, estranged from me, picked up an arm full of roses, walked towards the family line, tripped on a paver and fell on all fours at Christine's feet, spilling the roses all around her.

She says, without missing a beat, "Aww, you shouldn't have!"

He struggled not to laugh out loud. He looked like he was going to pee himself. I grinned. Is that a sense of humor I see in my brother? I checked my match with Christine's crown chakra and regrounded.

Naturally, I saved that plastic cork from the champagne, so after the ceremonies were done, I talked to the funeral director. I told him I had held a wake in honor of my mother's life, and how the rest of the family were not supportive of that kind of thing. I believe the word I used was "poopy." He looked at the crowd shuffling out of the cemetery, smiled and nodded. I told him my mother and I liked to party (okay, that's a tiny little stretch of a lie. She didn't drink alcohol after we moved to California, though I distinctly remember her filling a small green plastic cup from my father's bottle of beer and adding a pinch of salt to it when we lived in Ajo, Arizona).

I asked him if I could put this champagne cork in my mother's grave. He said he could do one better than that: he would place it next to her head in the coffin. I gave him my deepest gratitude!

We're the last ones near the gravesite. Christine and I start walking towards the exit of the cemetery and an old, nasty uncle of mine that used to pick on me relentlessly when I was a child, steps in front of us, blocking our way with his three-hundred pounds, nods at me, then gets all creepy-smiley at my beautiful girlfriend. Yeah. He did that.

And he stands up a little taller, which only makes his huge gut distend further, reaches out his hand as if to shake her hand, and says, "I'm his Uncle Lester!" like this answered all the questions in the air. This is the uncle that tried to pick four year old me up by my head and called me retarded in front of anyone who was around.

Christine glances at the ground, sees his foot is on top of a bronze grave marker with the name "Lester" showing next to his shoe, and says, "So, are you practicing?"

He gets confused. She's holding his eyes with her smile, then points down. He sees his name on the grave marker, turns bright orange in the face, and stumbles away.

Best funeral ever!

My Deer Hunt

O nce upon a time, I was in my mid-20s. Growing up, I heard about deer hunting. My parents were born in 1905 in rural Arkansas, a third world country. No electricity. No phones. No indoor plumbing. Hunting successfully often meant survival.

As a kid on vacations from either Arizona or California to Arkansas, I carried well water thirty yards up to the house so my aunt could cook and clean with it. There was a reason people only bathed on Saturday nights; it was too much word to bathe more often than that. I was fascinated by the long guns in the gun cabinet in my grandfather's farmhouse.

After a childhood of hearing about the deer hunting exploits of most of the adult men in my extended family, I felt incomplete. Something was missing from my life.

So, without any further preparation, I bought a deer tag for the fall hunting season in Tucson, Arizona, borrowed a rifle from my manager at the hospital, and drove my station wagon south into the Chiricahua mountains to camp overnight and hunt the next morning.

I had mixed feelings about all this, but there was this drive in me to fill the void of not having hunting experience. I was caught up in the momentum of that drive.

The first surprise was that the little stream that ran across the dirt road on the back side of the mountain was frozen. The car lost traction but slid to the other side and up onto the road again.

I parked in the clearing where I'd camped with my manager and his friends last spring for an epicly unsuccessful javelina hunt.

The second surprise was it was suddenly dark. I ran around gathering wood with a flashlight. I tried to dig a fire pit but the ground was frozen. I laid out my pad and sleeping bag and shivered for way too long before climbing back into my car, turning on the engine and heater, and napping as best I could.

At 4:00 a.m. I gave up on sleep. I got out of my car, made sure the borrowed rifle was safe, slung it over a shoulder, and began the steep climb up the mountain to the pass where my manager's hunting friends had said the deer liked to go through in the morning.

I was forty-five minutes up the south side of the mountain when all the hair stood up on my neck, and a shock of energy ran from the base of my spine all the way up. I turned around very slowly, trying to keep my footing on the loose rock and maybe not be seen by whatever made my body go on full alert.

Across the valley, over in Mexico, a red light stood still in the sky. It looked like hot wax slowly spinning. It pulsed once and three drops of "wax" fell downwards, their light extinguishing towards the end of their drop.

Then the ball of wax pulsed again, spun a little faster, and streaked east and out of sight in an instance.

My childhood hobby was studying airplanes. That was neither a plane nor a helicopter nor a rocket.

I stood dumbstruck for a minute, then yawned. The words "sleep deprived" and "hallucination" popped into my mind, and I turned back facing the mountain and began to climb again.

Five minutes later, almost sure that I'd put the swirly thing out of my mind with the exertion of climbing the steeper part of the mountain, the hair on my neck stood up and my spine went rigid. I turned around faster this time and saw two balls of red wax, taking turns spinning. First the right one spun, then the left one spun, then the right one spun.

I watched them spin and pulse for the longest minute of my life until several drops of wax fell from each, extinguishing on the way down to the earth. They streaked across the sky to the east and were gone in a second.

My mind was blank, not a single thought. My emotions were still. No fear. No nothing. This wasn't Zen. This was closer to something like paralysis.

I finally took a breath, realized I'd stopped breathing, and took another.

Well, there's nothing left to do about that. I guess I'll fulfill my purpose and complete this hunt.

After what seemed like hours, I settled down at the top of the ridge behind a tree, and faced east. The sunrise would signal the legal start of the day's hunt and any bucks traversing the pass below would be silhouetted by the sun.

Three hours later, after listening to gunfire on a different mountain in the distance, my butt freezing and my feet asleep from not moving, I gave up. The real hunters obviously knew what they were doing, and I did not.

The sun was up in the sky now. Maybe mid-morning. I looked around for what to do next. There was a meadow on top of the ridge to my west, a little below my position, so I headed there to see what was there and to wallow in my disappointment. The meadow had to be better than the sharp rocks I'd been sitting on.

There was no wind. Tall grass brushed against the knees of my jeans. It felt so peaceful. The sun was just beginning to shine into this little bowl of heaven.

So I walked in circles to flatten the grass into a bed. I laid my pack and rifle down at one side of the circle, stretched out on my back, pulled my wool cap over my eyes, and fell asleep.

Warmth on my chest woke me up. I opened my eyes to see the speckles of sunshine breaking through the weave of my cap and smiled. I uncovered my eyes, sat up, and looked straight into the eyes of a deer. I glanced at my rifle but dismissed that thought. This deer was a doe. The hunting season was for bucks only. That's when I noticed a bunch of does and their little ones all around me, all bedded down just like me, in little circles of flattened grass.

The doe nearest me held my attention. It was like she was waiting for my next move. I looked again to the right where my borrowed rifle lay. I looked back at her. She winked at me and made me smile.

I took a deep breath, said, "Have a nice nap," covered my eyes, and went back to sleep.

I woke up at noon and found myself alone. I was the happiest I'd been in a long time. I got my pack and the borrowed rifle and headed back down the mountain to my car. My deer hunt was complete.

I never experienced that drive to hunt again.

BUT WHAT ABOUT THOSE WAXY RED LIGHTS?

Years later, during the clairvoyant training program, I asked a few students to take a look at that experience. They could not see anything. They could not read my memory of it. They did get a bit upset, which was really interesting.

So, I went to a staff member, David Pierce, and asked him to take a look. He was British.

I told him the tale. He grunted, "Fucking aliens dumping their garbage!" and asked me if I had anything else for him to look at, LOL!

Between my laughing at his Brit accent and disgust, and the alien blank getting filled in, the fear and curiosity stored in my space just washed down my grounding cord in one huge release.

Yep! I'd seen aliens and it was no longer a problem.

Rose McLintock's Funeral

Or, the further adventures of my first day as Susan's assistant.

Note: Remember that story about me asking "What am I not looking at?" and then giving energy checks to Susan's assistants on the front porch of her cabin, reading everyone's fountains? Here's what happened next.

After the morning energy checks were complete, I was invited to stay for lunch. Simple sandwiches and good company. This was the longest I had been with Lewis in a non-teaching role and he opened up to me about his life before the institute. He gave me the tour of the property. He talked about meeting L. Ron Hubbard in a military hospital after stepping on a mine in WWII. He talked about some of the businesses he owned: watch repair, commercial laundry. He talked about traveling across China after the war.

He talked of how he always saw auras. Always, as in from birth. The ability just didn't shut down for him the way it did for most of us. We shared lots of stories and discovered some common interests outside of psychic stuff, like being machinists and traveling on whims.

Then the phone call came.

One of the ministers in the Church of Divine Man was found dead in her apartment. She was face down and clutching her chest. She had heart failure and was only in her 30s (?). She was legal counsel for the church, so worked closely with Lewis and Susan. Her name was Rose McLintock. She was also in the Trance Medium Program, where she would allow another being to come into her body to do readings and healings on guests at the healing clinics.

I'm just standing there, reading the energy of how people are reacting. From my perspective, this wasn't shocking for me. I'd worked in hospital ERs and saw lots of people die. I learned to recognize some of the energy signs of a spirit leaving the body. This news was bad but I remained grounded, mostly because I only knew *of* Rose McLintock. I'd seen her at the institutes and healing clinics. She and I never really spoke, been in readings together, or exchanged readings.

Susan asked me if I'm available for the rest of the day. She'd like me to accompany her and Lewis to the funeral services. I looked at the energy of the rest of my day and said that I just needed to make one call to my girlfriend. (This was the 80s. No cell phones yet. It was good manners to mention the need to call someone and wait for them to offer you the use of their land line. Back then, a long distance call cost a lot, unlike today.)

I am in the backseat of Lewis' old Mercedes. It's dark now and Lewis is driving us through the mountains of Calistoga to the chapel where the funeral will take place. I don't recall where that chapel was, only that it took us a couple of hours to get there.

No one is talking much, just riding through the dark in our thoughts. I'm staying grounded and out of trance. I don't really want to read either of my hosts right now. I'm not certain if they want me to read anything so I keep my awareness closed down.

Lewis says, "Wayne, I want to thank you for today. You stayed out of our spaces all day and that's very much appreciated."

Susan added, "Yes! Thank you!"

I ran through the possibilities for why they would point this out, but gave up and said, "You're welcome. You did teach me how to do that in the clairvoyant training program, you know."

He seemed thoughtful, almost pensive. I let it go and returned to looking ahead at the energy of the funeral and blowing my matching pictures.

Weeks later, Lewis would say to a group of us graduates/new ministers, "You know, I don't know what you learned in the clairvoyant training program because I never went through it!"

Then he told us how he founded the Institute.

He was meditating one day and a group of beings appeared above him and scanned his crown chakra. A few minutes later, they offered him the job of founding the institute. They showed him what the students would learn, and what he needed to do. He made his agreements with them. They showed him a map with hundreds of institutes on it. (Years later he realized those were not his institutes, but the institutes of his students.)

His first wife, Bunny, helped. He was complaining about how his students in his free classes in a room upstairs in a new age bookstore didn't stick around long enough for him to teach them everything he was able to teach them.

Bunny said, "If you don't charge for it, how much can it be worth to them?"

So, Lewis called ninteen (I think) former students and said, "I'm starting my institute. Six months. $2,000, all up front. Are you in?" Or something pretty close to that. They all wrote him a check and the Institute had its inaugural clairvoyant training program class.

The Mercedes slowed down and turned into the chapel parking lot, rolled over the gravel and into a parking place near the front doors. The engine stopped and Lewis almost collapsed over the steering wheel, wheezing and struggling to breathe.

He told me to go inside, and I left the car with all due haste. Just inside the chapel doors and to my right, I saw Tom Prussing running his energy on a bench. I approached him. He looked up at me and smiled, and told me to sit and run my energy. I sat next to him and did just that.

In a few minutes, Susan ran up to us. "Tom. Lewis is sick. Can you come to the car and give him a healing?"

Tom set his jaw and said, "I'll do it from here," and slipped back into trance.

Susan left. I stood and went into my control space, stood in front of Tom's body, grounded the area while I warmed up to grounding the building. Some energy started flying around as the non-psychic side of Rose's life started showing up. Conservative Christians. Not happy to see me or my control energy or any of it. I ignored them and maintained my control over the energy in my little part of the building.

Five minutes later, Lewis walks in, all smiles and laughing. He says, "Thank you, Tom!" Susan says nothing but seems to acknowledge Tom.

Lewis heads for the stage at the front of the chapel, and a room to the side to change into his purple robes and vestments.

I sit on the bench with Tom and realize that Tom and Susan have no love lost between them. Interesting. Tom's a favorite teacher of mine. What's up with that? And what did I just sign up for with Susan? No time for that now. The chapel is full and the funeral ceremonies are about to begin.

First up, this conservative Christian minister in a worn, black leather jacket and skinny jeans. He not only looks like a pimp, he sounds like a pimp. He actually sounds high, as in drugs. Rose's non-psychic family is all to the right of the minister. To his left, the pews are filled with psychic friends from the other side of Rose's life. Lots of empty seats on the right. Standing room only on the left.

All too soon, it becomes obvious that this minister never knew Rose. His speech was making Rose's family nervous and more sad. At one point, he dropped the three by five cards with his notes that someone gave him. He kneels down to pick them up, and his pants rip a little.

He stands. His face has the splotchy complexion of a street wino: broken capillaries everywhere, big red nose, swollen eyelids. Part of his hair broke loose from whatever gel or spray he'd attacked it with, and claims its freedom like a twisted unicorn horn. He tries way too many times to push it back in place, all while trying to talk about Rose. It's pitiful.

My memories of him are obviously biased. I have no idea what he was doing before he got the call, and then to be confronted with hundreds of psychics all reading his energy; he had to have been lit up in the worst way.

I'm standing in the back of the chapel, controlling. I look at the family side and their energy is a mess of heartbreak and embarrassment, their bodies shifting around, trying to get comfortable by taking up more space, even when no one sits next to them. I look at the psychic side and their energy is grounded, respectfully attentive, and expressing compassion for the families and friends on all sides.

Minister Pimp has moved all the way to the right of the stage. He's not acknowledged any of the people on the left at any time, which I find amusing, lol. He can't even look to his left. He's focused on telling the front row how happy and blissful Rose is now, kneeling at the feet of Jesus.

I can't help myself. I laugh out loud for the briefest moment. I may not have been Rose's friend, but the few times I saw her in action, I knew she bowed and knelt down to no one.

A few people at the back on the family side scowl at me. I just smile and return to controlling. Tom's got that mischief in his eye.

Minister Pimp seems to be nearing his climax. Thank God! I'm now looking at the whole stage and Wham! I see a bolt of energy form out of the air and slam into the back of Lewis' neck and head, knocking him forward, nearly off of his folding chair. I can tell who did it: a group of beings from the church of Pimp.

Now I'm on. I just saw someone attack someone I know, right next to his wife. My energy is ready for a fight and there will be few prisoners. Tom gently touches my forearm to get my attention. He says, "Be amused. It's alright. He's fine."

I look at Tom and take a breath. I look at Lewis and see him smiling broadly, running his energy like I haven't seen him do before. It's like

Lewis was waiting for that whack so he could blow his matching pictures. Rev. Pimp is done and Lewis is standing up to say his piece.

I don't remember the words Lewis spoke, not until the very end. While he spoke, I was aware of a wonderful healing energy flowing over everyone, calming everyone, as Lewis told us about his time with Rose and the wonderful things she did for everyone in her life.

Rose's coffin was center stage, just behind the podium where Lewis stood. He turned around, raised his arms in the air in a big "Y," and said the only words I remember from his speech.

"In love we met. In love we part. Hello, Rose!"

An arc of five stars appeared over her coffin, between his hands. Then it was like glitter just burst into the air under the stars and everything twinkled itself out. The service was over.

I rode back to their cabin with Susan and Lewis. They let me stay in their guest house office space on the floor, as it was past midnight when we arrived.

End of day one as Susan's assistant, lol!

EPILOGUE

I first met Rose at the trance medium healing clinic, where she was one of the trance mediums that brought in different beings into their bodies to give readings and healings. I was a shiny new control at the clinic and somewhat taken with her beauty and very much intimidated by how easily she could bring someone else in and give them control over her body while she took off to places I couldn't see. She also had the bearing of someone genuinely nice that you didn't really want to mess with. I found the combination alluring and terrifying.

A few days after Rose's funeral, I was back at the trance medium healing clinic, as a control. The clinic is supposed to start, but everyone is just sitting in their own thoughts, unsure of what to do. Rose's absence and the reason why was on the top of everyone's mind.

Lewis' assistant, Paul Ohmart, stands up and walks behind the line of readers that so far haven't changed their energy at all. Paul looks over the line of readers at the audience and says, "In case anyone's interested, there's an opening in the Trance Medium program."

Everyone breaks into laughter! The spell is broken. The energy in the room is moving and getting ready for the clinic to begin. Absolutely brilliant!

Paul is setting the energy of the crown chakras of ten trance mediums in the line in front of him. After he gets them tuned up, he breaks up the line into three smaller lines and gives me one. This is typical and how we were able to read and heal more people in one evening.

In front of me are a female in her twenties on the left, a middle aged male dentist in the center, and a thirty-something female on the right.

I'm standing behind them, grounding, looking at their energy, the energy on the ceiling, the energy behind me that says, "Don't ground!" I chuckle at that and ground with more gusto.

I'm looking at the energy of the part of the audience that chose to come get a reading from my line of trance mediums. It all looks good. I laugh out loud, recalling Paul's ice breaking joke.

The line breaks their grounding cords and goes up to silver-white. I'm helping by setting my palms to the silver-white vibration and holding my hands on either side of their crown chakras, one by one, helping them refine their match. They are starting to hum along, getting ready to bring in a being or two. (Technical note: I'm not healing their crown chakras; I'm providing a reference vibration for them to match. It's the "all abilities are mirrored in the hand chakras" thing, used to give them something to match their crown chakras to that is different from my crown chakra, which is at gold.)

My attention goes 100% on the female body in the right chair. Her energy had changed instantaneously, which is unusual. The center chair male is more nervous than I've ever seen him, scooting side to side on his chair, fidgeting with his fingers, and coming all the way out of trance and opening his eyes, clearing his throat, and going back into trance. His usual routine is smooth and free, and now he looks upset and out of control.

Interesting! So who has come knocking in that body to the right? The energy seems familiar.

I say, "Hello! Thank you for being with us tonight. What's your name?"

The body on the right wiggles just a little, then relaxes. Her mouth opens and closes a few times, and finally answers, "Rose."

The guy in the middle is having shivers pass through his body, and some jerks. His face is contorted, almost painfully so. I ask him if he's okay. He doesn't answer. I leave him to work on whatever energy he's working on and return to the lady on the right.

"Hello Rose. Your presence seems to be making our center chair nervous. Do you know anything about that?"

After a few moments, Rose answers, "We were intimate."

The way she phrased that revelation made the man in the center chair realize the being sitting next to him was Rose McLintock, his ex-girlfriend.

Friends, it doesn't get more real than that, LOL!

Rose came through that borrowed body and did some great readings and healings that evening. The guy in the middle just hung on for dear life, unable to read or even speak much. When the clinic was over, he ran out of the building. He was all right in a few days. The experience of seeing his ex in another body just lit up too many pictures for him to blow in one night. He blew them over the course of a few days, all while running his dental practice and attending more classes and clinics. Grounding and running energy works.

One takeaway from this story: the man in the center chair had been active in the church for years and he still got lit up and stuck. He was one of the few people that Lewis allowed to join the Trance Medium Program, which back then was $10,000 up front and a four year commitment, IIRC. You also had to take all the other programs as prerequisites to getting in, which was a couple years of classes after graduating from the clairvoyant training program. This guy knew how to manage his energy. He still got stuck.

There was a character named Rose in the romcom movie *Moonstruck*, played by Olivia Dukakas. There's a scene where she tells her unfaithful husband, "Cosmo, no matter what you do you're gonna die."

That's a true statement for everyone with a body. I would add that no matter what you've accomplished to date, you can still get lit up and stuck on pictures. So be amused and enjoy the process while you can, experiencing everything you can, and ground and run your energy.

Saving Momma Deer

There came a time during my last years in Tucson where I was lost in my head. This was well before I had much training in energy stuff, so I did what I did back then and got angry.

I had access to a friend's Jeep. I drove north to the backside of the Catalina Mountains around 3:00 a.m. or so. It was August and the night was still hot. I had a flashlight and a jug of water. I had no plan.

After driving through a couple of cattle guards, I ran out of dirt road and stopped. I'd hiked the trail near here before and was sure I could find it in the dark. I left the water and took the flashlight.

The arguments in my head were intensifying. They began to hurt. I was mumbling to myself, huffing and puffing up the steep path. This was not a reverie or an introspection; it was a fight.

My vague notion was to climb the mountain and over exert myself enough to burn out the conflict in my head. It was a bad plan. I realized it was a bad plan, but couldn't stop my boots.

Rattling broke me out of my stupor. My flashlight searched ahead and fell onto a really large rattlesnake, stretched across the path fifteen feet in front of me, tail up and rattling, head up and staring.

Mr. Snake asked me what the fuck I thought I was doing. Why wasn't I watching where I was stepping?

I stopped at the first sound. I was frozen with one foot still in the air. I lowered that foot after looking beneath it to make sure I was stepping only on the ground.

"I'm sorry! I'm really upset and wasn't paying attention. I'm really sorry."

He tested the air with his tongue, sensed I was telling the truth, turned off the rattle, and oozed off the trail into the dark.

For some reason, my head was now clear. The voices and arguments were gone. I wasn't sure what the fight was about. All I knew was the fight was gone, and the air was still, the night quiet.

I gave thanks to Mr. Snake for his help. I didn't know why I did that. It just felt right.

As I started climbing again, I realized I had no water with me. Huh. Why did I leave that in the Jeep? I should just go back and get the jug. There was plenty of time and I was in the best shape of my life. The extra distance meant nothing to me.

But I didn't. It just seemed like I could not delay getting up the mountain. So I pushed on.

The eastern sky was getting lighter. I didn't need the flash light. I found myself standing in a kind of saddle formed by the volcanic rock weathering between the mountain proper and a tower of rock.

I needed to get a closer look at that tower of rock. I took a dozen steps and something moved to my right. I stopped and listened and waited. I may have been a shit hunter, but that didn't mean I couldn't hear and feel nature.

A few minutes passed and a few dry leaves crackled. Now, I had a definite direction. Sound can be more accurate than light.

I stepped once and waited. Again, and waited. Three more slow steps, and I saw her.

The hooves of her baby stuck out of her birth canal, still and lifeless. She was stuck on the edge of the saddle where it turned into a cliff. Holding her there was a single bush about three feet high with a small tangle of branches with few leaves, parted down the middle by momma deer's body.

She tensed when I drew near. I said I was here to help and she should stay calm. She looked me in the eyes. The memory of all those does down on the Mexican border, sleeping all around me, came up into my awareness.

Her ears wiggled once and she took a deep breath. I took that as consent, and I knelt beside her rear end and stroked her hip and thigh.

She was exhausted. She was dehydrated. I thought about the water back in the Jeep but knew that was too long a hike. Blood and amniotic fluid stained the ground. She'd be coyote breakfast before I could get back.

So, I took hold of the hooves of the baby deer and pulled. Nothing. The baby was dried onto her birth canal. I spit on my fingers and started applying the moisture around the dead baby, trying to push it a little into her birth canal. I had no idea if this was a good idea but it was the only idea I had.

Twenty minutes later, after several failed attempts, I pulled and the dead body gave way just a tiny bit. Ten minutes of spit and pulling later, and I had a grip on the back and front hooves. That didn't help, but I was making progress.

I sat and rested, talking to momma deer with my hand on her thigh.

I kneeled on the sharp gravel again and pulled with all I had, and the hind legs came all the way out.

Something hurt inside momma, and she jerked a little, breaking the branches, and sliding down the rocks, coming to a stop ten feet below me on a tiny bush.

I looked at the situation. If I went down after her, and she lost the purchase on the little bush, we'd both go over the cliff.

She was starting to tense up again. I talked to her, tried to calm her. She looked at me. She seemed resigned. I said no. She said nothing. And I climbed down to her.

The jostling of her fall must have freed up some fluids. I pulled moderately on the legs of the dead baby and his torso began to move out.

My foot slipped and several seconds later I heard the rocks I'd kicked over the cliff hit other rocks. I sighed and looked her in the eye and said "no."

I scooched my butt closer to her side, trusting that little bush with both our lives. I pulled the legs again and almost all of him came out.

I was breathing hard, the sun now directly on us. I rubbed the sweat from my face and arms onto momma's rump, no idea if that helped, but momma seemed to smile at me.

On the next try, the whole body came free. Images of coyotes came into my head, so I picked up the dead body, held it to my chest, and spider-walked back up into the saddle. I stood up, picked up the dead body, and threw it over the cliff to the left. I thought that would give momma more time to recover and get away.

I needed water. Shit. Momma needed water. I crawled to within five feet of momma and told her I was going to bring her water. She wiggled her body and started to slip off the little bush. I screamed.

She settled, softening herself around the little bush, and sighed.

I scurried back up the loose rock and onto the saddle. I looked back at her and smiled. I turned to go back to the path and froze. There, on the ridge of the mountain, was a huge buck. The sun was rising between his antlers. He stood still and looked at me, not much more than a silhouette.

I couldn't move. I was in awe.

Then I heard him say *"thank you."*

I smiled. He didn't move. I ran to the path. He didn't move. I ran down the mountain, got the jug from the Jeep, and ran-walked back up the mountain.

From the saddle, I could see they both were gone. I tried to look over the cliff to see if she fell, but the rock was too loose, and besides, I knew she wasn't dead. I don't know how but I knew.

So I took a big gulp from the water jug, poured some over my head, and grinned all the way back down to the Jeep, skipping and bouncing like a fool.

Crayons for reading and healing

Coloring can be an amazing compliment to bed rest. A box of crayons and a notebook make wonderful psychic healing tools.

Let's say you have a broken leg. It requires surgery, lots of metal plates and screws, a huge cast, and the scars are gonna be epic. You're snowed under with prescription painkillers and anti-inflammatories most of the time. Life is not fun right now by a long shot.

No fun is a detriment to your healing, though. So you create some fun!

Let's have a little fun with pain as a first step.

Where is the pain? Doh! It's in my leg, you stupid fence post! There, there. I take no offense. Just play along with me for a bit. I promise it will get better.

So you say, "Okay, the pain is in my leg."

What color is your pain? You see it as dark blue. This confuses you, but just roll with it. Whatever color you see is fine. Find a crayon that is close to the dark blue that you see. Look at the crayon.

What shape is the pain? You see it as a jagged star shape.

How big is the pain? You see it as only three inches at its longest dimension, which surprises you a bit. You thought it would be larger. Go with it.

Draw a jagged, dark blue star about three inches across. Draw what you imagine your pain to look like.

If the pain could hold water, how much water would it hold?

WTF does that mean, "how much water would it hold?" when it's a flat piece of paper? Play along. In your imagination, it can hold somewhere between nothing and a whole ocean. So! How much can it hold right at this moment?

You've created a mental image of your pain.

Turn the page. The mental image is now destroyed.

Begin again.

Where is the pain?

What color is the pain?

What shape is the pain?

Draw what you see with the crayons, or a pen or pencil. Spell out the colors.

If the pain could hold water, how much water would it hold?

Turn the page. Repeat the four questions again and again. While it is possible for this not to reduce your pain, I've never seen it fail completely, nor has it failed completely when I've done it for myself. There's always some relief, and, surprisingly often, total relief.

So why does this work?

It focuses your attention and your healing energy by using your imagination. Imagination is part of your clairvoyance, which is how you create your reality and future. Clairvoyance is your ability to see energy and spirit. It's also a powerful healing tool. The saying is, "If you can see it, you can heal it!" This seems to be true. There may be exceptions, but it works almost all the time.

The crayons get around the filters and blockages that everyone has when they are in pain. By externalizing your focus by holding a crayon in your fingers, none of your thoughts that constrain your healing abilities get in the way. Crayons are a psychic lifehack!

Drawing the picture targets the pain. Turning the page destroys the image and releases the energy. Repeating this gains momentum for your healing energy.

This technique comes from a Silva Mind Control seminar that I took way back in the 80s. I don't know if Silva came up with this, or if it came with the Buddhist millionaire teacher of the seminar (yes, he made his money with two buddies in a garage, building a new circuit board thingy, and their little company was acquired way back when a million dollars each actually meant something).

The technique was taught without crayons and paper. You asked and answered the four questions, and with each iteration, the pain shrank away until it was gone. It was taught to us because one of the students complained about their headache. They couldn't do the meditation we were practicing. Two minutes later, they were headache free and the class was back on track.

When a raw beginner at BPI scribes in a student reading, they pick up crayons and color in the layers of the aura on a chart as the person reading the aura describes each layer. Sometimes, the scribe will pick up the "wrong" color, start coloring at some random place in that layer of the aura, see their "error" and switch crayons.

When the chart is presented to the house control, the house control doesn't see an error. They see an energy and quickly check the aura of the readee to compare the aura and the chart. Oftentimes, the house control will tell the readee to ask the readers about that off-color energy in their aura. Always, always, that "mistake" color turns out to be something significant to the readee.

The crayons focused the scribe's clairvoyance and got around the energies and thoughts and inexperience that constrain the scribe's ability to read energy. Isn't that cool!

Ghosts

L ike most things in our lives, when we find an answer that fits one situation, our lazy brains tend to apply it to every similar situation. This is true for people who read spiritual energy. It can create a blind spot. This has great advantages in the wilds of the bush, which is why our brains evolved it, but like most first chakra survival things, it's kinda blunt and simplistic.

Ghosts are spirits. The bodies they have are either the astral body from their last physical body or an image they've created for reasons of their own. Either way, if you see an ethereal looking woman floating at the end of the hallway and your only resource to draw on is *Ghostbusters*, your reaction might be a little inappropriate, lol.

Instead, just say hello to them. See if they can hear your spiritual hello. See if they can return it.

Spirit is energy organized around awareness. If their awareness has been compromised in some way, this can be the cause for them being stuck in between worlds, so to speak, but there are other reasons for them staying here. You have to take a look at the individual ghost, rather than a book of rules.

Ghosts are spirits, just like you and me. Spirits can get stuck on energy and ideas. If you talk with them, or even better, if you give them a reading, very often they can realize that they're stuck and get themselves unstuck. That process when they unstick themselves looks like waking up, so some folks say they were unconscious and then woke up and went away.

When you read a ghost, you are reading another spirit. When you read someone with a body, you are reading another spirit that happens to have a physical body. When you read a cat, they read you back, lol.

"Ghosts don't know they're dead." Think about that. The sentence is all wrong. Ghosts are spirits. Spirits know they are spirits, and spirits don't die. Bodies die. The more accurate sentence might be "Ghosts don't realize that their body has died." I have seen this. They're just be-bopping along in their astral body and don't realize that their physical body is no longer there. Not having a physical body causes you to lose your references to time.

Maybe they're missing some information. Maybe they're stuck on something. Maybe they didn't have enough energy to totally leave their body when it died, so they are waiting to gather up their energy. When you're out of the body, you don't know if three hours have passed or three centuries. You only realize the time when you return to your body, or get near someone else's body, and if you can't return, you can't observe the time.

I participated in readings of haunted houses and saw some really cool ghosts. One was in her fully formed astral body from a century before.

When we said hello to her, she looked confused. Saying hello brought her into present time. Things in our present were not familiar to her and she looked lost. In her case, it was like she was in a coma; a very long coma. She moved as if in a dream, but without a sense of time passing.

We asked her where her body was and how she died. As she began to look around her, her energy got brighter, then she said hello back to us, thanked everyone, twinkled as her astral body faded away, and disappeared.

We saw that she died in her sleep and lost her silver cord from her astral body to her physical body. When we woke her up, she gathered her energy together from everywhere, which made her brighter, then took her next step.

Dark energy

I've seen this many times. There's more than one possible cause for this. Foreign energy often looks dark in someone else's space. My energy in my aura might look bright and shiny around me, but stick some of my energy in another person's aura and it will slow down and eventually darken, but not always. Sometimes it looks like white static. Still just an energy that is foreign to that person's space.

Your energy in your space looks smooth and clear. Foreign energy in your space often looks opaque. Not always, but often.

I read someone that had an aura filled with the unconscious energy of a dead family member. It looked dull; just a bunch of unconscious energy that the person I was reading had taken on from their relative's space. The person I was reading was a healer and wanted to take on some of this energy from the dying family member to ease their passing. Then they didn't know what to do with all that foreign energy, and it stagnated in their space.

Another cause is called a *cosmic cop*. It's a spirit guide that's assigned to someone who needs to stay on a limited path this lifetime. It's assumed that this person screwed up royally in their last past life, but the cosmic cop never tells and won't allow them to be read. A good reader can read right past the cosmic cop's protections and knock such a person right off their path. They are on a path to redemption that is far more constrained than the average person they first appear to be. The times I've encountered a cosmic cop, the first clue was being blinded by the light. The CC beamed all the readers in the sixth and seventh chakras, causing pressure and headaches. To the readers, it was like a white out in a winter storm. Not necessarily dark energy, but totally opaque.

As soon as the house control came in and said hello to the CC, the pressure and pain disappeared. Then the house control introduced the readers to the CC, explaining why they couldn't see at first, and explained the ground rules. If the CC says "don't read that," you don't read whatever it was you were about to read.

The only reason the readee was able to walk into BPI was the CC either allowed it or directed them to come in. Someone with a CC has limited free will.

Another cause of dark or opaque energy is the secret energy of military agencies. People with top secret clearances often have agreed to have an energy from the group agreement reside in their space to protect and preserve the secrets. Some agencies assign cosmic cops to their key employees.

A rare cause is a walk-in. This is a spirit that has agreed to take over someone's otherwise healthy body and live out that body's life. They want to hide what's going on. Not all walk-ins do this. The few that came in for readings obviously did not mind us seeing them. One I stumbled across in the wild attracted my attention because they were hiding so much, it made them stand out in a crowd, lol.

Here's an interesting question: from the perspective of the body, does a walk-in represent a foreign energy? Technically, the answer is yes. It's also possible that the walk-in has been in this body long enough to make the necessary adjustments and to a non-psychic, their energy looks just fine.

Then there's someone who just has a lot of unconscious energy of their own stored for some reason in their aura. This is something I've read in many beginning clairvoyant students. As they get their energy running and start doing regular readings, they uncover stuff that looks dark and opaque. It's been in a kind of psychic deep freeze for too long and has no awareness in it at all, hence, unconscious energy. It comes up in layers, with people who are older and have more life experience generally having more of it than those who are younger and have less life experience.

How to read an aura

You can learn to read your own aura or anyone else's aura. The easiest way to start practicing is with your hands.

Pro tip: As you read this, you may get lit up in a big way. Auras are not supposed to be real. I ask that you be okay with taking more frequent breaks during this chapter. Take a nap. Take yourself out to eat. Ground and run energy for five minutes. If you feel uncomfortable and blowing your matching pictures doesn't yield relief, take a break.

WHAT'S AN AURA?

In ancient Greek and Latin, it meant breeze or wind. This is a rudimentary definition of life. If it breathes, it's alive. If it's not breathing, it's probably dead, meaning it contains no spiritual awareness.

An aura is made up of all the energy that doesn't fit within a body. This is a useful way to look at it. It explains why sleeping people don't have the same aura as when they're awake. Sleeping is like vacation time; you still own the home, but you're not there.

What does "doesn't fit within a body" mean? It means we find it more comfortable to surround our bodies with a bubble of our energy and awareness. It makes our body feel safer. It can help us identify threats. It can be how we sense the arrival of a visitor before they get to our door. It can be how we ground larger spaces.

The aura is often how we identify individuals in the dark; we can't see their clothes or faces, but we can sense their aura. Pro Tip for kids: you can pull your aura all the way inside of your body when you're playing hide and seek! Adults: you can try this when you're playing hide and seek with your dog.

The aura is a large part of what's missing from a dead body.

Seeing colors is using your clairvoyance, which is your ability to see energy and spirit. Knowing what color someone's aura is? That's using your claircognizance, which is your ability to just know stuff off the top of your head without any other input. Feeling your aura or the aura of someone else is using your clairsentience.

What makes your hands so powerful is all of your abilities from your seven major chakras are mirrored in your hand chakras. You can see, hear, feel, and know about any spiritual energy by using your hands.

Walk around at a psychic fair and you'll see maybe one or two people using the palms of their hands to read someone. Walk around at a psychic fair put on by the Berkeley Psychic Institute and you'll see almost everyone using their hands to read.

I mentioned the "clairs," which mostly refers to the four main ones we are training: clairvoyance, clairaudience, claircognizance, and clairsentience. I said *all* of the abilities in your seven major chakras are mirrored in your hand chakras. Look through the section called "A Useful Psychic Vocabulary" again. Abilities like telepathy and healing and grounding are also mirrored in your hand chakras. Imagine how useful that might be when dealing with injured animals, spirit guides that can't speak, humans that can't hear due to deafness, energy left in organic or inorganic objects. Your hands can feel and see and hear and know just by touching something.

Why using your hand makes practicing reading energy so much easier is even if you have a blinding headache (pun intended), you can still stick your hand out and read the energy directly through your hand. Even if there are people physically standing in your way, you can lift your hand and read the energy behind them until you gain the ability to skip by them with your attention. Even if you're living in your car with three cats and a dog, asleep in the thick fog around Yogi Beach near San Diego, and you hear something go bump in the night, you can open your hand, scan the area, ask if there's a threat, get the no answer, and go right back to sleep. It's useful to know how your hands work.

By the way, taking a healing class of any style will help you learn to read energy. For the most part, healing classes are safe and fun. How safe and how fun depends on the energy of the class. It's the partner practice that is valuable.

BTW, if you should ever have a blinding headache, you can read the energy that's causing it with your hand. Hold your hand, palm facing your face or head, and sense the cause. That's very handy, eh?

What do two psychics say when they meet on the street? "You look fine. How am I?" This is awkwardly amusing because, like all comedy, there's a bit of truth in it. It's more difficult to read your own energy than it is to read someone else's energy. We all learn to just push through the energy, rather than take the time to understand it and blow our matching pictures and heal ourselves.

WHY IS IT EASIER TO READ SOMEONE ELSE?

Their problems and emotions are not your problems and emotions. Your body will not react as strongly to their problems as it will to your problems. Reading these energies in someone else's space are no different, most of the time, than browsing a book. The exception is when you have really strong matching pictures with them, but you now know how to blow your pictures, so this isn't a problem. The only problem would be *not* recognizing that you have matching pictures lit up.

WHY IS IT MORE DIFFICULT
TO READ YOURSELF?

You aren't very neutral to what's in your own space. That's one thing. You can overcome this through practicing the tools in this book.

Some of the energy in your space does not want you to see it. That's another thing. You can overcome this by grounding and running energy, which accelerates making separations from energies that are not yours.

Because it's your problem, as soon as you see something, meaning as soon as you become aware of it, your healing energy tends to turn on to remove "the problem." That's another thing. You're trying to read an energy that your healing energy is making disappear.

When your healing energy is turned on, it's like you're painting over the pages in the book. As soon as you turn the page, you think "Oh wow! I see something fascinating!," begin reading the page, and then it's gone, painted over with healing energy. You're not sure you saw anything at all. You become invalidated, thinking maybe I didn't see it. You turn the page back in hopes of finding your place again, hoping to get a clue, but that one's gone, too. Now you're lost and invalidated. Healing energy gets in the way of doing readings, especially in the beginning.

The easiest way to turn off your healing energy is to imagine a valve on each wrist. Just grab that imaginary valve with the opposite hand and turn it to the "off" position. Turn it on and off a few times so you get used to how it feels in your hands and everywhere else when your healing energy is on. It's sometimes very subtle so practice slowly. Do this for both wrists.

The pattern is read first, heal second.

I just played a trick on you. You just read your aura a little bit. What color was your healing energy when it was on? What did it feel like when on vs. off? Where did it go in your aura? What did it do when it got to where it wanted to go? Did it all stay in your aura? The great Yogi Berra said, "You can see a lot just by looking!"

My interpretation of what Yogi said is if you ask a question, you'll get an answer. I apply the same interpretation to Jesus saying "ask and you shall receive." The kingdom of heaven is within, if you ask enough questions. Be curious, not judgmental.

Remember, just because you are no longer being judgmental of everyone else or yourself, this doesn't mean you have to take any shit from them. In fact, just the opposite happens. The less judgmental you are, the faster you blow your pictures, and the more energy you get back. The more your energy grows, the more it shows to those around you, and energy matters. You won't look like the easy target you might have been.

When you are just beginning to read your own energy, like your healing energy, it's really useful to be curious and ask questions. It's easier to ask good questions if you're a little amused by the whole thing than if you're terrified of what you might see.

Amusement makes things easier and safer.

Let's pretend you have seen glimpses of other people's auras. Sally has a pink aura. Fred has a blue aura. Jerrie's aura is purple. Your aura is gold. Well done. You're already seeing some colors. Right now you're seeing only the most dominant color in an aura. Well done. You're asking a good question: what color is their aura. Note that this question assumes there is only one color, which means the answer will filter out all the colors but one, which is why I say you're seeing the most dominant color. Still useful, but incomplete.

Try this. What is the color of energy in someone's aura that defines how they see the world? What is the color of energy in someone's aura that defines how the world sees them, or what they want the world to see? Those could be the same or different colors.

Notice the specificity of the questions. This can tell you more about a person's state of mind at that moment than just their dominant color. "Dominant color" may be something different to you than to another reader, and another reader may see the same "dominant vibration" as green while you see it as blue. Who is right?

You both are! Whew! That was a close one, eh?

Clairvoyance sees energy and spirit. All energy is clear. Our brains and a few other spiritual constructs translate clear energy into colors, based on their differences in vibration and intent. Even though our brains can count the cycles of vibration and may even be able to see the wavelengths and frequencies of different vibrations, it's just so much easier to say "blue" than to say "750 terahertz'." That's nine more syllables. Time can mean life or death, or prolonging suffering, so wasting time with too much detail is strongly discouraged by evolution. Shortcuts do have risks, but as long as you are aware of the risks, they are really useful.

Blue waves breaking on the shore means enjoy your nap on the sand in the sun. Blue waves with a lot of white on top means maybe move your towel higher up on the shore. Gray waves might portend a storm approaching, or might mean you're very far to the north where the light is different.

The pattern is read first, heal second. I repeat this so I can tell a story. Maybe also so you'll remember it.

In 1984, I completed the four introductory classes, two in healing and two in meditation. Each class was six weeks long with a week off before the next set of classes began. I began in January and completed this series in July. My next step was joining the clairvoyant training program, and I did.

A few months later, I'm reading all the time and taking more classes. My cohort of students all began around the same time as those basic prerequisite classes finished. The cohort ahead of us really got into healing everyone that came in for a reading, so much so that people that came for readings stopped signing up for classes; all their problems were solved during the reading/healing sessions.

So Lewis Bostwick gave an order that "no more healings" would be done in the readings. Reading only would be done.

This is useful to know because once you get into healing others and reading their energy changes as you heal them, it's really seductive and you'll want to stay there forever. Some of you reading this book will want to teach reading and healing, maybe you already are, and you need to know when to allow the students to figure the energy out for themselves.

This is healthy for the students. It prevents too much of a dependency in your relationship with your students. The institute managed this by having dedicated reading times and dedicated healing times; well not exactly, but that was the attempt. You can't heal without reading, but you absolutely can read without healing. As you read on through the book, you'll discover there are exceptions; you absolutely can heal someone without reading them, but doesn't that little sentence sound cool! Almost like a real rule, LOL!

You've got the abilities. You just need practice. So let's practice.

Notice how basic the questions are. Just seeing the basic outline of someone's aura, even your own, is valuable information. Does their aura surround all of their body, or are some parts exposed? Is their aura shaped like an egg, or a box, or a sphere, or something else entirely? What does the shape of their aura mean? Is their aura as full in the back as it is in front of them?

If your body is getting antsy or tired, blow some roses for any pictures that are lit up, fill in, and let your energy run for a bit. If that doesn't fully refresh you, consider putting this book down and taking a break.

Reading the aura can be intense, especially in the early days. Be patient. Some of this just takes time.

WHERE IS THE EDGE OF YOUR AURA?

You can find it with your hands or with a rose. First, let's tune up your hands and make things a little easier.

Check that your healing energy is turned off, then reach out your hand a few inches in front of your torso, palm facing your body. Notice the pressure, temperature, color, or sound that your hand picks up. If you held your hand over the middle of your chest, you did what most people do and held your hand over your fourth chakra. You could have picked any spot in front of your torso.

Slowly turn the palm away from your body towards the front of your space. Check your healing energy is still off. Notice the differences in pressure, temperature, color, or sound that your hand picks up. You may notice that your hand seems to reflect some energy coming off your body or coming out of your fourth chakra, and this feeling changes when you turn your palm away.

Repeat this a few times so that you can tell the difference between the energy closest to your body and the energy further away. If you can't tell the difference yet, don't worry. It will come with practice, and grounding and running energy.

Now take both hands and face the palms towards each other. Note what you pick up on. Move your palms further apart. Notice what changes. Move them close, a few inches apart. Notice what changes. Move them as far apart as you can but maintain the palms facing each other without your body getting in the way. Notice what changes.

I feel the intensity and focus of the energy change in my palms as I move my hands to different positions. It's like the pressure changes. Also the temperature can change on my palms. Not always, but often enough to be noticeable. Also, the surface area on my palm that feels the energy from the other hand can change.

Try this. With your hands far apart but your arms comfortable and relaxed, touch the fingertips and thumb of one hand together like making a little cone, focusing all the energy coming out of your fingertips into a single ray, and use that ray to touch the palm of the other hand. Now touch each fingertip on the target hand. Play with the distance between your hands and notice what changes. Now send energy with only your index finger. Notice the difference.

Check your healing energy. Is it on or off? Some finger positions can trigger your healing energy. Welcome to some of your past life healing information!

Notice your grounding cord. Check its connections to your first chakra and the center of the planet. Say hello to the center of the planet. Create a gold sun over your head. Fill it with your present time growth vibration to help your body stay relaxed and playful. Bring that sun down into your aura and body. Take a deep breath, yawn, and touch your fingertips to the floor. Stand up and stretch.

So far, you've felt the energies of your chest or torso, and your hands and fingertips. You've felt the difference between the denser energy near your body and the lighter energy in your aura further away from your body. Maybe some of the energy further away from your body wasn't so light. Cool! Maybe you noticed some energy that's not yours.

Your energy will feel light and smooth to you, almost always. There can be exceptions, but in my experience these are rare.

We can keep saying, "Check your healing energy. Is it on or off?" I think you've got this now, so let's just say, "Set your hands to 'sense'." A clear intention that implies sensing to read energy and healing to change energy. Sense and heal, the two modes of active energy in your hands. You can also shut them down, but that's not helpful in this context. You can also channel other energies through your hands, but that's not what we're doing now. Can be really fun, but not right now.

So! Set your hands to sense. Notice how that feels. It should be familiar now.

Find the edge of your aura. If you cannot feel a transition from inside your aura to outside your aura, it most likely means that your aura is either too thin or the edge is further away than you can reach.

What do you do if it feels too thin? Fill in with a gold sun of your own energy. Check your gauge and bring in gold suns until you are full. If your gauge is dropping almost as fast as you can bring in golden suns, check your aura for holes or rips. You've got leaky aura syndrome, lol.

If it's out of reach? Create a rose and have it mark the edge of your aura, then pull your energy closer to your body until that rose marking the edge gets close enough for you to touch with your hand.

Maybe your aura's edge is three feet away and your arm is only two feet long. Maybe your aura's edge is three city blocks away from your body. Meh. It happens. Just pull it in closer. Let your rose show you your progress.

You can reach out and feel it arrive with your fingertips.

Bring your aura in a little closer so you can comfortably reach outside of it, and move your hand back and forth from just inside your aura to just outside your aura. Notice the difference. Try sensing with just one fingertip, back and forth, inside your aura and outside your aura.

Create a rose, put any pictures that got lit up during this exercise into the rose and blow it up. Notice your grounding cord and fill in. Take a deep breath.

Note: the palms of your hands can be really sensitive, but using your fingertips seems to be easier for some folks to feel delicate details. Palms can also be like flood gates. Practice using both and learn how yours work. Fingertips are also very useful in psychic surgery, like when you need to modify one cell's DNA or some other structure inside the cell, test that change, then on success, propagate that change to all the other cells of that type. Wait! What? Meh. It happens. Reading and healing go hand in hand (see what I did there?).

With your hands set to sense, point at a hole in your aura. Point at one of your parents in your aura. Point at a sexual partner in your aura. Are we having fun yet?

Notice that the valves on your wrists now have three positions; healing on, healing off, and sense. Well done, setting them to sense without an explanation!

I picked those energies for the starting place because most everyone is familiar with them. You may not think you have an ex's or family member's energy in your space. In this context, what you think doesn't matter. We're just sensing energy with our hands and fingers, without judgment.

Point at a tear in your aura. Are your hands still set to sense?

Point at the energy of one of your fantasies in your aura. Now everyone knows! Just kidding!

No. Everyone knows.

I'm kidding. No one can see that. Or can they? Hmm.

Pro tip: Don't destroy what you don't understand. Take a look at that fantasy. Read it using the basic questions. Whose fantasy is it? What does it say? What is its intent? Is it in present time?

Can everyone on the planet see it? (Hint: not likely.) Can all of the psychics see it? If they are interested, sure. *But will they?* It's not likely. I once was assigned the "job" of helping a beautiful woman stay in control of her energy so that she could participate in the beginning meditation classes. She was a dominatrix. I could see all of those sex pictures in her aura, but that turned out not to be anywhere near as fascinating as the spirit guides that helped her do her dom-thing. Those were some *unusual* spirit guides, LOL! They wanted to get in everyone's spaces in the class and program them to become clients. From their perspective, we looked like easy marks to make into new and more interesting customers. My job was to "entertain" them and keep them outside of the class bubble. It was a hoot!

How did I do that? I created an image of bleachers, like at a football game, just outside the bubble of the class, and told them all that they could sit in the bleachers and observe, but if they came into the class they would be banned and unable to observe. Carrot and stick. As above, so below. It works.

There are no secrets in a psychic institute, but this book isn't an institute. Have fun. Learn all about your energy, all of your energy, and have fun doing so.

Holes and tears and whacks and blockages and lovers and others in your life show up in your aura. These are energy structures in your aura. Some of them, anyway. There's no urgent need to do anything about them. This is an exercise in becoming aware of them. Most likely, these have all been in your space for some time. That's why there's no hurry in fixing them.

In fact, once you become aware of them, just grounding and running energy, blowing a few roses, will release this stuff for you without putting much attention on it.

Just for fun, does that hole still exist in your aura? If it does, then set your hands to heal and fill in the hole with your own energy, all the way to the edge of your aura, and give it a quick fluff. Fluffy and nice! Fluffy, not stuffy. If there's a picture associated with that hole, blow that picture. Fill in again.

If the hole no longer exists, isn't that interesting. You healed it without thinking about it. Nice! Or did a guide heal it for you? Take a look for yourself. Ask why the hole changed or was healed or disappeared. Ask in your own words.

Set your hands to sense, hold out three fingers, and touch your fingertips to a cord in your aura. Feel and see where it enters your aura and follow it to where it attaches to something. That's most often a chakra, but sometimes it attaches to a body part, or is just left hanging like a floater. (I bet the younger ones reading "floater" thought of a toilet and the older ones thought of an eyeball. Both images work, lol.)

Obviously, you can do all these same things on someone else's aura. Just saying.

Check again if you need a break. The subject of cords can stir up a lot of pictures and energies, LOL! Blow your matching pictures. Release energy down your grounding cord. Allow the earth and cosmic energies to flow through your body, and breathe. Fill in.

Take your three fingers and slowly sweep them through your aura until you find a ridge. These often feel like a blade of energy, flatter on the side and sharper on the top. Other times they feel like a tube-shaped energy.

These are pain ridges that accumulate and stagnate over time until they become so rigid and dense that your energy has to flow around them. Find a ridge and then tap it lightly with the tips of the three fingers, and it will break up and ground out. Just tappity-tap-tap them. For this bit, you can have your healing energy on or off; it will work just the same.

What I notice when I do this three finger tapping is my body relaxes on a muscular level and my energy in my body begins to move with more life and vigor.

Find all the little and not-so-little pain ridges in your aura and tap them out of existence.

Where do these pain ridges come from, you ask? Great question. Take a look at one and ask yourself that question. Sometimes it's not even your pain. Sometimes it is. Ask the basic reading questions: whose energy is it? What was its intent? What does it say now? How does it affect you now? Where did it come from? And every other curious question that might come to mind, LOL!

If you need a short break, please fill in, dump out, and take a short break. You just covered a combination of topics that are introduced during three, six-week courses. The third one is only taught to clairvoyant students in the second half of the clairvoyant program. Take your time. There's no rush.

WHAT ELSE IS IN AN AURA?

Pictures. Pictures contain memories, information, and energy, all bound together by another energy that creates a unique vibration. What kinds of pictures can be found in someone's aura? Sex pictures. Past life pictures. Pain pictures. Death pictures. Relationship pictures. This life pictures. Every kind of topic, from silly to profound, can have an associated picture. Childhood trauma is a good one.

It's not the case that if you ground and run your energy long enough, you will begin to see pictures. You see them already but are not fully aware that you are seeing them. This gives them a little more influence over you than you might like in some situations.

As a senior clairvoyant student, I was asked to go from the Berkeley institute down to the San Jose branch and read that evening. It seems someone had overbooked some readings, so a group of us piled into someone's car and headed south.

The readings were assigned. Folks left to get to different rooms in the house and do the readings, leaving me and one other beginning reader in the living room. The director of that institute, John Fulton, told us to sit tight and run our energy.

We sat tight and ran our energy, lol. Five minutes later, he comes in with a man who looked like he didn't want to be there. He had driven his wife to the institute to participate in a women's healing class, which was happening just one door away, off the living room.

John sat him down in front of us and told him the reading was on the house. I introduced myself, as did my side chair, and I asked him if he'd ever had a reading before. "I don't believe in any of this stuff. I'm only here because my wife is taking this class and I got tired of waiting in the car."

I told him that was fine. We didn't have to give him a reading. The women in the class next door laughed at something, which seemed to jar him a little. He said it wasn't a problem. We could read him. He just wanted to set expectations.

So my side chair and I went back into a light trance and we read him. My side chair read the rose, the body clocks, the programmability gauge, and the chakras. She did a really good job.

Then I was up. Time to read the aura. The very first thing I see is my favorite airplane, the SR-71 spy plane. Sleek and all black, made of titanium, it held the record for fastest jet powered aircraft that still stands today.

My first response is that I must be lit up on my childhood hobby of airplanes. I blow roses for those pictures and the only thing that happens is the picture gets more detailed. Now I see two men, dressed in clothing styles from the 60s.

I haven't said anything so far. I'm supposed to be reading the seven layers of the aura.

Now one of the men is pointing to the fuselage and the other is pointing to one of the engines. OK. I tell the man we're reading everything I'm seeing and ask him if this means anything to him.

"The man pointing to the fuselage is my father. He was on the design team for that part of the aircraft. The man pointing to the engine is my father's best friend. He was on the engineering team that integrated the engines with the airframe."

I'm laughing now. Score: Wayne: 1. Guy that doesn't believe in this stuff: 0. LOL!

I open my eyes and this guy's body language is now more nervous than dismissive. I close my eyes and wonder what that's about.

And there she is! A picture of his mistress combined with lots of her energy is sitting on his left shoulder, humping his arm. She's thin and blonde. So, I play dumb.

I describe her and ask him if this means anything to him. He squeaks!

"Shhhh! Not so loud! My wife's in the next room!" My side chair starts describing the sex positions he and his mistress prefer. I'm laughing uncontrollably now. He is so busted!

He gets up and leaves the house to go sit in his car. The reading is over in thirty minutes instead of two hours, but it's a great success for us readers. My side chair can't get over seeing everything, the plane, the engineers, the lover, so clearly.

John Fulton comes back in to find out what all the noise is about and asks where the gentleman went. We tell him how things went down and now he's laughing as loud as us. It was a great evening, even though we got back to Berkeley after 1:00 a.m.

Are there seven layers in an aura? No. If you ask the same seven questions over and over, it will appear to you that there are seven layers. Some traditions teach that each layer corresponds with one chakra. Some other traditions don't.

At BPI, the pedagogy was to ask the same seven questions about the seven layers of the aura in every student reading. You might think of this like playing scales on a stringed instrument. There are seven notes in a scale and then they repeat. However, the notes depend on the habits of the player to exist. Without the practiced fingers of the player, there can be no scale.

The same idea is what happens when you read the same questions over and over. Without the reader asking the same seven questions, the layers just aren't there. To be clear, the layers are never there. So why do it? It helps the scribe color in the aura chart. It helps the students blow their matching pictures with those seven questions with every person they read. It's a wise consistency in that beginners learn to be confident because they match the energy of the more confident advanced readers.

BPI does this. Tarot layouts do this. Runes do this. The key is understanding that you're in a pedagogical technique and reality might differ from the scales you're practicing.

First layer: survival. What state is this person's survival in right now?

Second layer: relationships(?). How well does this person relate to others?

Third through fifth layers: I honestly do not remember the questions, LOL! I don't read seven layers anymore. I just look for the readee's most important spiritual question and read that.

Sixth layer: how does this person see the world?

Seventh layer: how does the world see them?

The seven layers and the implied seven questions were a ritual that provided lots of value to the readers-in-training, and quite often to the readee as well. Having a routine to follow is very useful. This leads us nicely to the next section.

Note: I said implied questions. The aura was often read by telling the readee, "First layer: this represents your survival information." "Seventh layer: this represents how the world sees you." The questions are not explicitly stated, but are inherent in the word, "represents."

Some traditions state emphatically that there are seven layers in the aura, each layer corresponding to one of the seven main chakras. There is some truth to this. For instance, the layer closest to your body probably is mostly about your body's survival, just like the first chakra. The outer layer of your aura is the first thing someone sees when they look at you, which correlates well with the implied question I mentioned above: the seventh layer represents how the world sees you.

However, when you just put your hands in someone else's aura, you don't find seven neat layers of energy unless you're looking for them. This sounds very much like a filter, and from working with Lewis Bostwick and Michael Tamura for four years, and hearing them explain that there really aren't seven layers, and looking at all the hands-on healings I've done where there weren't seven layers, I don't think it really matters. Practicing reading seven layers has clear training value. Realizing that it's just a teaching device has even more value.

You've used your hands to read and heal your aura. Previously, you've used the symbol of a rose to read and heal yourself and clean out the center of your head. You've learned to ground and run energy. You've learned to match and unmatch energy, and learned a bunch of details that might not mean much to you right now.

The following section shows you how we put it all together to train each other to read.

How reading
was taught at
BPI in the 80s

The clairvoyant training program taught us how to read by placing new students next to senior students in a line of chairs. We would ground and run our energy. We would close down our first chakras to just 10% open. We'd close down our second chakras to 10% open. Women would close their third chakras to 70% open. Men would close down their third chakras to 50% open.

The reason women did not close their third chakras down as far as men is they needed the little extra control that the third chakra provides over energy distribution to manage their female creative energies. These third chakra percentages were probably found by trial and error. The comfort level of female readers was the indication that the percentage was about right. Dialing it in to 68% or 71% was never mentioned, but women and men closed their third chakras down until they were comfortable, which tended to be around 70% and 50%.

When you were the control in a reading, you could see their energy change when they closed down their lower chakras. The readers often would not see this; they are focusing only on their own spaces, but to the control, the changes in the energy of the readers when they closed down their lower chakras was obvious. Their auras got less bright below their ribs and got brighter from their ribs up. Closing down the lower three chakras physically raised their energy up into their heads and their upper three chakras.

When the readers would ground and run their energy for a bit, and pull in their auras nice and tight, each reader's aura looked like a skinny egg shape. The energy was consistent throughout that egg.

As soon as they closed down their lower chakras, the energy moved up from their lower bodies to their head and shoulders, giving more energy and awareness to their fifth, sixth, and seventh chakras. This made it much easier to see energy and spirits.

The control didn't close down their lower chakras. Well, I studied martial arts a lot, and my third chakra energy could get overwhelming for others, so when I controlled, I would shut down my third chakra a little bit, just to keep my energy in my space while I was doing my job of controlling the reading and the room.

It was never mentioned in the beginning classes, but once you joined the clairvoyant training program, every class and reading began with grounding, running energy, pulling in our auras, and closing down the lower three chakras. Lectures were not lectures, they were show and tells where the instructor showed us some energy and we got to read it.

We would match our crown chakras to a gold, neutral energy. This was how every class in the clairvoyant training program began, by coming up to gold. The content of the classes would change this, because the students matched the teacher's crown chakra and the teacher would change as he or she would step us through the lessons for that class. Class always ended back at gold.

So, we all knew where the gold vibration was and could match it on command. Lewis Bostwick liked to describe "gold" as middle C on the piano. It was a neutral vibration, not the highest vibration. Neutral.

We'd match our crown chakras to the most senior reader, called the center chair, and each of us would do a part of the reading. The main parts of a reading were the rose reading, the chakra reading, and the aura reading.

Matching crown chakras with the center chair enabled the new students to begin to see what the center chair saw. It's the oldest pedagogical technique: monkey see, monkey do, but with a twist. We'd match the senior monkey, lol.

Then all the readers would match the readee's crown chakra and blow their matching pictures. Blowing their matching pictures automatically raised the vibration of their crown chakras to a slightly different color than the readee's crown chakra. In this context, this meant going from a dark blue to a slightly lighter blue, or from a grungy, moldy grayish brown to a less grungy version of that brown.

Sometimes the center chair would look at the readee's crown chakra and match the dominant color. They'd tell the side chairs what color they saw and ask them to match it. Sometimes there'd be some discussion because the side chairs would see different colors besides the main color that the center chair saw, but we'd all end up matching the center chair's crown chakra.

Being this close to matching the readee, but a half a step away, made it easier for the readers to maintain separation from the readee and continue to blow any matching pictures that came up, and still see the energy of the main reason this person came in for a reading.

Some center chairs would match the readee first, have the side chairs match them, and tell us to blow our pictures. Other center chairs stepped us through things a little differently, emphasizing blowing our matching pictures with each other first, then blowing our matching pictures with the readee. The point was to blow as many matching pictures as possible at the beginning to make it easier to see the readee's energy and be neutral to what we were seeing.

Another variation is the reading control would talk the line through the setup of matching the readee, blowing their pictures, and choosing a reading color. Most of the time, the control just stood back and watched, and didn't say anything unless there was a problem, like one of the side chairs losing their match with the center chair, or someone's lower chakras opening back up. Then it was reset time: come up to gold, blow your pictures, rematch the crown chakras to the center chair's reading color, and continue reading.

The center chair would describe the reading color to the side chairs, sometimes adding a stripe of a different color to help everyone maintain a more neutral separation: gold or turquoise or blues were some common stripe colors. Picking these came from experience and personal preference. Some center chairs could be quite complex in how they described the perfect match, lol.

Some would describe the stripe as "clairvoyant blue." This was an anchor vibration for that reader that they could always find and maintain throughout any reading. Is there such a thing as a clairvoyant blue energy? There was for those readers. Yours might look different.

TIME OUT.

Everything that you've read up until this point happened in the tiny amount of time that it took the center chair to say the following words:

"Hello! Please ground and run your energy. Come up to gold. Put up a rose and pull your auras on your side of that rose. Create separation roses between you and the people beside and behind you. Own the room for yourself. Close down your lower chakras, the first to 10% open, the second to 10% open, and the third to 70% open for females and 50% open for males."

"Let's match the crown chakra of the readee. Create a rose. Put any matching pictures you have with this readee into the rose and blow it up. OK I see their crown chakra at a medium blue. I'd like to read from a light blue today. Please match me. Is everyone OK at light blue?"

"OK Mary will read the rose. Tom will read the chakras. I'll read the aura. Mary, would you begin the reading please?"

TIME IN.

Once the line was matched and had blown their initial matching pictures, the readers came up to gold again and recited the Reading Prayer.

"As we read, we allow the cosmic and earth energies to flow through our bodies, opening the doors through which we become more aware of our spirituality and increase the communication with the god of our heart. Let us pray: May it be with the blessings of the Supreme

Being that whatever happens during this reading benefit each of us in our spiritual growth, awareness, and understanding. Amen."

BPI is the seminary for the Church of Divine Man. When clairvoyant students graduate from the clairvoyant training program, they are ordained ministers in the church.

Another student would act as the reading control. That person stood behind the line of chairs with the readers. They kept their crown chakra matched to a neutral gold. They kept their eyes open and did not go into the same trance that the readers in the line went into. They didn't read the readee. That was the job of the line of readers in trance. They did read the energies that came from the readee that affected the line of readers: spirit guides, family, gurus. Basically any energy that tried to tell the readers what to see and what not to see.

The key concept of a control is someone participating in the reading but not doing the reading. This was accomplished by them maintaining separations from the crown chakra reading color of the readers. The control just observed the reading. Reading the room, so to speak.

The control grounded their body. They lightly ran their energy. They blew roses and watched the energy in the room. They owned the room for themselves. They grounded the room, but not the readers or readee. If the readers got stuck on a picture or energy, it was usually obvious to the control. The energy in front of the readers' faces would stop moving and build up like a cloud of fog.

When this happened, and the readers did not notice it themselves and blow their matching pictures, or if the readers got stuck and stopped reading, the control would ask the readers to come up to gold, meaning match their crown chakras to a neutral gold, and blow their pictures.

The control would tell the line what energy they saw the line get lit up on. This was usually something simple like, "The line is lit up on a matching third chakra picture." That tiny observation of the most obvious energy was sufficient to enable everyone to blow their matching pictures. Sometimes only one person got stuck and needed help. Some controls or the center chair would notice and bring the whole line up to gold. Some controls would just speak quietly to the stuck person and help them blow their pictures and get their energy moving again.

The line would blow their pictures, the center chair would reset their reading color and have the side chairs match, and they'd go on with the reading.

The control would monitor the match of the crown chakras of all the readers sitting in line.

There would be another person in the reading: the scribe. This was typically someone who wasn't in the clairvoyant training program but was considering joining. They had maybe taken a few intro courses. Scribing was useful because it allowed prospective clairvoyant students to experience exactly what they'd be doing if they joined the program. Nothing was hidden from them. They might not have seen much, but we didn't hide anything from them, LOL!

The scribe would sit on a chair off to the side of the main action. They were not in line with the readers. They would be angled some way so that they didn't automatically match the readers and become overwhelmed. A lot of energy was flowing through the bodies of the readers. If the scribe matched that flow, they tended to just go unconscious. It was really cute to see someone's whole face glaze over, their hand holding a crayon just above the paper, not moving a muscle. Not useful, but cute.

The scribe listened and recorded what they heard the readers say on a piece of paper that had a space marked for the rose reading, a human outline around which to draw those layers of the aura, and a chart of sorts with the seven chakras and the psychic abilities held in each chakra.

During the chakra reading, the scribe would record how much the readee used each ability. This was recorded as a percentage, 0% meaning not used at all and 100% meaning used constantly. This was often referred to as percent open or closed, but its more definitive meaning was not openness or closedness, but how much they used each ability. A chakra opens and closes, similar to the iris in a camera lens. This is a different function from how much an ability in a chakra is used, though they are related in some ways.

For instance, closing down your second chakra does not shut off your clairsentience, but it can temper how much energy your clairsentience takes in.

Each ability's percentage was called out by the side chair that was reading the abilities in each chakra. So, something like, "Third chakra. Telekinesis: 3%. Energy distribution: 25%. Out of body experience: 90%. Out of body memory: 10%." None of the percentages were explained during the chakra readings. Just read and recorded. It's the combination of abilities that tells you something important.

In this example, it sure looks like this person spends a lot of their time out of their body on the astral, but they don't remember much of that experience when they get back. That is a hint but not a conclusion. The other abilities in the other chakras may change the meaning, so interpretation was done during the break at the one hour mark by the house control, who was usually a staff member. Each part might confirm or call into question some other part of the reading that, by itself, appears obvious, but taken all together, did not mean what you first thought it meant when seeing it by itself.

The house control could see the whole chakra chart, the whole aura chart, and the rose reading. The house control also had the readee in front of them, and could see what was most important to this readee. This is how they suggested what to ask about during the second half of the reading, which was reserved for the readee to ask all their questions. A whole hour to ask questions.

The order of reading was first the rose reading, then the chakra reading, and finally the aura reading. The scribe was a busy person. They had a pen or pencil, and a bowl of crayons. They would draw the rose that the reader described with crayons. They would fill in the chart with the percentages the chakra reader read with pen or pencil. They would color the seven layers of the aura with crayons.

WHAT'S MISSING?

You probably already read the section about Rose Readings. There's a whole section on Chakra Readings, though it's just a listing of the main abilities in the seven chakras. There are two more elements that were read by either the rose reader or the chakra reader. These were the body-being clocks and the programmability gauge.

Body-being clocks were just two clock faces, one for the body of the readee and the other for the spirit of the readee. The reading was super simple: "I see the body clock at 3:30 and the being clock at 6:00." That's it.

The two clocks were super useful. In this case, the body and the being are in the same quadrant of the clock, which indicates this person has good communication with their body. Each quadrant has its meaning.

1 to 3 was just beginning to be aware of energy. 3 to 6 was starting to focus more on spirit. 6 to 9 was actively working with energy. 9 to 12 was completing a large cycle of their spiritual growth.

When the being and body clocks were far apart, the spirit was almost always running ahead before their body was ready to handle that kind of energy. Body-being communication was compromised or even ignored. This isn't healthy.

I recall only one time seeing someone whose being clock was behind their body clock. It was very confusing until someone with more experience in the line pointed out that they were just that far ahead of their body and about to lap their body, to use a race analogy. Really bad body-being communication, lol.

The programmability gauge was useful because it was faster than interpreting the rose in multiple ways, i.e. the blossom being too open could represent the readee being too programmable and might believe everything they heard without questioning it. The blossom being wide open also means the reading is done; the readee has heard all that they're capable of hearing at that time. Having two meanings for the same symbol gets confusing.

The programmability gauge only meant one thing. The values were zero to 100, with the higher number meaning the readee was more programmable.

It's a really useful tool, especially with gullible people and with spies. Yes, spies from different schools or government agencies would show up to get a reading and see what we were up to. Spies would try to disguise their energy, LOL! Imagine that!

Spies would have programmability readings of zero. This conflicted with their rose reading and their chakra readings. During the break, the house control would ask them if they were getting everything they came for, and leave that hanging. Sometimes they would out themselves and apologize. Sometimes they would lie, making up some issue with the readers as a distraction from themselves.

The second half of the reading, spies would ask really contrived questions, and we'd answer them and laugh. I recall the vivid changes in one spy when the center chair said, "That's not your question, lol. What you really want to ask is…" Their aura then turned bright green.

One spy ended up taking some classes. I don't recall if they took the clairvoyant training program.

THAT'S WHAT WAS MISSING.
BACK TO THE NARRATIVE.

Someone on staff was the house control. They grounded themselves, grounded the house, set the reading energy for the building, decided which readers would read each readee, and visited each reading during the first hour. Sometimes a senior student or graduate would be the house control, but that was rare.

Readings began near the top of the hour. A reading lasted two hours from the point of view of the readee. If their reading was at 10:00 AM, they'd show up a few minutes before, pay their $20 or hand the house control a business card or coupon for a free reading, take a seat and be given a five minute healing by a clairvoyant student. The readee would be grounded, have their energy called back to them, and have their chakras cleaned and spun a little, their aura fluffed a little, and filled in again with a gold sun of their own energy. This made the reading easier to do for the readers because the readee's energy was not as scattered.

The person doing the five minute healing was either a clairvoyant student or a beginning healing student. This was silent practice for the most part. The healer was not talking about what they saw, or at least they were not supposed to, lol. Everyone did read and heal at the same time because it was so much fun, but mostly the job of the healer was to get the readee closer to their body before they got their reading.

One staff member, Tom Prussing, would chide us gently with, "Remember. If your five minute healing takes longer than five minutes, it's not a five minute healing!"

This also removed the energy of everyone in the readee's space that also wanted a reading. Everyone who wanted a reading generally had to bring their body through the door of the institute. Some exceptions were the healing clinics and special circumstances. Sometimes long distance readings and healings would be done in the clinics or ad hoc by the staff and students if the staff saw a great opportunity for the students to read some energy that didn't show up at the institute that often.

If someone in the readee's space didn't want them to get a reading, that was usually left in place because more than likely that was one of the energies that the readee wanted to get a reading on. It was a five minute healing, not a reading. Just ground them, call back their energy and fill them in, fluff their aura, floss their chakras, and fill them in again.

After the five minute healing, the reading assignments were made by the house control. A group of clairvoyant students would be assigned to each readee, and then assigned a reading room upstairs. The readers and readee would then go up together and get settled. The readee would sit there and watch and listen to the center chair walk everyone in the reading line through grounding, running energy, blowing some roses, filling in, seeing the dominant color in the readee's crown chakra, matching that color and blowing their matching pictures, and finally setting the reading color and having everyone match their crown chakras to the color.

The reading assignments were made based on crown chakra matches between the readers and the various readees. The house control could see who was already beginning to read who. It was quite easy to make the assignments because most of the time the house control was just getting out of the way, LOL! The house control could say, "Who's going to read Carolyn?" and the center chair and their side chairs would all light up, meaning their auras would flash a bit brighter for a second.

That first half of the reading, there were no questions asked by the readee. This was just training for the readers and was always the same structure and sequence. Once the three big parts of the reading were complete, everyone took a break. It was called a five-minute break, but it usually lasted fifteen minutes on busy nights.

When the center chair said it was time for the break, the scribe handed the paper with all that the scribe had recorded to the readee. The readee would be escorted by the scribe or house control back downstairs to the kitchen and offered coffee, tea, or water. The house control would meet with each readee and review that piece of paper. The house control might suggest a question for the readee to ask the readers in the second half, or might just let the readee talk about the reading or anything else on their mind.

The main point was to allow the readee, who usually was not trained in managing their own energy like the clairvoyant students were trained, to blow off a little steam and relax. Sometimes, when the center chair had nailed all the readee's major issues during the aura reading, the readee needed some gentle hand holding because of nothing more than the realization that they really could be read by a total stranger. People in general take comfort in their belief that their inner lives are private. That their energy can't be read without their permission. That their secrets are safe.

Auras don't work that way. Auras are about as private is a billboard in the desert. As long as no one's in the desert looking at the billboard, it's private, LOL! As soon as a car comes along, well, you get the picture, eh?

I don't see this as an ethical issue. I see it as a misunderstanding and misplaced fear. 99.99% of the time, we psychics just do not care what you've got tucked away in your aura. It's background noise, and we have our own lives to worry about. I mean no disrespect, but you just aren't that interesting to us.

Besides, like in real life, the stuff in your psychic life is mostly mundane and boring. There's some red energy in your aura. You're pissed off about something. Big whoop! Everyone's pissed off about something, even psychics. It gets boring to look at auras all day most of the time.

The second half of the reading saw the same group of readers and readee go back to the same room. The line of readers would go back into trance and check their crown chakra match with the readee and each other. The control would reground themselves and the room, and establish their control space and separation from the line of readers. The scribe just sat and listened and watched.

The readee would ask their questions for about another hour.

If the first half was structured the same way every time, the second half of readings was always a surprise, often in delightful ways. The energy was different. The questions sometimes were already answered in the first half and the readee struggled to come up with more questions. Some readees brought in printed lists of questions.

Some readees would shock us, asking about some personal trauma that they had hid from us in the first half, but now trusted us enough to let us see it. (Surprise! Psychics do not see all and know all! Not every time, anyway.)

Some readees requested healings during the second half. Some did not. Sometimes the house control would come in during the second half and ask the readers to heal something specific for the readee. This was a benefit to the readee and an opportunity for the readers to see something new.

Every segment of the two hour reading was designed for just one thing: to blow our matching pictures and practice reading while giving to ourselves. We were giving a ton of information to the readee, AND we were grounding, running energy, and blowing our pictures, and filling in.

HERE'S THE NEATEST THING: WE WERE GETTING OUR ANSWERS TO OUR SPIRITUAL QUESTIONS, TOO.

These two hour readings were not just a healing for ourselves, where we blew our matching pictures. In a few short weeks or months after joining the clairvoyant training program, we were capable of mocking up a readee that had the energy of an answer to one of our questions. Questions like how does someone heal themselves from this specific kind of trauma. Or, how does someone create this specific kind of experience. Or, what does the energy of seeing specific kinds of events look like in someone's space? We were on the lookout for energies that could help us understand and grow.

If a particular topic was talked about in the clairvoyant class, readees with insights into that topic would start showing up for readings the next day. Once we saw this happening, we couldn't unsee it, lol. In fact, we consciously began mocking up specific kinds of readings.

Maybe we saw something in our own space while meditating. We asked a question about the energy of what we saw but didn't get a satisfying or complete answer. Sure enough some readee walked in for a reading later that week and they had the same traumatic experiences that we had. We could read their trauma, how it impacted their life, where it was stored in their body, how they tried to manage the energy of that trauma and succeeded or failed. They had the answer to our question.

Questions like how does someone create *this* kind of relationship? How does someone create *this* kind of career change? You get the picture. The readees were not just our spiritual books; they were Life's cheat sheets.

The readees all got wonderful readings. Don't get me wrong. It was not a take on our part. But while different readers were doing their parts, the rest of us were reading, too, and answering our questions.

From the readee's perspective, a reading was two hours. For the readers, it was always a minimum of three hours. We got to the institute at 9:30 a.m. for a 10:00 a.m. reading, and ground and ran our energy for thirty minutes to match the energy of the institute that the house control and staff had set. This ensured that we made separations from work, school, and everything else that could have our attention on it so that we could bring all of our attention to the reading of someone else.

When the time was up, the center chair would send the readee back downstairs, sometimes with the scribe accompanying them, and then do a short cleanout with the "team" in the room. Sometimes it was the reading control that did the cleanout. This was a quick, formal guided meditation of a minute's length.

We brought our crown chakras up to gold. We blew any remaining matching pictures. We mocked up a gold ring with a piece missing. This represented our communication with the readee. We mocked up the missing piece and put everything we wanted to say to the readee, but didn't get the chance to, into that piece. We threw the missing piece into the ring to complete it, then blew the ring up in a rose to complete our communication with the readee. This was called completing our communication, or hanging up the phone. Another ritual.

Sometimes, a readee would be so fun to read we would not want the reading to end. That's us as spirits talking. Bodies needed the readings to end so we could pee, eat something, go to where we needed to be next.

Hanging up the phone released our attention from the readee and all of the pictures we had read. It also stopped whatever telepathic communication we may have started with the readee.

BEGIN NOTE: ENDING A READING IS IMPORTANT.

The two images accomplish the same thing; completing a ring, or *cycle*, and hanging up the phone. Actually visualizing these was a critical part of ending a reading. Why? Because if you didn't complete your communication with each person you read, the telepathic energy could build up in front of your face, clouding your vision. For me, this ongoing, semiconscious reading would manifest as sinus headaches. Some of the telepathic channels run parallel to the sinuses.

I think this tendency to keep reading after the reading is over either comes from or is reinforced by our healing abilities. Man, if I had just said this one thing a little differently, I am sure they would have heard what I was trying to say, and that would have resolved so many things for them. That would have been so cool. That kind of thing.

This is important. Create the image of a ring with a piece missing that represents everything that transpired during the reading. Create the missing piece from the energy of everything you wanted to say but didn't or couldn't, any telepathic connections, any chakra connections, then throw that missing piece into the ring to complete it. Put the ring into a rose and destroy the rose and ring.

END NOTE.

After the readings were done and the readees had left the building, we gathered in the main room downstairs with all the other readers from the other readings for a group cleanout. All the readers and controls and scribes gathered together to ground and run our energy for five minutes, usually with a guided meditation from the house control. The house control would ask each center chair what they had seen that stood out. This was always fun. Sometimes all the readings had the same theme. Other times each reading met the different mockups of each group and there was no common theme. The house control might ask if we'd noticed some specific energy that interfered with some of the readings and we'd volunteer our experiences about that. This was useful in training us to recognize these kinds of energies.

Most times, our experiences were confined to the reading we were in. Sometimes, a cop or military person or someone with a lot of energy would flow through the whole house and this would affect all of the readings. The house control would make the rounds, visiting each reading and helping the readers clean out that energy and make separations, but different energies would come back up when we were doing the final group cleanout. A different group of psychics means a different group energy, which means different matching pictures likely get lit up. When the center chairs described their readings, it created an opportunity for everyone not in that reading to blow their matching pictures.

Once the house control saw we'd blown the majority of matching pictures and our energy was moving and smooth, they would say bye-bye and leave us to clear out of the institute. Some students would leave the institute right away and go back to their daily lives, but almost always there would be a few that would trade readings to dig out a few more matching pictures or get questions answered and heal themselves. Some would do energy checks. All were reading to deepen our understanding of what we'd just experienced.

At the end of it, the readers had been there for three to three and a half hours, grounding and running energy, blowing matching pictures, getting stuck and unstuck, recovering more of our energy, and healing ourselves.

HOW IS THIS STORY USEFUL TO YOU, THE READER OF THIS BOOK?

This thorough description of the student readings at the Berkeley Psychic Institute from way back in the 1980s probably is not exactly how BPI or its many offshoots do it forty years later. Classes are online now, as well as in person. How does this trip down my memory lane help you in your spiritual growth, awareness, and understanding? How is this relevant?

On one level, it's not relevant at all. Your situation may not allow you to take classes, do readings and healings.

On the other hand, this illustrates something really important that I want you to see and understand.

There is very little judgment at any point in the three hour process of doing a student reading. That whole time, you are giving to yourself by grounding and running energy and filling in. Giving to yourself for three hours while reading someone else took almost all of the fear off of being in a reading. You had no time for imposter syndrome when all of your attention was being taken up by matching energy with the center chair, losing that match, blowing the pictures that caused you to lose the match, rematching the center chair, finding the center of your head, seeing what the other readers were talking about, blowing your matching pictures, trying not to leave your body or go totally unconscious, LOL. There is a lot going on for beginning readers!

Focusing on the mechanics took almost all the fear off of reading some-thing specific. Something like past life death pictures. Something like you playing the role of an exorcist in a past life where your space was totally owned by some being that you errantly thought was Satan. Something like a soul that was torn in half. Something like a guru that takes over the lives of their followers by taking over their crown chakras. And pain. Lots and lots of pain pictures. Cancer pictures. Dismembering pictures. War pictures. Rape pictures. Pillaging was fun, but the rest was all pain. ;-)

All of that became a part of blowing our matching pictures and giving to ourselves, and after a year, we could do it anywhere at the drop of a hat. Hospitals. Funeral homes. Churches. Haunted houses. The back of a moving minivan. Ashrams. Public transit, which honest to god was probably *the* toughest reading environment, LOL!

It was magical, and we were the source of the magic. This is relevant to you because you can be the source of the magic, too.

The institute reading space worked like this: find your space, get in a reading, and see what you see. There was no overt policy or energy that said, "Don't look at *this*."

Now. The house control did set the house vibration, which did filter or influence what we could and could not see. This was also part of what we were learning, though. We didn't know we were learning that until we got a different house control that was substituting for the regular staff. They set a different energy for the house, and that allowed a different set of pictures to light up for us to see and read.

This minimal judgment and the focus on using the tools to find your space, blowing your matching pictures to heal yourself, and giving to yourself throughout the three hours of giving to the readee, made our life better outside of the institute. I had more energy after doing a reading. I had more energy after doing healings for others, some with some serious spiritual damage. Grounding, running energy, and blowing matching pictures is the opposite of being drained.

Six months into the clairvoyant training program, I'd be walking home late at night after a class or reading, matching crown chakras with people walking on the streets of Berkeley, California, and blowing my matching pictures. The homeless. The mentally ill. The shady actors. I'd match their crown chakras and blow my matching pictures. Sometimes, I freed up a lot of energy.

When trouble bubbled up at my job, no matter whose trouble it was, I'd match it and blow my matching pictures. When a substitute teacher showed up to teach our clairvoyant class, I'd match their crown chakra and blow my matching pictures.

With more energy and more awareness from giving to myself, the problems of life faded and mostly disappeared. What remained wasn't a problem, but a decision, and those decisions became fun!

Prove to me that you are a psychic

It should be obvious. We cannot really tell someone all about auras and prove auras exist. They have to experience auras for themselves. We cannot really prove to someone that spirit exists. They have to experience spirit for themselves.

We can't tell someone something they are incapable of hearing. Ooo! Hearing is a spiritual ability. Spiritual hearing is called clairaudience. Hearing is, therefore, an energy. You can read the energy of someone's hearing and see what they can and cannot hear about spirit. That's useful.

Without preparation, then someone might hear the words describing auras, but they can't do anything with the information. If they can't hear the information yet, why would you tell it to them? It can only invalidate them, and that's unkind.

When I asked questions during classes or during and after readings at BPI, I almost never got a direct answer. What I got instead was "Let's take a look at that!" and I'd be paired up with one or more readers with more experience than me, and we'd take a look at the energy of both my question and the answers.

There was only one time that I heard Lewis Bostwick, the founder of BPI and my clairvoyant teacher, give a direct answer to a question. It was at the Female Trance Medium Healing Clinic in San Rafael, California. Lewis and I were the only spirits in a room with forty people in it that had male bodies. One of the women asked Lewis, "Are spirits male and female?"

It took Lewis a good minute to reply. Most of the women in the room were into discovering everything they could about their female energies, and many saw the planet as being female. Some participated in rituals from our pagan times, worshiping the goddess energies.

"No," Lewis said.

I'm standing in the back of the room. I was a control at the clinic. I already came to the same conclusion from the readings I'd done, but for this lady, it was new information. I was expecting a bit of a rumble, but it never came.

No energy flew around bouncing off the walls and everyone's heads. No one was being rude or indignant. Everyone with a female body was integrating this information into their space, adjusting their energies as they went. Nice and calm and female. Blowing their pictures and enhancing their awareness.

It was delightful. No one gave up their seniority or power. They just looked at the energy of the answer for themselves and changed their energy. A few did get stuck on this and I bet you can guess what happened next: after the clinic was over, they asked someone to take a look at them and tell them where their pictures were lit up. This helped them blow their pictures and get their energy moving again.

So what can you do when someone asks you to prove that you're psychic? You can take a look at their energy. Can they hear what you're talking about? That's a good first question to ask yourself and their energy. Are they working up to asking you for a reading? Are they setting you up for a logical debate that only they can win, even though their position is ill informed? Is it a setup? Are they a friend? Do you care whether they get an answer or not?

You don't have to answer them. If you're just beginning to explore your abilities and someone gets wind of what you're doing and challenges you to prove it, unless you're ready to rock their world without incurring any harm to your world, just say you're playing, that's all. It's a fun hobby and it entertains you.

I've proved it many times, but I was rolling through my version of the clairvoyant training program. You don't have to prove anything to anyone, unless you want to. You might learn a lot, or you might be invalidated. If you are invalidated, it's just matching pictures lit up in your space, and you know what to do with those, eh?

If they really want to know, then give them a five minute healing. Ground them to the center of the planet and call back their energy. Fluff their aura. Floss their chakras. Clean out their energy channels. Fill them in with their own energy, and kick back.

They either become aware of their energy changing or they don't. They either feel your energy or they don't. Either way, it's not your problem.

My best friend and training partner from Aikido in Tucson was on a tour of all of the Aikido dojos in California that he could fit into his vacation. He was sleeping in the back of his small pickup truck. He stopped in to see me in Berkeley, and I put him up for a few nights. The truck was really uncomfortable. We had trained and tested together in Aikido for three years.

He asked why I wasn't practicing Aikido anymore. I said I found something more in line with my interests in energy and healing. We talked at some length and he kept calling it BS-I instead of BPI. After about the fifth insult, I'd had enough.

I asked him if he'd like a healing. At the Tucson dojo, we had a shiatsu practice along with a form of energy work called Kiatsu. I had done a lot of healing work with him when he got too sick to work or train for six months. So when I asked if he'd like a healing, he said, "Sure!"

Instead of having him lie down like at the dojo, I had him sit in a chair and I gave him the five minute healing. He could feel some of it but was still dismissive and disrespectful.

Sometimes a mind should be left alone. It really isn't my place to judge, or attempt to influence someone else's path, but at this point he was being a prick. We were best buds in Aikido and he was being Mr. Pricky-Prick.

So I had my healing masters plug into his right arm.

He bolted upright. "What the fuck was that?"

I told the truth. "It's just my healing masters plugging into your arm channels. No biggie really. You okay?"

"I can feel that!", and his face looked troubled.

I had my healing masters walk up his arm. "Hey! It's changing. What's going on? Stop it! That's enough!"

Okay. Enough fun for me. I was beginning to be mean. Just because he was being a prick did not justify me turning into a prick, too. I sat back into my space, grounded and ran my energy, blew my pictures, and just looked at him, smiling. I gave my healing masters a nice vacation in the Bahamas and went to bed.

He left earlier than planned the next morning. He was obviously still shaken and not stirred. In Aikido, we talked for hours on end, drinking sake and waxing poetically.

In Aikido and Kiatsu, we talked about energy and universal ki and healing and spirit and The Dao. We talked about coordinating mind, body and spirit, but we didn't talk about spirit guides. This was the new experience that shook his space, and he needed to leave and settle himself down.

Notice that upsetting him proved nothing. This was the tragedy that made me learn something new. He was not ready to hear about spirit guides. He was not able to hear the BPI perspective on how energy works. He retreated to his comfort level, and I saw him one time decades later when I visited Tucson. We had almost nothing to say.

He's a really nice man. This could have been different had I been more patient. He died in 2016.

Be patient with yourself and the process. Every time you ground and run energy, you are uncovering more of your abilities. Some people will progress faster than others; don't compare. They didn't start where you are starting from.

BUT I WANT MY FRIENDS TO
KNOW THE REAL ME!

There's a risk of losing your friends. There are reasons why this is so.

Imagine what your friends have seen on TV, how people with psychic abilities are depicted. *Heroes* was a really popular series and psychic abilities were not presented in a positive context. Many of the "psychics" were stone cold psychopaths.

The Mentalist depicted all psychics as frauds. Most movies depict them as supernatural and perverted.

The only positive examples that come to mind are Deanna Troy and Guinan on *Star Trek: The Next Generation*. Total acceptance by the crew. Held in positions of influence and in high regard, AND, approachable normal human beings. Yeah, they were not human in the story line, but the human audience totally got them and accepted them.

In the absence of any other first hand experience with psychics, the energy that will dominate someone's impressions of psychics will most often be negative. This is the energy your friends will have to deal with when they discover that you are psychic.

As you read in the previous section, I lost a good Aikido friend by playing "prove it" with him.

Let's say you "came out" to a close friend and now they are keeping their distance from you. What's going on?

Your friend is scared. You can recover the relationship, but you will have to be in command of your abilities and explain them in words that norms understand. Words like sensitive and empathic are more accessible to norms. I've told strangers that I read auras and watched their eyes glaze over, LOL. To be clear, the context was not psychic. Like sitting at the counter in a diner. At psychic fairs, it's all OK.

The glaze over their eyes is the energy and pictures that light up in their space when they find out they have a psychic in front of them.

From the perspective of most norms, just telling them you are psychic is an invasion of their privacy. They shut down primarily because of this. We have to expect this reaction and respect it because in their world, it really is an invasion of their assumed privacy.

If perception is reality, then telling them you're a psychic is, in their minds, an invasion of their privacy.

Everyone has secrets they do not want to share. They assume that if they keep their mouths shut, their secrets are secure. Breaking that assumption disrupts their energy in what feels like destructive ways to them.

Do not attempt to prove your abilities to your friends. That would be selfish on your part. You want them to be open so that you're not as lonely, and I understand that to my core. But trying to prove your abilities are real is often like trying to explain the music of Chopin to someone born deaf, or explaining the joy you feel in your heart when you see a Rodin sculpture to someone born blind. It doesn't do either of you any good and risks compromising a perfectly healthy friendship.

Allow them to have the version of you that they love and let them take the lead on what they want to know or not know about your abilities. If you love them, then be patient.

Okay, I get it. Patience doesn't sit well with you and you're going to tell someone no matter what I say about the risks. Let's be smart about it, then.

What do you share with them? How about something small? Something that in their minds is just you playing around and having some fun. Tarot readings are, for some reason, easier to accept than just looking at someone and telling them about themselves. My opinion is the cards remove some of the fear of losing their secrets in a semi-public setting. The cards can be interpreted in several different ways, and this provides them with an easy out.

Maybe you had a vivid dream about someone. That might be safer to share with them.

I don't know what you can and cannot share. There isn't a guide sheet on this topic in the Akashic Records, LOL! The best I can recommend is to pick something and imagine it playing out.

At this point, you know about rose readings, so consider creating a rose for your friend and another rose to represent the energy of what you want to tell them. Put the second rose next to the first and see what happens. Let that play out over time and see what happens. You can create a third rose to represent your relationship with them and let that rose travel along a timeline of a few months or years and see what happens.

You've introduced a new facet of your life to them, one they may not have been aware before. Give them the time they need to process this revelation. In a positive sense, you've opened them up already. What you may not realize is they are dealing with the worms in the energy can that you've opened, and that takes time. Being more aware, which is all opening means, almost always stirs up some shit, and if someone has little or no energy management, the experience can be overwhelming.

Here's a really useful question: You've been grounding and running energy and blowing roses for several weeks now. Maybe several months. And, you've spent time with this close friend you want to open up to. How much have they learned about managing their energy just by being around you during this period of time?

Mock up a rose for their ability to handle changes to their energy. Put their rose on a timeline from when you first met them to when you started reading this book to now. Has their ability grown along with yours?

Spirits still see energy, even if they don't know it in their bodies. Your friend has been watching your energy this whole time. If they can match your energy, they are probably grounding and don't yet know it, lol. Isn't that neat?

So you tell your friend that you are learning to read and heal energy. They will respond to this. If they respond badly, don't despair.

Energy often fades over time. It's one of the big advantages of having a body; we get to experience the healing brought about by Time. This is why being patient is useful.

Don't be afraid of what you've done. That's not useful. Be yourself. That's who they know and love. Them becoming curious and wanting to know more should be their choice. Be there for them as best you can. That's what friends do.

More reading tips!

Questions have energy. Very cool! You can read energy. Therefore, you can read someone's question, see where it's coming from, see if it really is their question, see who is really asking it. This is very useful, not just in readings or meditations, but especially at work or other political settings.

You don't even need to ask someone what their question is. You can go into a light trance, ground and run your energy, get into the center of your head, match their crown chakra, and look at their spiritual question for yourself. You can use a rose to represent their question. You can look in their aura for their question. Your intent lights it up. You can say hello to them, spirit to spirit, and ask them directly what their question is.

Oftentimes, when asking them spirit to spirit, they will point to something in their space. Just read the energy they pointed out. Describe out loud what you see and watch how happy they and their body get. It's really cool!

One of my instructors, Tom Prussing, did this for me. My question, or one of them, lol, was this: does spirit die? It's a good, basic question.

The answer, depending on what your beliefs have been before asking it, can really rock and roll your energy. Tom didn't answer it for me. He smiled and said that I'd figure it out soon enough.

He did warn me about something. Many of the other clairvoyant students in my class were not ready to look at questions like that. They were not reading as often as I was reading, so they hadn't dug as deep into their space and blown as many pictures. He said if I got stuck, to come back to him and he'd give me an energy check. He's a generous man.

So questions have energy. Neat-o! Reading the energy of someone's question led to students asking better questions. First better question: "Would you take a look at something for me?" This became as lovely and polite as asking someone to dance.

Then, we'd have a question and after a class or a reading, we'd glance around the room and spot the one person in the room that had our answer. We'd run to them and ask them to take a look.

The questions then became some version of, "What is the <random painful energy description> behind my left scapula?" or "What energy gets between me and advancing at work?" or "Why can't I see the back of my aura?" or "Who's zoomin who?" That last question is about energy sex games, not just physical mating. Looking at the energy of sex games opens up a whole new can of wor... I mean a whole new perspective on human relations, LOL!

Notice the neutrality in the second question. It's not "*Who* is in the way of my big promotion?" That implies several questions have already been asked and answered. It sounds personal, doesn't it? "Who" is always more personal. "What" is less so. More neutral questions can help you remain more neutral to the answers, which helps you blow your pictures faster! You may perceive a coworker is in your way, blocking you from advancing, when it's actually a picture in your space from a family member that envied your abilities and wanted to set limits on you so you didn't make them look bad.

But! LOL! Don't make a rule out of this pattern of questioning either. You'll create your own dogma and stop taking a look at stuff that your intuition tells you to take a look at. Rules, or dogma, are anathema to a psychic growing their awareness. Just ground, run your energy, blow some roses, and be curious about what you're seeing or not seeing, and ask questions. Sometimes the right question really is "Whose energy is getting in my way?" Sometimes you already know who it is.

When you see whose energy is in your way, ask why. To stop right there is to judge someone, potentially unfairly. You can match and unmatch energy with anyone, which means you can see things the way they see things for a while. Be curious and ask why being in your way matters to them. Are they even aware of being in your space, or is someone else coming through their space and into yours?

Each time you go to read some energy, ask what color it is, whose energy is it, what is its intent, what does the energy say. The intent can be different from what the energy says if that intent is no longer in present time.

You may one day run into an archangel and get to read them. One of at least two outcomes are possible, both of which are valuable. You may see they are a fraud, just posing as a biblical figure to impress and deceive, or, you may find they are initially an archangel but quickly meld into something more pure and wonderful when you blow your matching pictures. Just a very capable spirit that decided to visit you, the other very capable spirit in the room.

Did I just imply that you have matching pictures with archangels? Hmm. Take a look for yourself.

Spirits get lonely. We like to get hellos from kindred souls. It brightens our lights.

Whenever two spirits say hello, healing occurs.

SHIFT HAPPENS!

All psychics pick up on big energies. One of the biggest is the planet we live on. The planet is the body of a spirit. Hmmm. If the planet is a spirit and spirits can go into growth periods, then the planet can go into a growth period.

The majority of the time, whenever someone asks about *a shift in the energy,* they are experiencing the planet's growth period. "Does anyone else feel like something big is about to happen?" Take a look at the person asking this question and where they are on the planet. The planet is always in motion, and when the energy of the planet changes, we pick up on it. The person asking this may be in a volatile area of the planet's spiritual energy.

If you match the growth period of the planet, your energy really can look and feel like shit. When you look and feel like shit, and after you've run your energy for a bit and don't feel any better, ask yourself whose energy you are matching. Sometimes, it's someone you know. Sometimes, it's some random stranger, or a non-human energy, or alien energy. Sometimes, it's the Earth's growth period.

You unmatch usually by blowing your matching pictures, but in the case of the Earth's growth period, just becoming aware of what you're matching is often enough to enable you to unmatch.

PSYCHIC TRAPS!

If you believe that emotions that get stuck in your body can cause disease, you will look for stuck emotions and release them. Cool beans! Well done.

What happens if, several years in the future, you have a pain in the same area of your body where those emotions were stuck? Do you invalidate your healing from the first time? Do you get emotional and dive in to see what's going on? None of these steps are inherently bad. So where's the trap?

If you're still placing more faith in what others say, and those others are saying something traditional like, "All disease can be traced back to emotions that got stuck in the body," you may go on a snipe hunt. The pain may be caused by something totally different. You are trying to find and heal an energy that is no longer there. That's an impossible task. That is the trap of a cultural or traditional assumption.

If you simply say, "Ow! What energy is causing that pain?" and read a rose for the energy in present time, you leave yourself open to learning something new instead of looking for only what you've been told to look for. Trap avoided.

Assumptions are filters. The more specific the assumption, the more information that gets filtered out.

If you're very ill, see a doctor. This isn't necessarily an assumption. You are managing your risks by ruling out infection, blood clots, hormonal weirdness. It could be energy, but it could also be a staff infection.

Besides, looking at the energy of your blood when it's drawn gathers a lot of information for you to read.

Lewis Bostwick said, "You know those headaches where everything you do just doesn't help at all? You try all your healing techniques and your head still feels terrible? I just say "fuck 'em," and take two aspirins!"

CONSPIRACY TRAPS

Yes, in the United States, the American Medical Association is a monopoly. The AMA has a distinct energy that is all its own. That energy can filter what you see sometimes, but it's just one more energy that if you blow your matching pictures and find your neutrality to it, it doesn't matter.

In the 80s, there was a strong backlash against the AMA in the press, in New Age circles, and at the Berkeley Psychic Institute. It was bullshit. People totally forgot that this was just energy, and began imbuing it with alien invasions, class warfare, etc. Does this sound familiar?

This *conspiracy energy* creates a judgment, which creates a filter, which limits what you can see, what questions you can ask, and what pictures you can blow. It's a trap. We see this going on today. For humans, history doesn't repeat itself, but it rhymes.

Did I just equate history with matching energy? Maybe.

Does everything happen for a reason?

O f course it does! The thing to know about reasons is we make
them up.

We say "everything happens for a reason" as a coping mechanism for
the most fucked up parts of our lives. Our brains cannot picture a story without an end, so our brains make up endings. The benefit to us
by our brains making shit up is it allows us to carry on with our daily
lives, which we have to do to manage life's risks. If we don't show up
for work, or don't look after each other, or don't take out the trash, bad
things begin to happen.

Yes, there can be spiritual reasons for some bad experiences, but that is
not universally true. Yes, there almost always is a picture or an energy
associated with some behavior, sometimes even causing that behavior,
but not always. There can be bad experiences that absolutely deny us
the value we wanted to have in our lives. It wasn't a mistake. It wasn't
a bad choice. It wasn't Satan. It wasn't the hand of God.

It was just bad. Random and bad.

Look at what your mind is doing right this second. It is piecing together an explanation for you that makes "random and bad" manageable and less of a threat. It's building a way out of the emotional hole in the universe that my previous words created in your mind. Technically, it's changing the picture I painted with my words so that it's not a threat to your points of view, whatever they may be.

This is why everything happens for a reason. How you reframe an event can often determine how the rest of your life goes.

To be fair, there is another explanation for everything happening for a reason. This phrase is applying meaning to an event. Meaning is retrospective. We create meaning for our failures and our achievements. Our experiences have no meaning until we create one.

So our minds input an experience in real time and then let it soak, eventually assigning some meaning to that experience. This is another way of describing the reasons that things happen: it's our source of meaning in life.

Pro Tip: Reframing applies to arguments, perspectives, problems, etc. As an energy, reframing means changing the picture! Once you see and understand a picture, you can blow it up, or you can change it any way you choose. Make a copy and change the copy. This allows you to experiment with different changes and see how your energy reacts to each change. Very cool!

You can put the copy of the picture on a timeline and see how it plays out in the future. Also very cool!

Can something happen because of nothing else but karma? Of course. This doesn't mean that everything happens because of karma.

Can something happen because of agreements we made before we incarnated? Of course. This doesn't mean that everything happens because of soul agreements.

The Big Question: Can something happen because it's destined to happen? Yes, but destiny may not mean what you think it means. Take a look at all the players involved in the event. This might include the supreme being, or it might not. If not, do you still call it destiny? What if a group of beings saved you from certain death? What do you call that?

My friend Paul was in Vietnam during the war. His platoon came under fire in the jungle. He was behind a tree. He looked around and saw that his best option for survival was to run up the hill to the other side.

He braced himself to run and just before he started, a voice said, "Stop!" He stopped, and machine gun fire tore through the jungle right where he would have been. He took a breath and the voice said, "Go!" and he made it over the hill.

This happened again, a voice telling him what to do, and following its instructions saved his life again.

Then he was offered a command of his own. Big promotion. Something to build a military career on. The voice said, "We saved you twice. There won't be a third time."

He declined the offer and left the service, returning to the States with a ton of questions, LOL!

Was that fate? Destiny? Do we have the right word to describe Paul's experiences?

Was it fate that brought Paul and I together at the Berkeley Psychic Institute? Is destiny really adequate to describe how, after fifteen years without talking to each other, and a few cross country moves, a contractor gets hired at my place of employment, and on his fourth day working four desks down from me, looks over and asks, "Do you know Paul Ohmart?" It turns out he was a mutual friend from twenty years before and had Paul's contact information.

I call it "getting lucky!" It's what happens to psychics. Paul and I have stayed in touch ever since.

You have to take a look at the individuals involved in the event, with or without bodies.

As a psychic, just take a look at the energy of the event. What color is it? What does it remind you of? Whose energy is it? How did this energy function during this event? You can read all these energies in a single rose, and watch it change colors as you ask more questions.

That last question: How did the energy function? is really useful. It doesn't assign blame. It seeks understanding. This curiosity often leads you to see the energies beneath this obvious one. This is often a rabbit hole worth going down.

Remember my story about my first day on the job as Susan's assistant, and giving energy checks to all her workers at the cabin? That energy check came from asking, "What are we not looking at?" and then following the breadcrumbs down the rabbit hole.

Be curious, not judgmental. Thank you, Ted Lasso!

A friend in need

Many decades ago, before I had much development or training as a psychic, I dated a beautiful nurse. We'd been on a few dates, just getting to know one another. I worked days. She worked evenings. We couldn't get together frequently, but we were happy with how it was going.

One morning on the way to work, I started grinning. I knew I had to be late to work that day. I knew I had to go to my friend's home and see her. Both of these things that I just knew were what made me grin. I had no idea why.

Then a kind of dread came over me, I pulled a u-turn in traffic in the middle of a busy street, and sped up.

I knocked on her door. The door opened. She looked like she had slept in her clothes. She was crying, her shirt soaked down the front, her eyes red and swollen.

I stepped to her and held her in my arms, trying to find the right pressure that would reassure her. Her arms were squeezed between us.

I asked her a few times, "What's wrong?" She couldn't speak through the sobs and tremors.

After some time, we moved away from the doorway. I closed the door and held her again. She looked up into my eyes and said, "John Lennon was killed!" and cried.

After some time, we laid down on the carpet where we stood. I held her close for an hour, trying to feel what she felt. I didn't have that kind of connection to John so the news didn't affect me the way it affected her, but her upset made me think of nothing else but helping her. I had the thought of blanketing her in warmth. I didn't know where that thought came from.

Eventually, I called in sick to work. I stayed with her most of the day. We parted in the afternoon, after she thanked me and said that she needed to get ready for work.

My abilities had informed me and I made me turn my car around. My intent focused my abilities on healing her. I was at once both very sad and very happy, almost joyful. This was the first time this kind of thing had happened to me and just knowing what I did validated my suspicions about who and what I was, even though I had no words to express that. It was awkward, wanting to comfort someone I was just getting to know who was hurting, and at the same time wanting to celebrate what I discovered. I'm grateful that I didn't act the fool in her presence.

Here's the odd part. We never saw each other again. This made no sense to me at the time, especially how I was okay with it. My response to never hearing from her again was mellow. My interest in her didn't fade; it disappeared, and I was okay with that. This surprised me. We looked like we would be really good together, and then, nothing.

Every time I thought of contacting her, clear as a bell that thought was replaced with leave her alone.

Looking back now, I see it as one of my early experiences of finishing my spiritual business with someone from a past life. She called out. I answered. The news of the day was a catalyst.

I also see now that there were other influences in my head, telling me to leave her alone. I don't know what influences were in her head, but back then, I was clueless about "other influences."

I've done a lot of work on myself since then. I put in a lot of hours, getting to know those "other influences," and sorting out which ones could stay and which ones needed to leave.

But mostly, I learned to recognize my own energy. This was the key to recognizing my own abilities and what I wanted. The rest fell into place through reliable practice and having fun being a psychic and a healer.

There are as many ways to express our spiritual abilities as there are people on the planet. I'm pretty sure you will find your way just fine. Enjoy your self-discovery. Really enjoy it. And when you can't, then enjoy not enjoying it. It's just energy after all.

Healing a knee

In the early 80s, I was a dojo rat, training and teaching Aikido pretty much full time. Tucson at that time had no high ranking resident teacher. John Takagi would come down once a month from Phoenix to teach the Friday night and Saturday morning classes, and one of his newly-promoted blackbelts had moved to Tucson to get a masters degree from the University of Arizona. He taught Mondays, Wednesdays, and Fridays in the evening. I had been a brown belt, the highest belt before black, for almost two years, and I taught Tuesdays and Thursdays; three 6:00 a.m. classes, three days a week; Saturdays; and an intro course, Monday through Friday, at 5:00 p.m. I covered the other nights when school interfered with the black belt teacher. Why I wasn't a black belt is a story for a different time.

I went to weekend seminars every few months, usually traveling from Tucson to somewhere in California where the special teachers taught.

Terry Dobson had lived and trained with the founder of Aikido for ten years in Japan. His take on the art was very different from Bob Nadeau, who had also trained for several years in Japan, which was different from Frank Doran's, who had lived and trained a shorter time in Japan, but had taught hand-to-hand combat in the US Army. Then there was this fireplug named Bruce Klickstein that lived in a dojo in Japan as an understudy of a disciple of the founder, a man named Morihiro Saito.

The first three direct students of Morihei Ueshiba always spoke in terms of energy and flowing motions. Klickstein didn't speak much at all during class. He came up in a strict, traditional style of Aikido with lots of high falls and a lot of athleticism. No talking during training, except "Yes Sensei!"

I'd trained with them all separately at their individual seminars. I loved that they were not all the same in their explanations, not all the same body types, not the same styles, and taught the exact same techniques emphasizing very different principles. I had been thrown by all of them and their techniques all worked. They were just different.

The Japanese word for different is *chigau*. It was Frank Doran who would emphasize, "It's not right. It's not wrong. It's *chigau*." This is a useful way to keep your curiosity alive and well.

I'd spend a weekend with one of them and then back at home, I'd become one of them for a month in my classes, teaching in their style, while I integrated everything I'd learned over the three-day weekend of all-day classes.

Then I heard about a weeklong retreat with all four of them teaching every day, starting at 6:00 a.m. and ending at 9:00 p.m. This was held at Dominican College in San Rafael, CA. Friday night through Sunday morning. Sleep in the dorms. Eat in the cafeteria. Live on the mats. Heaven.

I sent in the grand sum of $200 for the whole week and made my arrangements for flights.

During lunch, an older man would accompany our eating by playing classical music on a baby grand piano. He played beautifully. I spoke with him and made friends. He was having some issues with his back and wasn't enjoying the training as much as he could have. I gave him a healing and he was better.

One evening, Bob Nadeau was having a meditation class after the last Aikido training session. Fifty brave souls hung out for this. I had no expectations of what a meditation class would be like in this context.

Bob brought out a single, metal folding chair and sat it at the front of the mat, facing us. We all sat on the mat. Bob said we were going to take a look at some energy. We needed a volunteer to sit in the chair. I raised my hand.

I was taught by a senior student in Tucson, Mr. Jim Davis, to run to the front of the class whenever a teacher was going to demonstrate something. You see more from the front. You catch nuances from the front. You learn more from the front. This is true. You also get picked to demonstrate techniques sometimes. When this happens, you learn even more.

So I raised my hand from my front row seat and got picked. I walked over and sat in the chair.

There was no prep or instructions. Bob just asked the class what their first impressions were of me. Some folks that seemed to have practiced this with Bob before started describing my energy. It was all very general stuff until someone mentioned getting an image of a crusader, a knight.

I thought this was the first interesting thing they had said. It resonated with me and I put my elbows on my knees, interlaced my fingers together, palms down, put my chin on my fingers, and smiled.

Well this shocked everyone. They now saw the sword that my hands were resting on. They saw my helmet sitting on the ground beside me, some banner blowing in the breeze behind me. Not the mat of the real room. The helmet was on the ground of the scene that I'd stepped into. Bob remarked that when I took that position with my chin on my hands, my energy had just "thumped" down around me. The funny thing is I felt it go thump.

They described the white vestments and the red cross on my chest, bits of chainmail peeking out here and there. I began to grin.

Then Bob asked me if he could ask a question. I nodded my head.

"If you're such a Christian and all-loving and stuff, why are you going around chopping off people's heads?"

I didn't speak. I looked him in the eye, still grinning, and he jumped back. He said that he got, "If you have to ask that question, you can't understand the answer." That felt about right to me, so I shrugged.

I was told to sit down back in my place on the floor and they'd read another volunteer.

I believe this was the first time that I was aware of someone reading me and one of my past lives. I had no words for what they did or said, other than "meditation class." It was all new.

This retreat changed me. Everyone in the Tucson dojo noticed the difference when I got back. Everything was easier for me. My teaching began to be my teaching instead of mimicking others. I could help a student solve a technique problem with ease, picking the most appropriate method for them from my now-deeper repertoire of pedagogical techniques.

The next year, three other members of the dojo in Tucson went with me to the retreat. Same energy. 200 people on the mat, flying through the air for a week.

On Wednesday of that week, there was a meditation class with Bob Nadeau. This time, we partnered up and sat in front of each other, staring into each other's eyes, looking for what we "got" from them.

My partner went first. She said she was getting something from me. Her eyes got bigger. She said I was god. This resonated, even though a lot of things went through my mind, like "Who is this crazy woman?" LOL! but it struck a chord, and little by little my awareness started to fade.

It was my turn to read her, and the shadows that I slipped into receded.

I said something about how beautiful her energy was and she cried. I don't recall anything after this.

Class was over. Most folks went to their dorms. I was left by myself, sitting in the stew of being a god, feeling my insides get bright and then go dark, over and over.

At some point, I became aware of a man in a white *gi* standing beside me, talking to me. I almost recognized his voice. He was saying something about his knee hurting so bad he thought he'd have to leave the retreat. He said something about me healing him last year.

My only thought that rose above the turmoil on the inside of me was, "I don't have time for this. Let god handle it."

I glanced up at his face. It was the piano player. My left hand reached out and touched his knee with my palm. That was it. Two seconds. My hand came back, and I slipped under the murky waters inside.

Time didn't exist. Thought didn't exist. The murky water, quiet and reflective, it was everything.

And then a man in a white *gi* was jumping up and down right next to me, shouting, "See! See! My knee works! You healed my knee! Thank you, thank you, thank you!" He kept repeating his gratitude.

I was barely able to come out of my dark, comfortable space to say something like, "Glad I could help."

Slipping back inside, the waters got deeper and darker, and I was the light.

Forty years later, this memory still makes me smile. I don't know what the lady was looking at when she told me I was a god. As I reflect on this, I recall her saying that I told her I was God. I think that's an accurate memory, but she woke up a piece of me that had been missing from my life, right up until then. It's never left me. She also woke up a piece of her own.

It was over so fast and had such a big impact on both of us. Before that few minutes of staring into each other's eyes, we had never spoken or trained together. I'd seen her around the mat, and I'm tall and loud and hard to miss, but we'd never trained together before then. It's also interesting that with half a week left in the retreat, we didn't train together or speak again.

I think at that stage in our lives, it was all we could do to hang on and handle the changes to our separate energies. Seeing stuff is easy. Seeing stuff and still managing your energy, well, that is a different thing. The latter takes a little more practice.

Male and Female
Energy

Everyone has both male and female energies in their bodies. The ratios of male to female energy vary from one person to the next, but the ranges tend to have the following properties. I do not propose any rules or perfect settings for these energies, mainly because if there is a rule somewhere in the universe, all I've read are exceptions to it, LOL!

Here are some general patterns that can give you a starting point for what kinds of questions you might ask when looking at male and female bodies, and how their energy differs. And! How those differences affect the body in which you see them.

Male bodies run more male energy than female energy, for most people.

Female bodies run more female energy than male energy, for most people.

How much more? I have big thumbs, so my rule of thumb might be different than yours. If a male body is running around 60% male energy and a female body is running around 60% female energy, I don't expect to see some glaring issue jumping out of their auras. So, 60/40 male-to-female, or female-to-male, in the cis population. Lesbian and gay populations follow this pretty much as well, but when it doesn't follow, it's obvious.

Here's an interesting situation. When doing relationship readings between a male and a female, when their communication is going into the toilet, I have seen this disconnect caused by an unexpected behavior.

The male and female both empathize with each other, so they adjust their male and female energy to try to "meet in the middle," as if that were a good thing. The male runs 50/50 and the female runs 50/50. When they talk to each other, they can't hear the other person. It sounds like they are lying: "I love you, sweetheart." "*Lies! It's all lies!*"

When I point out why it sounds like lies, and they adjust their rations closer to 60/40, it instantly turns to: "I love you, sweetheart!" and "I love you, too!"

Play with that. It's a really interesting unintended side effect of compromise. They sound like they are lying, or hiding something, because they are not being themselves on an energy level. Their vibration on a sexual level is not true for them in that relationship.

There are variations of this for non-heterosexual relationships that may manifest in different ways. The question to ask when reading a dysfunctional relationship is what has changed since the relationship was functional. That's how I found this male/female ratio side effect.

It absolutely helps to have both parties in the same reading. It takes two, and how each party sees each other during dysfunction is not always how it is.

Case in point: we were doing a relationship reading on a woman I used to date and her on-again, off-again boyfriend, who I also knew. We were all in the clairvoyant training program.

I was the control for the reading. The line of readers were all staff. The woman had paid the $100 fee for a professional reading.

We're barely three minutes into the reading when Richard Lawrence, one of the side chairs, asks the man, "So who's the blonde?"

The woman's eyes showed that she realized everything, and she's pissed off. The man is looking totally busted, so admits to everything. The woman storms out of the building. The man tries to act dumb for a minute, then we're all laughing at him and he realizes he really is dumb, so gets up and leaves the building.

Shortest two hour reading ever, LOL!

Grounding can be different for male bodies than for female bodies.

Male first chakras ride a little lower in the body than female first chakras. The reason has to do with childbirth. A woman's first chakra is closer to her second chakra, like half an inch or so. It's not much but really makes a difference in how comfortable a body feels.

If a male is matching a female on this level and has his first chakra a little higher in his body, he typically feels more antsy. Blowing whatever pictures had him matching that way settles his body right down. This benefits all his relationships because it's easier to relate when you're comfortable where you are.

The opposite is the case for women who carry their first chakra a little too low. They often feel sluggish and uncomfortable.

This is a pattern in the position of first chakras that expresses matching energy in a compromised way.

The two energy centers of the first and second chakras combine to make a pitch, just like a tuning fork. The distance between them affects this pitch, making the pitch either more in harmony with the body or less in harmony with the body.

A video that approximates this tuning between the first and second chakras is this:

https://www.youtube.com/watch?v=qoDAue56LXM

Play with this in your own body. Raise and lower your first chakra in the vertical plane, and see how it feels.

Grounding for male bodies is the grounding you've already learned in the opening to this book.

Grounding for female bodies is, too, but there's something extra that women have that can benefit from modifying their grounding cord.

In front of the uterus, a few inches in front of the body, is a diamond-shaped energy that is female creative energy used in the creation of a new body. Men don't have this unless some woman gives them theirs. Weirder things have happened.

Females can create a branch from their grounding cord and attach it to the bottom point on that diamond. Grounding this diamond helps own this energy for the spirit that owns this body. This cleans out foreign male energies from past sexual partners, real and imagined. This enables this really powerful energy to be repurposed to other pursuits, like healing themself or focusing on a career or something else entirely. It's just energy and owning it for yourself keeps you healthier.

This also enables a female to control this diamond of energy. Sometimes, women and girls will lose energy through this diamond to the people around them. Some families or cultures have the picture that females serve males, or serve the family, or serve the community, and the implementation of this picture is owning all the diamonds of all the female bodies.

I've read this in ex-Mormon women, some Asian women that immigrated away from Asia, several women in Indian cults with powerful male gurus. Just something to be aware of, not something to be afraid of. The truth shall set you free, but first it will piss you off.

For some women, just grounding this diamond changes everything. For others, grounding this diamond begins a longer process of healing. Everyone's different.

Grounding this diamond helps maintain separations. Imagine this really powerful creative energy running sideways through a crowd. Now ground that diamond and watch the energy run up and down through their body.

Men: be aware of a game. Some women have weaponized this female creative energy to control others, but especially men (because we are so easy, lol). You might easily misinterpret this energy as having something to do with sex, and may blindly do someone's bidding with a grin on your face, buying drinks all night, followed by another night at home, all alone. It's but one game, and once you are aware of this kind of energy running sideways, the game is easy to spot.

Do not judge the player. She probably learned the game by copying someone she admired, or was trained this way by her mother and knows nothing else, and has no awareness of what she's doing on an energy level. Be curious, not judgmental. Ground yourself and be amused. Amusement sheds all other energies from your space.

Women: men play games, too. Learn to see the energy of the game and not judge the players. It helps you maintain separation and avoid getting caught up in the games. Neutrality is a tool. Ground yourself and be amused. Amusement sheds all other energies from your space.

For everyone: see the energy. Ask what it's saying. Read the game and maintain separations.

In other words, keep your rose up.

Teenagers are an extraordinary group. Males and females sometimes play a game where they dump a bunch of their energy into some other teen or a teacher, and then just watch what happens. They don't have to have a goal, they just need to see how their energy works in someone else's space.

Those boys or girls that you just can't stop thinking about, day or night? They're in your space.

It's sometimes useful to ground your reproductive organs with branches from your grounding cord. Ovaries. Testes. Falopian tubes. Prostate glands. You get the idea. Experiment with this and see what changes. You might find it useful.

DO MEN GET PREGNANT?

Yes, they do, and it happens when they match the pregnancy energy of a nearby female. They are not physically pregnant, lol, but matching the pregnancy energy of a female causes men to problem solve for things they cannot possibly solve. When pregnant, everything seems like a risk, which makes it a problem. Pregnant men lose their perspective and are less effective in their daily lives.

Men: unmatch the preggos!

Speaking of pregnancy, some men don't match the energy but are impacted by it in another way. They feel useless. It's like their lives have become one agonizingly long waiting room. All that female creative energy zooming throughout the house also zooms through the male bodies in the house.

Women: ground your female creative diamond. You don't need your energy zooming around the house, lol.

Men: unmatch the waiting room. You still have jobs to do. Check that your first chakra is low enough on your spine. Blow any matching pictures with the feeling of the waiting room.

Women: none of that is your problem, LOL! Ground yourself and your creative energy, and enjoy your pregnancy.

You can talk to the men in your life, or your partner, tell them about matching and unmatching energy. Sometimes, just asking them if they feel a little bit pregnant can cause them to sort themselves out and get back on track, lol. We cis men are mostly simple. We want to know if you're OK and if there is any trash to take out.

If your partner is female, take a look at a rose representing her energy and ask the rose to show you any problems she's having.

When you ask your SO how they're doing, it tends to put their focus momentarily on themselves, and sometimes that's all the attention they need to sort out their energy.

A case study in reading and healing yourself to improve your love life

Someone posted a really important question on Reddit. I responded to it in depth and the following is a version of her post and my response.

The value of this section to you is sharing some of my considerations for healing intimate, personal energy issues, i.e. what I would look at if I were reading this person. There's lots of information about keeping yourself safe while reading and healing strong energies in yourself or others.

Her post is used with her permission. Yes, Reddit is an anonymous, public forum, but I didn't feel right using it without asking her first. She graciously agreed without any reservation.

I've made minor edits to her post for clarity. I've added a few sentences to my reply for the benefit of the readers of this book. I've thought of a few more energies that are useful to look at in this complicated situation, and I've included them in this version of my comment. They don't exist in the original comment.

Please keep in mind that I'm writing to someone who is on a different continent in a different culture. I have no idea of her background with healing or reading. You, on the other hand, have all the tools in this book at your disposal now.

I'm going to take some time explaining things before we get to her actual post. There are reasons for this, especially for people with female bodies.

You are a psychic and you are reading ahead on an energy level. This is lighting you up on levels you may not be aware of, so all of this explanation is 1) explaining stuff, and 2) buying you and your body time to dispose of its matching energies, if any. Please create and destroy roses all through the reading of this section. You may get a little stuck, and that's useful. Getting totally stuck wastes time.

If I were guiding you in doing this healing, I'd ask you to create a rose for the next energy that this healee was ready to release *at this time.* Have the rose show you where in her space that energy was, and then you'd be able to take it from there, grounding her body and assisting her in releasing whatever energy your rose showed you.

This way, you'd also know something absolutely critical: when to stop healing her and allow the changes she's made so far to consolidate into their new configurations in her space. You'd finish with one energy, then create a rose that answers the question, "What energy should be removed next at this time?" "At this time" helps you see the stopping place for this healing session. With practice, you won't need to ask this so formally, but in the beginning it's necessary.

Another way to see when to stop is the openness of the bloom on the rose. If the bloom is fully open such that the pedals look like they're ready to fall off, she's done. Make sure she's filled in completely. When doing two hour readings at the institute, we'd call that "baked" and stop the reading or healing. Not often but sometimes, we'd stop a reading before the two hours were up because the readee just couldn't take in any more information.

I would sometimes stick an image of a fork in the readee's aura as a joke. That's how you tell when a roast is done, eh? Some side chairs would laugh out loud when they saw me do that. Some readees would see me do it and laugh. After sitting with us for two hours, they'd match our reading energy and their awareness would open up without them trying. They would laugh out loud.

And no, I didn't leave the fork stuck in their aura. They were done. Why waste a perfectly good fork?

What if the bloom goes the other way and closes up? That means they're not ready as a spirit to let go of any more energy or receive any more communication about it. They're choosing to stop there. You'll be tempted to continue. I won't tell you to never do this because you need to learn what it's like. Just be careful.

In either case, you can say, "You're done. That's it for today," or come up with another way to ease them out of the reading or healing, then suggest things they can do for their body to help it heal: hot bath, massage, spa day, extra sleep, exercising, comfort food, grounding and running their energy and filling in.

Yes, at your stage now, you can give to your body by grounding and running your energy. No need to push it or release any chunky energy or blow up more pictures. Just relax and run your energy for the joy of it. Bodies like joy, too.

Trigger warning: trauma induced by child sexual abuse. Blow some roses. Fill in. Maybe create a new grounding cord. Run your energy.

I sometimes suggest a healee have sex. Sex is another way to help a body adjust to changes in your energy. Dopamine is a spiritually helpful energy, but not in this case study where sex abuse is at the core of the energy problem.

You'll see how often I suggest that she, the woman who posted the request, take a break. I have some idea of what size and shape the energy is that she's going to uncover at each stage of my response to her post. I'm not fully in trance and reading her as I typed my response - sub rules and all that. Still, every psychic picks up on energy.

She'll need prodding to take breaks. She's a strong, capable spirit who knows her own will, can keep her own council, and will be capable of pushing through more energy changes than her body can take. This could set her back. She's no victim anymore and is asking for advice about healing herself on an energy level. Her energy reminds me of a combination of stubborn and gentle.

Much better to allow the body to have its space to heal at its own pace, than drive through all the energy in one go and be unconscious of anything else for a few weeks.

Use your rose to know when to stop reading or healing someone else or yourself. Know when you're done, stick a fork in you, and go do something else physical.

I had someone read me into the ground at the Berkeley Psychic Institute, just before I graduated from the clairvoyant training program. Not a healing, a professional reading only. Professional readings from the staff were $100, which was a lot for me, living almost paycheck to paycheck.

He read only one energy in my space for two hours, and it was the energy from all the women in my extended family that said, "he's not good enough."

They had their reasons for saying and thinking this. My parents were forty-seven when I was born. Surprise! I was tall, extremely skinny, with a big head, and painfully shy. Aunts and uncles would whisper when I was around, glancing at me sideways. Animals loved me and spoke to my face, as well as a few cousins, but the adults seemed to think I was retarded, to use the word from the 50s and 60s, when I was a kid. One uncle, Lester, yes the one who stood on his own grave marker, *that* Lester, told my mother I was retarded to her face while he was holding the top of my head in his meaty hand. I was four years old. That's my earliest memory of seeing my mother enraged, lol.

This reader was the director of the institute, Michael Tamura, and he only read this one energy. No uncles. Not my father or older brother. Just the collective female energies in my extended family that said, "he's not good enough."

Two hours of hearing about this one energy in every corner of my space and I disappeared from the institute the last three weeks before graduation. I did no readings at all. I slept. I walked to work. I walked home and I slept.

Two years of grounding and running energy, and the best I could do was get out of bed and show up at work. I remember nothing else from those three weeks before graduation. Everyone knew I was a little over-done by this reading, but we also knew that I'd recover. I had the skills to manage these changes eventually. I viewed this as my graduation gift to myself. One final plunge, lol.

I was over-read. I released more energy from my space than I could take in stride, and therefore had to slow my life way down for three weeks, but I knew how to do that.

Did that need to happen? No. There is always the option for a follow-up reading or healing. Always. Especially remote on the phone.

Did I need that to happen? No. Lighting up the initial layer of energy that said, "he's not good enough," gave me enough information to continue to work that energy on my own. Grounding and running energy an hour a day and focusing part of that time each day on this specific energy would accomplish the same thing without the upheaval in my space.

Two years earlier, on my first day at the Institute at the free psychic demo, I'd received a healing from Hanna Jane that put me in a growth period with a deep green color. It felt like the beginnings of motion sickness. "Green behind the gills" is the old-school description. I was semi-conscious for a few days, but happy for the first time in months.

Looking back, that healing from Hanna Jane wasn't that dramatic. It was just a small repair to a crack in my fourth chakra and some descriptions of the energy my ex left in my space, and yet it changed my life for the better, just not right away. The weird feelings of the growth period were because I didn't know how to manage my energy any better than that.

Don't underestimate how your readings and healings can transform someone's life, including yours. Every reading is different. Keep track of how much more information they can take in and how much more change they can make. I favor using the bloom of the rose. It's the easiest for me to keep an eye on.

You will quickly develop the ability, if you practice, to over-read or over-heal somebody. Keep track of their energy with a rose and know when to stop. "Quickly" will mean different things to different people, but it happens before you fully know it. You'll find your enthusiasm for reading going up and up, and you can just keep going on with nothing but a smile and the next layer of energy.

Check your reading rose.

As you begin a reading for someone, check the bloom on the rose. Maybe it's half open. Maybe it's fully closed like a brand new rose just coming into the world. As the reading progresses, check the rose a few more times. What you're looking for in the bloom is when it opens all the way. That's when you want to stop reading. If the petals are falling off the bloom, you've probably read too long.

It's perfectly OK to give them a little more than they're ready for. This helps build momentum in their growth curve. It's not OK to over-read them because it does them a disservice. The reading will leave them in a less-functioning state and can impact their daily lives in negative ways. Yes, there are some gung-ho folks that want to take everything they experience to the max, but even they can be abused. They're just too cocky to realize it.

Know when to stop reading. You can know this by monitoring a simple rose for how it opens during the reading, and stopping when the bloom is fully open but still fresh.

Trigger warning: trauma induced by child sexual abuse. Blow some roses. Fill in. Maybe create a new grounding cord. Run your energy. This message is an intentional repeat. Please blow some roses for pictures that have lit up due to you reading ahead on an energy level.

Now for the case study. Keep your rose up between you and the book. This will be good practice for you. Watch the bloom and let it tell you when to stop reading and take a break.

Allow me to repeat: Trigger warning: trauma induced by child sexual abuse. Keep your rose up.

HER POST'S TITLE: *EFFECTS OF GROOMING AND SUGAR BABYING*

Her post: "Hi all, I'm looking for advice on something quite personal that I'm yet to share with anyone, even my therapist.

I was groomed by an older man (23) at the age of 14 and had sexual encounters with him for nearly half a year. My parents were divorcing around the time and being an only child, it took a toll on me.

Later at 20, I moved abroad to study in one of the most expensive cities in the world. While in university, I started dating sugar daddies to maintain an income, and I slept with just under 10 men, mostly older. Never had the courage to talk about this with anyone, feels like I have hurt myself and my inner child a lot that I didn't value my body and sexuality.

I feel like I can't connect sexually with the men I love. Although I enjoy it, there's an intimacy block. I have an amazing man in my life now and I want to bond with him more but I could never share these incidents with him.

Any advice on how I can energetically work on myself? I'll eventually work with my therapist when I'm ready but I would like to start from within myself first.

Much appreciated."

MY RESPONSE TO THIS WOMAN:

I think working on the energy in reverse chronological order would be safest. Start at the most recent energy and work backwards to your relations at the age of fourteen. This is safer because our life experiences tend to accumulate like layers of sediment. Removing something from an early layer almost always affects all of the layers on top of it. This can release too much energy all at once and overwhelm your body. The one exception to this layer rule of thumb would be past life energies. Those can come into play anywhere because they are not accumulating this lifetime the same way your life experiences are accumulating.

I'm not going to read your energy. That's against the rules on this sub. Instead, I'm going to tell you where to look. If you have some kind of energy hygiene practice, do it before and after looking to keep your energy moving. Healthy energy moves. This hygiene practice could be meditation, dancing, yoga, martial arts, painting, drawing, gardening. Any activity that helps you feel better and does that consistently will work. It doesn't need to be a formal energy work practice.

I'll provide you with my basic energy hygiene technique at the end. Since this energy work involves all of your major chakras, I'll provide the definitions I use for these chakras in terms of the psychic abilities they hold.

You will likely find cords or remnants of cords from your past lovers in your chakras. Do not cut them. Remove them like this: gently push them into the chakra, give them a slight twist to free them, and pull them out. Tie a simple knot on the end of the cord to prevent it from leaking someone else's energy (this is just good manners). Push the cord all the way out of your aura, which is a little less than arm's length away from your body. Seal the hole in the edge of your aura and heal the path that the cord made through your aura by gently swishing your hand back and forth across the path, like wiping away something written in the sand.

The following instructions are a treatment plan that you can execute at your own pace. Your body will tell you if you're going too fast, so listen to your body. Don't be surprised if one step seems complete in the first session, but the next step takes you several weeks of daily energy work. This is your life, so far, that you are remediating, and you've had a rich life full of experiences. Don't judge the energy that you find, just release it. It's just energy and releasing it spares you reliving the memory.

So. First things first. Well done. You are a really capable spirit. You have a strong will, as demonstrated by posting this information here and your life story itself. Your will is also demonstrated by your control over your body over your lifetime. Again, well done. Some people would not handle the energy that you've been through as well as you have.

Sugar daddies. Ten or so of them. Sugar daddies are usually at the peak of their careers with a lot of expendable income, but they are only men. Even though they know that their relationship with you is an arrangement they are buying, some of them will take ownership over you. This probably isn't conscious on their part. It's more instinctive. They want you exclusively to themselves as long as they are paying you.

This kind of monogamous drive is primitive. Look into your first chakra at the base of your spine. This chakra holds your survival information. You may discover traces of sugar daddy energy in your survival information, which blocks parts of your ability to create long term relationships and career steps. Typical long term relationships that have first chakra cords are parents and children. Take care with treating this one. You might find energy from your parent's divorce, too, as at fourteen a divorce is a life changing/threatening event.

This would be a good time to do your energy hygiene practice :-) Really. I suggest you stop here and notice how your body feels, what parts of your body are uncomfortable, and work on your energy to release those discomforts. Maybe take a bath or have a small meal. Then come back and read more.

Lovers create cords between their second chakras. These cords focus and reinforce the sexual experiences you both have together. Look for damage to your second chakra and its ability to send and receive cords.

Deep breath. Maybe take a break and walk around.

Look for energy in your second chakra that says, "you're mine." When the sex is good, the desire to repeat the sex is instantaneous, even though the ability of both parties to repeat it is physically limited. This energy of "doing it again" gets stuck in your second chakra, gets stale over time, and turns to static. Static energy doesn't move. Energy that doesn't move appears darker and more opaque than energy that's moving. This is sometimes interpreted as a blockage. It's just energy. Do your hygiene practice while thinking about removing this energy. The static energy is in the way. It's accumulated over time. When you remove it, you may think of some of the individual men that it came from. That can be terrifying or loads of laughs. If it's terrifying, laugh at it anyway. Laughter breaks up static energy. Your memories can't hurt you from the past, but they can make your body respond to them, and laughter breaks up your body's responses as well.

Break time, anyone? Coffee and a donut?

Look for energy from your second chakra that you left in your lovers' spaces. Women create a similar control energy to men in the second chakras of the men. This energy says things like, "you're mine," or "I'm the best you've ever had," or similar basic mating ideas. We may be way smarter than this, but our bodies are not. Pull your energy back from your former lovers. Don't judge what you did with that energy. It may have kept you out of harm's way. Lovers control each other on some level. Lovers are collaborators and these exchanges of energy are agreed to.

Some of those sugar daddies may have cared for you, maybe even loved you in spite of the impossibility of the relationship ever continuing. Look in your fourth chakra, which is the heart chakra, for any energy from your former lovers. Some of this energy may say obvious things like "I think I could love you," "I wonder what kind of a wife she would be," or it may say something less curious and more deliberate like "Don't you dare fall in love with me. I'm taken and I will not allow you to become attached." Imagine how that last statement might affect your relationships now, even if your current partner is technically not taken by someone else. This could create doubts in your mind. This could block a deeper relationship from forming now.

Break time.

Take a look at your fifth chakra. This holds your spiritual communication abilities of telepathy and clairaudience. It also holds your inner voice. Sugar daddies do not want to be found out. Their fears of you exposing them will create some energies in your fifth chakra to block you from saying anything, verbally or telepathically, with their family, friends, coworkers, bosses, peers, parishioners, your friends, your family, your peers... This can be a debilitating energy for your relationships. This can be debilitating for your inner voice, which can compromise your self image and confidence.

Break? Really. Take a break if you feel the least bit uncomfortable. Working through this much energy might take an energy worker with a lot of experience and really sound energy hygiene habits several months, or it may take you a few moments' thought and it's done. It's your call. Just listen to your body. It's the one that has to deal with the release and replacement of all of this energy. It's your call.

Deep breath. Only two more chakras to go, LOL! Read some jokes. Find your amusement. These last two can be real pissers.

Take a look at your sixth chakra. On the surface, it has one ability: clairvoyance. After the fifth chakra with its many abilities, this might seem like a let down, but it's not. Your sixth chakra influences how you see the world and how the world sees you. This is a big deal.

Look for any energy from your sugar daddies that says, "don't look at this." This is the energy that lovers create to hide secrets from their partner or anyone else. If there was anything a sugar daddy wanted to hide from you, they would most likely have put some energy into your head and sixth chakra that hides what they do not want you to see. This energy becomes a filter on your reality, preventing you from receiving all of the information that is coming your way and making it much harder to make decisions for yourself. Release all the energy like this that you find, then come back every day and look for more.

Continue this process of looking for more until you find the energies that your groomer placed in your fourteen year old head to hide what you could see and understand about what he was doing. I said it would get worse, but at least now you are prepared by the practice you did on the lighter layers from the sugar daddies. I say lighter only because they are more recent and they were not buried as deep, not because they were any better energies.

You may also find the remnants of cords into your sixth chakra. This is a more active kind of control over what you are allowed to see. Remove them as described at the beginning.

Big breath, LOL! But don't worry. This isn't even the worst news.

Take a look at your seventh chakra. The big deal here are cords. If someone wants control over your life, a cord here can accomplish that. If someone wants you punished if you behave in certain ways, a cord here can do that. If someone doesn't want you to know something, a cord here can do that. Basically, controlling your crown chakra with a cord disables your ability to know stuff off the top of your head, which is the spiritual ability called claircognizance. A cord in your crown chakra can mess with your precognition, which is your ability to predict the future, which is absolutely necessary for you to keep yourself safe and to control your own destiny. Remove all the cords from your seventh chakra. Return to this task every day until it becomes second nature.

Look for any energy in your crown chakra that says, "think about this," or "don't think about that." Look for any energy that says anything about death. A common control is keeping your body in fear, and the easiest way to do that is with an image or memory of death. Bodies don't like that and it will keep you off balance.

Note about death pictures. Putting a death picture in someone's crown chakra, or anywhere else, is an effective technique to prevent someone from looking at that specific space. Ew! Death picture! I'll look someplace else. A death picture can convince you to stop looking for cords. This prevents you from finding and removing cords from your chakras, especially your seventh.

You can review the other six chakras for death pictures and energy as well. Release it all and fill in with your own energy. Now you can review the other six chakras for similar kinds of energies, but energies from your groomer. Fear. Punishment. Lies. Controls. Release these energies and fill in.

Consider having a spa day: massage, sauna, the works. Your body has been working hard, trying to keep up with your energy work. Make friends again with your body.

Sex energy work. Look at your ovaries, vagina, clitoris, anus, breasts, nipples, and any other erogenous places on your body. Release any energy from any of the prior men in your life.

Note: also look for the energy that your lovers placed in what they assumed would be erogenous zones. These often have nothing to do with your actual erogenous zones.

There are switches in a female body that control your arousal. You'll find them in your breasts and ovaries. Release any energy there from your former male relationships. Re-own these switches for yourself. Just place your female creative energy over them and own them.

Note: These switches are for reproduction. Some folks have learned how to turn them on in others in order to get laid.

Deep breath. Look for and release any energies put on your switches by your father or other male relatives, or your mother or female relatives. You're on a roll, so look for stray energies on your switches and erogenous places from primary school teachers, parents of friends. Stray energies? These are energies created when an adult looks at a child and starts to wonder, then quickly suppresses the thoughts. The suppression relieves them of their guilt but doesn't necessarily stop the energy of those thoughts from going into your young, childhood space. Again, don't judge. You're looking for energies in important places in your space and not all of it was put there with ill intent. Just release it and fill in. The intent could have been as simple as, "I wonder if she'll look like her mother when she grows up?"

If any of your prior men had a fetish for a body part, look for their energy in that body part of course, but also look for any energy associated with that fetish that they put into your chakras. Releasing the fetish from your chakras will help ensure that you got it all and that it doesn't come back. The energy of "be my foot fetish for the rest of my life" is a wish that can come true, even after the two of you have separated for decades. Clean the energy out. Look for their fetish energy in your switches.

Take a break.

Time to clean out your aura. This is a bit different. Touch your pinky fingertip to the tip of your thumb. Take the tips of your three fingers and slowly move them up and down through all parts of your aura. Feel for ridges.

Ridges feel more dense than the energy beside them. You may feel a temperature change when you touch them. You may feel them buzzing or feel a mild shock. These are pain ridges.

Pain ridges change the normal movement of energy through your aura. The way to get rid of them is to simply tap them with the tips of those three fingers and they will break up and disappear.

Can't reach the back of your aura? Decouple your aura from the surface of your body, grab the front with both hands, and give it a good turn until you can reach the back and sides. When done, bring it back around where it was and couple it back to the surface of your body.

Look in your aura for machines. These are energy constructs. They might look like boxes or wheels or random geometries. The geometry doesn't matter. If you look for a machine in your aura, if there is one there, you will find it.

Machines are designed to keep programmed behavior in place. Do those pictures and energies that you removed from your fourth chakra start showing up again the next week? Look for the machine that is keeping them in place by replacing what you remove.

Breaking those machines into pieces and destroying the pieces inside a rose ends the cycle and deprograms you from the person that placed the machine in your space.

(I then shared the brief inventory of the chakras, the grounding exercise from the start of this book for her energy hygiene practice, and the modification to the grounding for female bodies and the female creative energy diamond.)

Are There Scary Beings Out There?

Everyone has something that scares *them*.

What scares us can be found in pictures in our auras. Spirits without bodies can see these pictures and learn what scares you. If you are from certain forms of religions, demons are real and will scare you when you see the image of a demon, or throw you into some kind of hyper defense mode.

If demons aren't part of your pantheon of spirits, that image is not going to work on you.

That's one part of the game.

The other part is this: what in your space scares spirits without bodies? You have a body.

That can be scary because having a body enables you to use many of your powers. Having a body is also your home base, or safe place. Like the game of tag, when you're in your body, spirits without bodies can't touch you. Fortunately for the spirits that are more devious, most folks don't know this about themselves, lol.

There is some part of you that spirits can see that makes them not play their "let's scare the shit out of <your name goes here> and see what happens!"

Before I got some training for my clairvoyance, spirits would show up looking like Darth Vader or T-Rex or those aliens that tried to eat Sigourney Weaver. After I trained up my clairvoyance, I could see that those images were just that, images created by some spirit, meant to manipulate my emotions.

Once I saw that, the pranksters just stopped coming around. Perhaps they see something in you that affects them in a similar way. When you begin to ground to the center of the planet and run your energy, the pranksters back off. Why? In part, it's because they can't be in the flow of cosmic energy. In another part, it's because you can tell the truth from the lie, which breaks up a lot of games that spirits play. You can read that spirit's energy in a rose. You can ask questions and get answers about that spirit from your rose. They can't lie to you anymore.

You can tell when you have a picture lit up and you can blow it. The little deviants can't manipulate you anymore, and they move on to easier targets.

Even nice spirits, like our spirit guides, create images, but do it to facilitate communication with us. What would be easier to understand: an image of a sweet grandma that smiles a lot or a small ball of light with no face and no other context? The latter is what all spirits look like, including you and me. The former is what we're shown.

When you get scared by some spirit, come back to your body, ground and run your energy, blow whatever matching pictures that spirit lit up in your space, and watch your body settle right back down. Then you can thank that spirit for helping you find another picture to blow so you can grow your energy. They get really bored and leave soon after that.

Endnotes

Ground. Run your energy. Blow roses. The trifecta of psychic hygiene! Filling in is assumed to occur at the beginning and end of every meditation, reading, and healing, of course, but check your gauges regularly, just in case. Fill in during your work day. It just takes a second.

Learning to be in a control space, meaning grounding, lightly running energy, and blowing the occasional rose, while not being in a light trance with your eyes closed, is how you take all you've learned into your daily life. Being a control is the most useful combination of skills you can learn. Once you can tell when your energy is running, when you're grounding, when your separation rose is no longer there and create a new one, you can be anywhere doing anything and protect your space while giving to yourself.

Being a control is what makes work more fun, more tolerable when work isn't fun, and makes you more resilient in the job market when it's time to look for something new. You'll come home from work with more energy than you used to, and most of it will be your energy, LOL!

Being a control allows you to practice reading the energy of a room, or a conversation during a business meeting when the communication breaks down. You may not have the words to fix the problem, and that's OK. You are contributing on an energy level and people notice. Ground the room but let the individuals choose if they want to ground themselves.

It depends on the group, but I've been in meetings that were way too rough and going nowhere. I grounded and matched my control space, and before I grounded the room, everyone grounded themselves. They matched the energy of what I was doing and it wasn't even my meeting. The energy just smoothed out and work started getting done.

In a control space, you can more easily identify when you're healing someone instead of just listening to them. You'll be able to save your energy. When you do choose to heal someone, you'll have more awareness and energy available to you, and the healings will happen easier and faster. You just need practice, and not as much practice as you might think.

Blowing your matching pictures and filling in is giving to yourself. You can give to yourself all day long in a control space. You can get through the worst news and still have more energy at the end of the day. That's an advantage everyone can use.

And here we are, at the end of the book. I'd like to hear from you. What did you find useful? What questions went unanswered? What needs more explanation?

If you email me at nottoodeep@nottoodeep.net and let me know, I will make every effort to put your feedback to good use.

If you want to see how some of your feedback gets used, you can sign up for my newsletter here: https://tremendous-designer-4185. ck.page/e74f7ba6a8

I'm going to make my very irregular newsletter into something more useful now that the book is done. I'm not sure what that means. Perhaps you can help define that.

My editor is talking about Volume 2 of *The Psychic Bedside Reader*. There is so much that we couldn't squeeze into this first book. We had to stop and focus in order to complete the book this year, and doing so in a good, quality way. I'm super pleased with my experience working with my editor, Dawn Wirt. She's a psychic with a similar background to mine in terms of the tools we both use, and she's a professional editor. Her style of feedback improved my writing tenfold. It also pulled up more useful memories, which is always great fun for me. Our working relationship enriched both our lives. Ain't that a hoot!

Is there any interest in a volume two of A Psychic Bedside Reader? Writing this book has been the most fun I've had in a long while. If you want more, please let me know.

———•———

How does one describe what happens that enables us to see energy and spirit? "Open" is often used, but that also describes lots of things that are not necessarily part of what happens when we see energy. There are lots of metaphors used to describe the process: opening the drapes; looking past the veil; changing to a higher dimension (math metaphors miss the point IMO); raising your energy or your vibration; hanging out with people that already see energy and spirit and waiting for it to rub off on you; getting into your higher chakras; and my least favorite, "Don't bother. It's a gift from God and you either have it or you don't". Such piss and vinegar, LOL!

In my experience, what I've seen is a slightly more complex process than one word or metaphor can describe. Metaphors are particularly prone to creating dogmas that say, "you must do these seventeen things before you can truly achieve x, y, and z." You must master kneeling quietly from 5:00 a.m. to 7:00 a.m. every morning. You must master full lotus position. You must see like I see.

So a Redditor asked, "Another serious question: how do you open? What does this entail?"

I used to think I had "the one answer" to this question: learn to ground and run your energy, do this long enough that you clean off your sixth chakra, and you're good to go. In short, do what they teach at the Berkeley Psychic Institute and its many offshoots.

It does work and it is predictable, but it is only one training approach.

I thought BPI was the way, because it was exactly what I needed at that time in my life, but then a very interesting thing happened a few years after I left BPI.

Back in 1992, my wife and I were hired by a businessman to help him set up a 900 psychic line, similar to the now-defunct Psychic Friends Network. Our job? Find fifty really good phone readers to launch the service. Our method? We took out a very small ad in a few newspapers and got 500 applicants. We scheduled them to give each of us short phone readings, dividing them up between my wife and I.

We asked the same interview questions of every reader: how long have you been reading? What do you like to read? How did your abilities begin? And then they read us.

We asked the same reading question of each candidate. Mine was "what's my relationship with my father." Yes, it's a trick question. We thanked them for their time and the reading, saying we'd be in touch for those we wanted in a few weeks. They knew we couldn't hire everyone, and also knew that this first round was a first round, and the intent was to grow the business fast, so more readers would be needed.

Every reader answered the trick question correctly. All 250 of my readers got it right. The very few readers that were offended by the trick question were removed from further consideration. An angry response was not appropriate for the business. The rest we ranked.

I had to narrow 250 readers down to 25. This sounds impossible, but it was actually quite easy.

The best readers, considering their voice, manners, accuracy, amusement, rapport, and ease with reading, stood out from the rest. Their energy was brighter and more in their control, and was up around their heads. Their joy in doing the reading was obvious; they loved reading. They were not easily flustered. The really good ones also knew that I was reading them, which was cool!

So, how did they open up? The only factor that the best readers all had in common was how long they had been reading. Who they studied with, what methods they learned, was all over the place.

My favorite that gave me the best reading? She bumped her head when she fell off her bike at age five and when she stood up she could see auras. Imagine being the only child in public school and in her family who could see energy. When she read me, she was in her late 30s, so that was 30-plus years of reading energy and figuring out how it works and how to manage her reactions to it, all on her own.

She had a steady clientele that included celebrities and read full time. She wanted to take an extended break from full time reading to complete her book, but she thought reading strangers on the phone would be fun and keep her engaged while she wrote.

Note that if she was your only point of reference, it might be easy to believe that you're either born with these abilities or you were not. Bias is often an outcome of incomplete data.

I don't recommend getting your head bumped in order to open up, LOL! If it was a consistent method, then all the players in the NFL would be seeing auras, LOL!

What I recommend is doing your own version of tryouts. Try different methods of psychic development.

Go onto meetup.com in their Religion and Spirituality section and see all the groups that do energy work, both reading and healing, and go visit all of them at least once. Those that catch your attention, even if it makes you a little uncomfortable, visit twice.

After doing that tour of little groups, you have some first hand experience and are building an inventory of experiences with your energy and the energy of others. Being able to distinguish between your energy and other people's energies is really useful in keeping your space healthy for doing readings and healings, and living your life.

Check out social media platforms for more little groups that are near you. Visit a meeting with all of them. Blow your matching pictures. See what their energy is like. You can do this for online only groups as well.

Taking a healing class is a wonderful next step. Energy gets real quickly in a healing class, and you start to open up on your own. Everyone is different; the students in a healing class all have different life experiences to draw on, including past life experiences. Comparison is the thief of joy, so be curious, but not judgmental, especially of yourself.

If you see another student do something different, ask them about it. If they are aware of what they did, they might give you a really useful answer. We are not always aware of what we do in the beginning, so ask politely but don't push if they don't know. They're just being honest.

My methods may not click with you, and that's OK. There's more than one way to crack this egg.

Just remember this: your experiences are always real; it's all the competing explanations for your experiences that are suspect. Go with what works for you. Understand that it might change.

So that Redditor asked, "Another serious question: how do you open? What does this entail?"

This entails getting enough of your energy and awareness into your sixth chakra to use your clairvoyance. This often means pulling some of your awareness up from your lowest three chakras. You don't have to be grounded, but it sure helps. You don't have to have your energy flowing, but it sure helps. You don't even have to know what you're doing, but being around others that do know sure helps. For the most part, you already know how to read and are now in the process of remembering what you know.

I never thought books could help someone learn to read energy. BPI encouraged us to use people as our books. BPI also had us sign a contract stating we would not write a book about our experiences until ten years after we left.

I took seminars and classes, but I never bought a book in a new age bookstore. I did buy my first psychic development book this year. Evaluating the competition, lol.

I didn't believe anyone could learn to read energy from a book, and I was wrong.

A Redditor DMd me to thank me for teaching them how to read auras. I responded that I did no such thing!

He replied that he liked the grounding technique that I often share so much that he combed through my comment history and pieced together all the techniques and steps needed to read an aura, then gave a reading to his friend. He gave a really good reading, too. Simple and to the point. His description of the steps he put together was, indeed, exactly how I would teach someone to read, LOL!

He grounded. He ran energy. He found the center of his head, created a rose, and blew his matching pictures. He sent a hello to the friend sitting in front of him and saw his friend sparkle over his right shoulder. He saw one dark, static energy in his friend's aura and described it and what it said, how it compromised his friend in some ways. His friend's energy popped and started moving that dark static out of his space.

That Redditor's DM to me is the reason you now have this book. My wish is that you found something truly useful by reading it.

Be well. Do good work. Have fun.

Thank you.

Made in United States
North Haven, CT
21 October 2024

59288113R00245